WITTGENSTEIN
STUDIES

THOEMMES

Printed and bound by
Antony Rowe Ltd., Chippenham, Wiltshire

WITTGENSTEIN STUDIES

The Danger of Words
and writings on Wittgenstein

M. O'C. DRURY

Edited and Introduced by
David Berman, Michael Fitzgerald and John Hayes

THOEMMES PRESS

This edition published by Thoemmes Press, 1996

Thoemmes Press
11 Great George Street
Bristol BS1 5RR, England

US office: Distribution and Marketing
22883 Quicksilver Drive
Dulles, Virginia 20166, USA

Wittgenstein Studies
6 volume hardback set : ISBN 1 85506 494 4

Paperback : ISBN 1 85506 490 1

Publisher's Note

CONTENTS

Maurice O'Connor Drury, about age 10

EDITORS' PREFACE

Maurice O'Connor Drury, like his mentor Wittgenstein, did not publish a great deal. Most of his publications – and, we believe, the most valuable of them – are reprinted in this volume. Probably best known are 'Some Notes on Conversations with Wittgenstein', which originally appeared in *Acta Philosophica Fennica*, vol. 28, in 1976, the year of Drury's death, and was then included in a volume edited by his friend, Rush Rhees, *Ludwig Wittgenstein: Personal Recollections*, published by Blackwell in 1981, which also contained the first printing of Drury's 'Conversations with Wittgenstein', a longer work from which 'Some Notes' were drawn. In 1984 Rush Rhees's volume was again issued, this time by Oxford University Press, with corrections and some new material. The present reprint of Drury's 'Some Notes' and 'Conversations' is taken from this later, corrected edition.

However, Drury was more than merely the biographer of Wittgenstein. He was also a student of philosophy and a respected psychiatrist, and his most original work, *The Danger of Words* (Routledge and Kegan Paul, 1973), reprinted here, brings together these two dominant elements of his life-work: the philosophical and the psychiatric. As an addendum to *The Danger of Words* we also reprint Drury's 'Fact and Hypothesis', which appeared in the journal *The Human World*, vol. 15–16 (1974), in reply to a review of his book by Ilham Dilman (*The Human World*, vol. 14, 1974).

The final item in this collection is a hitherto unpublished lecture which Drury gave at University College, Dublin, to the student Philosophy Society – probably, judging from a letter of Rhees to Drury of 24 May 1968 – on 9 November 1967.

vii

We are grateful to the Drury family for their generous cooperation – for example, in making available the typescript of Drury's lecture as well as two photographs of him reproduced in the present volume.

David Berman and Michael Fitzgerald
Trinity College, University of Dublin, 1996

WITTGENSTEIN'S 'PUPIL':

THE WRITINGS OF MAURICE O'CONNOR DRURY

I

Maurice O'Connor Drury (called 'Con' by his friends) was born in Exeter in 1907, of Irish parentage. He attended the grammar school of that city and then went in 1925 to Trinity College, Cambridge, where he took the Moral Science Tripos. In 1929, Drury met Ludwig Wittgenstein, a newly appointed lecturer in philosophy at Trinity College. Wittgenstein had taken up a fellowship in that College in 1926 following strenuous efforts by Frank Ramsey, Bertrand Russell and Maynard Keynes to bring him back to philosophy from self-imposed obscurity as a primary school teacher in remote mountain villages in Lower Austria. Drury and Wittgenstein met at a meeting of the Moral Science Club, in C. D. Broad's rooms. There began a friendship between student and teacher that was to last through the many vicissitudes of their lives until the philosopher's death from cancer in 1951 in the home of a medical friend of Drury's.

Drury made several attempts to give an account of this friendship. The first was a brief intervention in a symposium, which is recorded in a book published in 1967,[1] in which he disputed the popular conception that Wittgenstein was a 'rather cantankerous, arrogant, tormented genius' rather than

---

[1] In 'A Symposium', in K. T. Fann (ed.), *Ludwig Wittgenstein: The Man and his Philosophy* (Sussex: Harvester Press, 1967), pp. 67–71.

the man he knew to be 'the most warm-hearted, generous, and loyal friend anyone could wish to have'.[2] His most substantial account, however, was 'Some Notes on Conversations with Wittgenstein' and 'Conversations with Wittgenstein', edited by another member of Wittgenstein's circle of close friends, Rush Rhees.

Taken together, these texts offer perhaps the most intimate portrait available of Wittgenstein for the last twenty years, or so, of his life. The point of view is initially that of an impressionable student-disciple, who admits himself that he neither had the quick-wittedness nor the emotional resources necessary to stand up to his teacher – and who, even when he was in his maturity, had to take steps to avert undue influence from Wittgenstein's powerful, even domineering, personality. They also give us a unique depiction of Wittgenstein's religious sensibility and suggest, in particular, that at least at the time when Drury was his student, the philosopher's religious concerns and attitude to metaphysics were still akin to those originally recorded by Paul Engelmann,[3] whose friendship with Wittgenstein was especially active for a decade after 1916. Drury's personal record challenges – self-consciously so – what he saw as the common misunderstanding of these and some other aspects of Wittgenstein's personality and philosophy within the analytic tradition.

Prior to the publication of this record, Drury had made other attempts to outline his view of Wittgenstein's thought, adopting a different format. One of these was a lecture given at University College, Dublin in 1967, which has not been published previously, in which he tried both 'to turn the attention away from certain common misunderstandings about the man and his work' (instancing J. L. Austin, A. J.

---

[2] *Ibid.*, p. 67.

[3] Paul Engelmann, *Letters from Ludwig Wittgenstein with a Memoir* (Oxford: Blackwell, 1967). The Engelmann/Wittgenstein correspondence began in 1916 and virtually ceased in 1925. Contact with the Engelmann family and its circle of friends re-activated Wittgenstein's latent sense of his own Jewishness.

Ayer and Gilbert Ryle) and 'to see his writings from a new point of view'. On the positive side, Drury wanted to show that in an age marked most of all by scientific progress the central Wittgensteinian philosophical project was to prevent us 'being dazzled by what we know'. Another – his first effort – was made in 1954 in the form of 'Letters to a Student of Philosophy', eventually published in 1983.[4]

To a lesser degree, one can also find in the Drury material Wittgenstein's views on modern psychological approaches to the human personality. Drury was to become a psychiatrist – a choice of career in which he was strongly influenced by Wittgenstein, whom he reveals as sharing an interest in the mentally ill as well. We shall have occasion to indicate later what Drury himself made of his Wittgensteinian inheritance in relation to psychiatry, chiefly as recorded in *The Danger of Words*, his most important work. This book is a collection of lectures on the general theme of what philosophy can bring to medicine, especially psychiatry.

---

[4] 'Letters to a Student of Philosophy', in Desmond Lee (ed.), *Philosophical Investigations*, vol. 6 (1983), pp. 76–102, 159–74. Prior to this edition of the letters, they were copied and circulated privately in America. The 'student of philosophy' was Drury's then two-year-old son, Luke, who is imagined as having entered his second year of University. Luke is perplexed by the lack of a positive doctrine among his philosophy teachers who offer only analytical criticism of other writers' metaphysical theories about the 'great' questions such as the destiny of man, the nature of the real, of goodness, of truth and of beauty. The burden of Drury's advice to his son, for which he claims Wittgenstein's authority, is that the widespread understanding of Wittgenstein as a fellow-traveller and even inspirer of the enemies of metaphysics is fundamentally erroneous. Wittgenstein's critique of traditional metaphysics was designed to protect (not, as commonly understood, undermine) the metaphysical passion for the absolute by locating it where it can be fulfiled – beyond the boundary where language fails us. Access to the metaphysical is indirect: the philosopher is in the same Janus-like situation as a cartographer who in the process of mapping the outline of an oceanic island *pari passu* indicates the expanse of the sea which surrounds it. Many of the secondary discussions that take place in these letters are more fully developed in *The Danger of Words*.

II

The account of their conversations shows Wittgenstein and Drury quickly becoming friends. Wittgenstein questions Drury about how he had come to have an interest in philosophy, enquires about his childhood and confides feeling 'morbid fears' himself during that period of his life. The only cure for such fears, Wittgenstein said, was 'religious feelings'.[5] As the reader can see, quite a lot of their conversation centred around religion. It is clear from the unpublished correspondence between Drury and Rush Rhees, who was one of Wittgenstein's literary executors, that Rhees regarded Drury as Wittgenstein's special intimate in matters religious from the 1930s onwards.[6]

Wittgenstein related to Drury certain crucial incidents connected with the evolution of his own religious sensibility. To begin with, there was a line in Ludwig Anzengruber's *Die Kreuzelschreiber*, a play which he attended in 1910, and which, although not obviously distinguished, spoke directly to him. This Wittgenstein rendered in his *Lecture on Ethics* as 'I am safe, nothing can injure me whatever happens'.[7] Then there was the influence of Tolstoy, whose short version of the Gospels (*The Gospels Briefly Stated*) he read in 1915, during his period of military service in the Austrian army in Galicia (where, incidentally, he met Engelmann). Tolstoy presented Christianity as a radical moral doctrine, summed up in the Sermon on the Mount. The message of spiritual purity as a basis for human community had no need of the

---

[5]   Maurice O'Connor Drury, 'Conversation with Wittgenstein', in Rush Rhees (ed.), *Recollections of Wittgenstein* (Oxford University Press, 1984), p. 100. Henceforth, this is referred to as *C* (cursively in the text mainly). The companion piece, 'Some Notes on Conversations with Wittgenstein', from the same publication, is henceforth referred to as *N*.

[6]   Rhees to Drury, 10 July 1971. This correspondence is in the Drury family.

[7]   Ludwig Wittgenstein, 'A Lecture on Ethics', in *Philosophical Review*, vol. 74 (1965), p. 8. This was Wittgenstein's only formal public lecture and was delivered on 17 November 1929 to the Heretics Society in Cambridge.

scaffolding of dogma. Later, while living as an elementary school teacher in the village of Trattenbach in Lower Austria, Wittgenstein had read *The Brothers Karamazov* aloud to the local priest. Now, he had Drury read it also and *Crime and Punishment* too, as well as Tolstoy's short stories. Wittgenstein told Drury that Tolstoy and Dostoevsky were 'the only two European writers in recent times who really had something important to say about religion' (N, p. 86). It is clear that the important thing to say about religion was that it concerned ethical action – what Wittgenstein customarily referred to as 'decent' behaviour. When a student of Wittgenstein's wrote to tell him that he had converted to Catholicism, Wittgenstein replied: 'If someone tells me he has bought the outfit of a tightrope-walker I am not impressed until I see what is done with it' (N, p. 88). On another occasion he said to Drury: 'If you and I are to live religious lives, it mustn't be that we talk a lot about religion, but that our manner of life is different' (C, p. 114).

Wittgenstein was radical in his views on the basis for Christian faith. When Drury and he discussed the fundamental texts of the Christian tradition, they could agree that the Old Testament canon was 'no more than a collection of Hebrew folklore' (C, p. 100). However, Wittgenstein disagreed with Drury's view that the New Testament books had to be a historical record; it did not really matter, he thought, whether Jesus was a historical figure or not. Indeed, as he later put it, it would be impossible for him 'to say what form the record' of the miracle of God becoming man should take (C, p. 164). Nevertheless, he could not relate to the person revealed in St John's Gospel and preferred St Matthew's Jesus. Similarly, he could not see that St Paul's epistles were 'one and the same religion' (C, p. 165) as that of the Gospels – although he changed his mind about that later in life. If religious belief is not grounded in historical fact, neither can it be based on rational considerations – as the contemporary Cambridge theologian, F. R. Tennant, was trying to do (in his *Philosophical Theology*) by reviving the argument from design, for example. Wittgenstein did not accept that for a religious believer the existence of God, could ever be merely a probability (however high), as Tennant considered it to be. Wittgenstein wanted to steer his friend to Kierkegaard, whom Drury had already come across in quotations in the writings of the Catholic modernist, von Hügel. According to Drury, what Wittgenstein found in Kierkegaard and also in Augustine was a vein of 'negative theology'. This vein is already adumbrated in the last lines of the *Tractatus* – now so often quoted that they seem trite – that 'whereof one cannot speak, thereof one must be silent'. Drury's primary intention in publishing his journal was to alert us to Wittgenstein's views on what religion was – and its importance, so understood, in impelling him to live a decent life. In so doing, Drury also alerts us to the surprising depth and extent of Wittgenstein's acquaintance with classical religious thought and to the remaining ganglia of the religious sensibility of a man once known to his fellow-soldiers as 'the man with the gospels'.

If religious belief is not based on historical fact or philosophical (or indeed theological) reflection, neither is it based on science. James Frazer in *The Golden Bough*, a book Drury obtained at Wittgenstein's request in 1931, had understood the primitive rituals he described as arising partly from the scientific errors of the peoples who celebrated them. This, Wittgenstein said, was itself erroneous. These rituals were created by technically advanced civilizations. In the UCD lecture, Drury asks us to consider, for example, what such people had discovered about agriculture, metal working, architecture, the use of the wheel, and the making of fire. Rather than being a symptom of some lack in their knowledge of how the world works, their rituals expressed their awe and wonder at it. Wittgenstein shared this 'primitive' feeling. As he put in his *Lecture on Ethics*: 'I wonder at the existence of the world. And I am then inclined to use such phrase as "how extraordinary that anything should exist" or "how extraordinary that the world should exist".'[8] He was, in general, disinclined to privilege any religious tradition, finding a

[8]   *Ibid.*

common fundamental experience to respect in all of them, and recommending William James's *Varieties of Religious Experience* to help Drury to see this. Yet, in religion, as in all other areas of life, Wittgenstein wanted to 'teach people differences' – especially where what they wanted to see were similarities.[9]

Wittgenstein's own religious background encompassed many differences. His paternal grandparents were born Jews but both were baptized before their marriage in the Lutheran church, the grandfather perhaps at an early point in his life. His maternal grandfather was reared a Catholic by his mother, who had converted to Catholicism from Judaism. His maternal grandmother was Catholic. Although the family did not see themselves – nor emphatically did they want to see themselves – as Jewish, a relict of that identity still attached to it. Wittgenstein himself was baptized a Catholic and received instruction in that faith. This instruction was not much reinforced in his home and he gave up standard Catholic religious practice as a teenager after discussing the matter with his sister, 'Gretl' (better known as Margarete outside the family). The particular Catholic position that offended him, he told Drury, was that it is possible to prove the existence of God by natural reason. This, he said, involved conceiving of God as just another being, like himself and outside himself – only infinitely more powerful. If this were God, he would regard it as a duty to defy it. Nevertheless, he admired the Latin collects, thought the symbolisms of Catholicism 'wonderful beyond words' (*C*, p. 102) and, unlike Franz Brentano, could even conceive of a meaningful infallible Papal declaration (*C*, p. 130). He himself had prayed during his military service and said he was happy to be compelled to attend Mass during the Italian

---

[9]   *C*, p. 157. Wittgenstein adopted this phrase from *King Lear*, Act I, Scene iv. Drury in a note to Letter 14 of his 'Letters to a Student of Philosophy' says that 'the *Philosophical Investigations* are concerned with insisting on differences where we want to see similarities' (p. 169). Note, however, how in *The Danger of Words* Drury writes: 'it is not given to any man to be an honorary member of all religions' (p. 133).

campaign. Instead of writing, he prayed, when in 1931 he went to stay in Norway, in the hut he had had built there in 1914.

While in Norway, he also wrote down his sins and on his return disclosed them to his friends. Like all the others who read or heard this particular confession of 1931, Drury did not reveal what Wittgenstein confessed to. From a remark Drury later made to Rush Rhees, the latter inferred that Wittgenstein confessed, *inter alia*, to having denied to his headmaster that he had hit a child while teaching in an elementary school in the village of Otterthal in 1926. There was, in fact, a formal investigation of an incident in which Wittgenstein struck a boy of eleven following which the child collapsed. Although Wittgenstein was cleared, he insisted on resigning, which was wise since this appears to have been part of a pattern of abusive behaviour of his pupils. According to Rowland Hutt (who heard a later version of the confession in 1938), Wittgenstein said he had told lies at this investigation as well as simply to the headmaster.[10]

It appears from the testimony of his teacher of Russian, Fania Pascal (to whom he confessed in 1938) that Wittgenstein was also concerned that he had been deceitful to his friends regarding the details of his Jewish family background. He believed he had allowed them to assume that he was one-quarter Jewish and three-quarters Aryan, rather than the reverse – as was to be the technical position, at least, for a family with his bloodlines under the Nuremberg race laws. It is implausible that this 'deception', in precisely these terms, was a live issue in 1931 – but it is clear from other writings that his Jewish identity and its supposed effect on his intellectual style (which he thought he shared with Freud, among others), was already preoccupying him at that time. In his diaries he recorded his struggle with the concept of *'den judishen Geist'* – in which he was probably influenced by his reading of *Sex and Character* (*Geschlecht und Charakter*), by

---

[10] Cf. Ray Monk, *Ludwig Wittgenstein: The Duty of Genius* (Jonathan Cape: London, 1990), p. 370.

Otto Weininger (who killed himself in Beethoven's house in September 1903, four months after his book was published). From the point of view of Wittgenstein's religious sensibility, this feeling of Jewishness seems to have manifested itself in a strong belief in the Last Judgement as a young man and, as an older one, in what he called the 'hundred per cent Hebraic' (C, p. 161) sense that what we do makes a difference in the end. Such a perspective compels taking our actions seriously; there is only one chance at life and an accounting at the end of it. Wittgenstein seems to have had an abiding sense of guilt which he constantly counter-balanced by a renewed resolution to live life decently.

Although clearly imbued by the Gospels and various thinkers within the Christian tradition, Wittgenstein waged what can only be called a campaign to have Drury change his plan, originally influenced by the example of an Anglo-Catholic priest in Exeter (Fr. E. C. Long), to go to Westcott House, the Church of England Theological College, in Cambridge, after graduating, with a view to taking Anglican orders. This plan was shared by at least two of his contemporaries, who were also students of Wittgenstein – John King and Desmond Lee. When Wittgenstein heard of Drury's intentions, he said, 'I can't approve; no, I can't approve. I am afraid that one day that collar would choke you' (C, p. 101). What he seems to have objected to specifically was the 'narrowness' of the Anglican clergy for which William James was a good antidote. Drury probably did not know that Wittgenstein had himself considered taking orders in 1919 – at least, according to a fellow prisoner of war, Franz Parak.[11]

Nevertheless, when Drury did graduate with a First Class Honours degree in 1931, he went to Westcott House but after a year told Wittgenstein that he was abandoning his plan. Wittgenstein, who had undermined Drury's view of a future leading a small village community as its priest, had ready advice for Drury. He was to leave Cambridge now that

---

[11] Cf. Brian McGuinness, *Wittgenstein – A Life: Young Ludwig, 1889–1921* (London: Duckworth, 1988), p. 274.

'a separation had occurred' in his life and 'get among ordinary people of a type that you at present know nothing about' (*C*, p. 121). He cited approvingly the case of another student who had left Westcott House (probably Desmond Lee) who had taken a job in Woolworth's Stores.

III

Drury took his mentor's advice and volunteered to help the Archdeacon of Newcastle to run a club for the unemployed on Tyneside, then in the throes of the Depression. After several months, Drury was no longer needed as the club could survive without him. In imminent prospect of unemployment himself, Drury applied for a job teaching philosophy at Armstrong College, now the University of Newcastle. Wittgenstein agreed that under the circumstances it was the only thing to do and gave him a reference. When Dorothy Emmett won the competition, Wittgenstein was very relieved and later used to say to Drury that he 'owed a great debt to Miss Emmett, in that she had saved [him] ... from becoming a professional philosopher'.[12]

Drury found a position as an assistant to the warden of another unemployment scheme in Merthyr Tydfil in South Wales. Moved by the plight of a friend who had to be admitted to a mental hospital, he determined on becoming a psychiatric nurse. On receiving his application, the Medical Superintendent tried to dissuade him and urged that in view

---

[12] *C*, p. 123. In Fann, *op. cit.*, Drury reflected on why 'Wittgenstein constantly urged his pupils not to take up an academic post and become teachers of philosophy'. Professional philosophers were *ipso facto* under the pressure of:

> having to go on talking when really they knew in their heart that they had nothing of value to say ... Kant said that a great deal of philosophy reminded him of one person holding a sieve while the other tried to milk the he-goat. Wittgenstein wanted above all things to make an end of sieve-holding and he-goat milking.

The reality was that good philosophy emerged only after 'long periods of darkness and confusion when one just had to wait' (p. 69). If a philosopher possesses a marketable skill, he should practise it during such periods. Wittgenstein envied Spinoza, the lens-grinder, for this.

of his education he should train instead as a doctor and later on, presumably, specialize in psychiatry. Drury wrote to Wittgenstein giving an account of these events and received, in reply, a telegram summoning him at once to Cambridge. On his arrival, Drury found that Wittgenstein had already arranged for the financing of his medical education. The money was to be raised by Wittgenstein and 'two wealthy friends' (C, p. 124) – Maynard Keynes and Gilbert Pattisson.[13] Wittgenstein and Drury decided together, after reading the available prospectuses, that Drury should study in Trinity College, Dublin and in due course he enrolled there in 1933.

Drury's brother, Miles, an architect practising in Exeter, had a holiday cottage at Rosro, Salruck, on the Co. Galway side of Killary Harbour, and in September 1934 Drury invited Wittgenstein and his friend, Francis Skinner,[14] to stay there for two weeks. They took the Galway-Clifden railway to Recess, some twenty miles from Rosro. Drury's mother was ending a holiday there and the plan was that the car that took her to the station would provide transport for Wittgenstein's onward journey. Perhaps not surprisingly, Drury's mother had been suspicious of Wittgenstein's influence over her son but was quite won over when she met him at the railway station. As Drury's record shows, the friends ate simply, and were forced to stay indoors (because of rain) where they read aloud to one another and discussed what they had read. In general, Drury makes clear that Wittgenstein had a catholic interest in books – from history to literary fiction to detective stories etc. It is also clear that Wittgenstein was passionately interested in, and knowledgeable about, classical music.

Drury and Wittgenstein shared the Easter holiday of 1935 with Drury's family in Woolacombe in North Devon and Wittgenstein came for a stay in the Drury family home in Exeter in 1936. Wittgenstein, who had earlier told Drury that 'one of the things you and I have to learn is that we have to

---

[13] Ray Monk, *op. cit.*, p. 335.

[14] Skinner was a young, extremely talented mathematics student when Wittgenstein got to know him. He died of polio in 1941.

live without the consolations of belonging to a Church' (*C*, p. 114), now encouraged him to attend church services. Again, in 1949, he recommended to Drury, as a kind of religious experiment, to attend what Wittgenstein considered the more awesome Latin masses in Dublin in comparison to the predominantly low-church Anglican services – even though as a group he preferred the Protestant clergy because they looked less smug than the Roman priests! In August 1936, Wittgenstein (accompanied by Skinner) came to Dublin to holiday with Drury. One diversion was taking photographs with cheap cameras purchased at Woolworth's. Appositely, Drury refers to his journal entries of his conversations with Wittgenstein as 'an album of snapshots taken by an amateur photographer with a mediocre camera' (*C*, p. 98).

That same year, 1936, Wittgenstein wrote to Drury with a most surprising request. He and Skinner were seriously thinking of taking up medical studies and he wanted Drury to enquire at Trinity College, Dublin what the formalities connected with enrolling in the medical school were. In another letter, Wittgenstein suggested that if he did qualify, Drury and he might practise together as psychiatrists, as he felt he might have a 'special talent' for that branch of medicine. From an extant letter to Maynard Keynes, it appears that the plan to become a medical student was originally hatched in 1935 as a means of fulfilling a wish, very difficult to realize, of living in Russia.[15] Nothing came of these enquiries. Later – it is not clear whether this was an explanation for the abandonment of the plan – Wittgenstein told Drury that 'he would not want to undergo a training analysis' (*C*, p. 137).

Although this remark is difficult to understand, because training in psychiatry did not then (no more than it does now) require undergoing a psychoanalysis, it is clear that Wittgenstein's interest in mental illness and its treatment was

[15] Wittgenstein to Keynes (30 June 1935), in *Letters to Russell, Keynes and Moore*, G. H. von Wright (ed.) assisted by B. McGuinness (Oxford: Basil Blackwell, 1974).

sincere and persistent. On the theoretical side, this is shown, for example, by his long-standing engagement with Freud's writings, begun when he read the *Interpretation of Dreams* in 1919 and had his sister Gretl enquire of Freud whether the symbolism in a picture Wittgenstein had seen at an exhibition was, as he believed, oneiric. The interest in Freud is further documented by G. E. Moore, who records two lectures given in 1932 by Wittgenstein on Freud as part of a series on aesthetics.[16] Wittgenstein's interest in Freud is, to a degree, also documented by Drury himself (whose birthday present from Wittgenstein in 1936 was the *Interpretation*) and, most of all, by Rush Rhees who wrote down the substance of a number of conversations he had with Wittgenstein about Freud in 1942, '43 and '46.[17]

Perhaps more revealing of the sincerity of Wittgenstein's interest in psychiatry was his visiting of mentally ill patients during a stay in Dublin from 8 February to the middle of March, 1938. He asked Drury, now a resident at the Royal City of Dublin Hospital, Baggot St., to arrange for these visits.[18] Drury approached Dr R. R. Leeper, the Medical Superintendent of St Patrick's Hospital.[19] After interviewing Wittgenstein, Leeper allowed him to visit long-stay inmates two or three times a week. Of one such inmate – 'certified and chronic' according to Drury – Wittgenstein said memorably: 'this man is more intelligent than his doctors'.[20] He was also

---

[16] 'Wittgenstein's Lectures in 1930–33', *Mind*, vol. 64 (January 1955), pp. 15–21.

[17] In Ludwig Wittgenstein, *Lectures and Conversations on Aesthetics, Psychology and Belief*, ed. Cyril Barrett (Oxford: Basil Blackwell, 1966).

[18] It was probably during this residency that Wittgenstein wrote to Drury the encouraging letter given in *N*, pp. 95–6.

[19] St Patrick's, James's St., Dublin 8, was once popularly known as 'Swift's Hospital' after the Dean who inspired its foundation. Elizabeth Malcolm, in *Swift's Hospital: A History of St. Patrick's Hospital, Dublin, 1746–1989* (Dublin: Gill and Macmillan, 1989) mentions Drury on p. 276 and *passim*.

[20] Maurice O'Connor Drury, *The Danger of Words* (London: Routledge and Kegan Paul, 1973), p. 136, reprinted here. Henceforth *DoW* in text.

very supportive of Drury, who was so lacking in confidence as a young resident that he suffered a disabling tremor when he examined patients.

On one point, Ray Monk finds Drury's account of this 1938 visit 'to the say the least, somewhat strange'.[21] This concerns Wittgenstein's reactions to the events leading up to the *Anschluss*, which finally occurred on 12 March. When Drury told Wittgenstein on 11 March that all the newspapers were reporting that Hitler was poised to invade Austria, Wittgenstein said: 'This is a ridiculous rumour. Hitler doesn't want Austria. Austria would be no use to him at all' (C, p. 139). Monk finds Drury's account strange because it is clear from an entry in Wittgenstein's diary for 16 February that he was already considering changing his nationality in view of a 'further compulsory rapprochement between Austria and Germany'[22] that had taken place on 12 February. Again, when the annexation had in fact taken place, Wittgenstein told Drury that he believed his sisters were quite safe although it is clear from his diary that he was already debating whether he should visit them to check their situation and, furthermore, that he had consulted with his Cambridge economist friend, Piero Sraffa, about whether it would be prudent to do so in view of his Jewish ancestry. In addition, he had enquired of Sraffa about what a change to British citizenship would entail. On receipt of a letter dated 14 March from Sraffa on these matters, which invited him to further discussion, Wittgenstein immediately left Dublin for Cambridge.

It may be, as Monk speculates, that Wittgenstein 'did not wish to add to Drury's burdens'[23] and, further, that this is an example of Wittgenstein's tendency to compartmentalize his friendships. Thus, 'with Drury he discussed religious questions; it was Keynes, Sraffa and Pattisson upon whom he relied for discussion of political and worldly affairs'.[24]

[21] Monk, *op. cit.*, p. 390.

[22] Quoted in Monk, p. 389.

[23] *Ibid.*, p. 391.

[24] *Ibid.*

Leaving aside the fact that Wittgenstein's discussions with Drury are manifestly farther ranging than religion, it seems clear, at least, that Witttgenstein did not intimate to either Drury or Sraffa the deeper concern that (on Monk's account) made him hesitate before going to visit Austria, viz., that he did not want to leave his friend, Francis Skinner. In the event, Wittgenstein managed to reconcile both ties in that he first visited his sisters and on his return to Cambridge moved into Skinner's lodgings.

The foregoing raises a question as to the extent to which Drury had (at this stage) a mature friendship with Wittgenstein rather than a dependent unquestioning relationship that served corresponding needs in his teacher. This leads on to questions about the value of his record, questions that become more insistent in the light of the following: While Drury did not disclose what was contained in Wittgenstein's confession of 1931, he does say that 'it contained nothing about the sexual behaviour ascribed to him in a recent writing' (C, p. 120) – a matter confirmed by the other confessors. When writing that remark, Drury had in mind a then recently published book by William Warren Bartley III, alleging that Wittgenstein was homosexual.[25]

Bartley's thesis was difficult to evaluate at the time for a number of reasons. Firstly, he relied on 'confidential reports from ... friends'[26] – who were unnamed and not directly quoted – to the effect that on Wittgenstein's return from the army to Vienna in 1919 he went compulsively to a known resort of homosexuals to seek partners and that he suffered feelings of guilt on account of this behaviour. Secondly, Bartley wrote that this was corroborated by what he alleged was a successful trawl of the homosexual bars of London and Vienna for erstwhile 'rough young men' and 'tough boys',[27]

---

[25] William Warren Bartley III, *Wittgenstein* (Philadelphia: Lippincott, 1973); the quotations in what follows are from the revised second edition (London: The Cresset Library, 1986).

[26] Bartley, *ibid.*, p. 160.

[27] *Ibid.*, p. 40.

who might have known Wittgenstein – fifty years after the event! Thirdly, Bartley found confirmation in two of Wittgenstein's dream reports, from that period, that he was preoccupied with a conflict over his homosexuality – but Bartley's dream analysis seemed unconvincing to many. Fourthly, Bartley ascribed certain psychological conditions to Wittgenstein , viz., agoraphobia and acrophobia, and ascribed them to conflicts about his sexual behaviour. However, the evidence for attributing these conditions to him was so slight that it would be unreasonable to even have begun to consider an aetiology, which is itself highly questionable in any case.[28] Fifthly, although Bartley did name names – David Pinsent (a young man whom Wittgenstein met at Cambridge, who served as a test pilot in the First World War and was killed in May 1918), and Francis Skinner – there were problems with his evidence: He himself admitted that with regard to the relationship with Pinsent, 'which is often supposed to have been a homosexual one', one could not 'judge with certainty whether [it] involved active sexual relations'.[29] There was no question that Pinsent and Wittgenstein had been friends at Cambridge, and there is some confirmation that Wittgenstein was thought of as homosexual at Cambridge in the shape of

---

[28] *Ibid.*, note, p. 28. Bartley's evidence of agoraphobia is F. R. Leavis's account in Rush Rhees, *Ludwig Wittgenstein: Personal Recollection* (Totowa, N. J.: Rowman & Littlefield, 1981, p. 73; 1984 ed., *op. cit.*, p. 60). Leavis wrote:

> The agoraphobia he more or less avowed to me. We were walking one day on the Grantchester footpath when he said: 'Let's sit down.'... I sat down at once. Wittgenstein said: 'No, not here'. Getting up, I looked at him, and he explained: 'You'll think it strange, but I never sit down in the open'. I said, pointing, 'Look! there's a hawthorn tree halfway down ... That should be all right'. It was, and we went and sat under it.

His evidence for acrophobia is Drury's recounting of Wittgenstein's childhood fears which do not appear to bear on acrophobia at all (cf. p. 115 of the 1981 edition and p. 100 of the 1984 edition). Even Bartley did not agree with A. W. Levi, who attempted to make the case *inter alia* in 'The Biographical Sources of Wittgenstein's Ethics', *Telos*, vol. 38 (Winter 1979), pp. 63–76 that Wittgenstein's philosophy reflects a homosexual orientation in its insistence that 'nothing is hidden'.

[29] *Ibid.*, p. 165.

a reported remark by Bertrand Russell that 'Wittgenstein was witty but a homosexual'[30] – which is remarkable in itself for its baffling disjunction of two attributes not necessarily related in the first place. With regard to Skinner, Bartley was clear that 'active homosexual practice was involved'[31] but there was the counter-evidence of Drury. Sixthly, some members of Wittgenstein's family, many of his friends and most crucially of all, his literary executors, joined in dismissing Bartley's views.

The reason why the position taken up by the literary executors – Rush Rhees and Elizabeth Anscombe – was significant is because Bartley stated that his assertions, both regarding Wittgenstein's general preoccupation with homosexual desire and specific homosexual activity, were verifiable with reference to two notebooks/diaries in coded writing in the archive (to which he had had unexplained access) and which had survived a destruction of such material ordered by Wittgenstein in 1950.[32]

---

[30] Irina Strickland (letter to the *Times Literary Supplement*, 22 February 1974, p. 186) recalled Russell saying this. However, Russell wrote to Lady Ottoline Morrell on 2 May 1912 that Lytton Strachey and others were 'thinking of electing' Wittgenstein to the Cambridge Conversazione Society (the 'Apostles') but that 'I told them I didn't think he would like the Society.... It would seem to him stuffy, as indeed it has become, owing to their practice of being in love with each other...' (quoted in McGuinness's *Life*, *op. cit.*, p. 118). Again, it was difficult to be convinced by Bartley's adducing as evidence of Wittgenstein's homosexuality a question to G. E. Moore by Richard Curle and Iris Wedgwood about Wittgenstein's 'being normal (about women)' (Bartley, p. 164).

[31] Bartley, *op. cit.*, p. 165.

[32] Further to a review of Bartley's book in the *Times Literary Supplement* (17 August 1973), Elizabeth Anscombe wrote (16 November 1973) asking Bartley to indicate (*inter alia*) the nature of his sources. An exchange of letters with Bartley ensued, involving in addition to Anscombe (who wrote again on 4 and 18 January 1974), Brian McGuinness (18 January 1974) and F. A. von Hayek (8 February 1974). This correspondence is more notable for the heat generated than the light shed on the question of Bartley's sources. In similar vein to Anscombe, Rush Rhees introduced a long and diffuse review of Bartley's book in *The Human World*, vol. 14 (February 1974) with the rhetorical question: 'what standards guided the publishers and the editor when they brought this book out and sponsored it?' (p. 67). Wittgenstein's sister, Margarete Stonborough, also got involved. She interviewed Bartley's interpreter, Helmut Kasper, regarding

There the matter stood until the appearance of Ray Monk's biography. Monk has found evidence that seems to corroborate Bartley – at least in one respect – and this bears directly on Drury's testimony. During the time that Drury knew them, it appears that Wittgenstein was indeed sexually attracted to Skinner and that according to a 1937 entry in Wittgenstein's diary, he 'lay with [Skinner] two or three times. Always at first with the feeling that there was nothing wrong in it, *then* with shame.'[33]

Drury stated in a letter to the *Times Literary Supplement* that, as a psychiatrist, it was 'in the nature of my work to be alert to problems of homosexuality whether latent or active', that Bartley was 'in error when he supposes that Wittgenstein was at any time "tormented by homosexual behaviour"' and that 'sensuality in any form was entirely foreign to his ascetic personality'.[34] Perhaps Wittgenstein compartmentalized that part of his life from Drury, who was not, of course, at the time of Skinner's friendship with Wittgenstein, a qualified, not to say, a practising psychiatrist. However, the case that Bartley makes about the younger Wittgenstein remains moot and Monk is probably right in thinking that Bartley overstated the degree to which Wittgenstein was sexually active at that point in his life. On the other hand, it must be said that Bartley did

---

Bartley's research during a six week stay in Vienna in 1969 but these enquiries too shed little light on the basis for Bartley's assertions. Bartley wrote that another family member, one of Wittgenstein's nephews, took a different view of his work. This nephew had written to congratulate him on his 'superb job in ferreting out sources' (*TLS*, 11 January 1974, p. 32). It may be that Bartley was referring to Margarete's son, Thomas Stonborough, with whom (as his mother had ascertained from Kasper) Bartley had had a short interview.

[33] Monk, *op. cit.*, p. 376.

[34] Drury to the *Times Literary Supplement* (22 February 1974), p. 186. Wittgenstein's nephew, Major John J. Stonborough, commenting in *The Human World* (*op. cit.*) on what he called Bartley's 'farrago of lies and poppycock' also wrote of Wittgenstein's asceticism: 'L. W. was an ascetic and that is as yet no crime' (p. 84). Rush Rhees, in his review (*op. cit.*) noted 'Wittgenstein's regard for women and, at certain times, his love for a woman' (p. 78). Monk, *op. cit.*, recounts that one of Wittgenstein's friends, Rowland Hutt, understood Wittgenstein to tell him that 'as a young man he had had sexual relations with a woman' (p. 369).

make a valuable attempt to link Wittgenstein's life and thought – and that he was successful in this project at least in regard to the connection between Wittgenstein's activities and interests as a primary school teacher and his later interest in language acquisition, primitive languages, and private languages.

IV

On qualifying as a doctor in 1939, Drury worked as a general practitioner for a few months in the Welsh Rhondda Valley and was playing host to Wittgenstein and Skinner on the day that war broke out. Soon, Drury joined the Royal Army Medical Corps, serving first in England (at Yeovil) before he was posted to Egypt. Wittgenstein and Skinner came to Liverpool to wish him farewell and Wittgenstein presented him with a silver cup, remarking that 'water tastes so much nicer out of silver'.[35] The war years separated the two friends; they tried to keep in touch through correspondence. From November 1941 to April 1943, Wittgenstein added weekday work as a laboratory assistant in Guy's Hospital, London, to his regular duties as Professor of Philosophy at Cambridge (which he discharged on alternate Saturdays) and thereafter, until early 1944, went to Newcastle to work on the physiology of shock in a psychological laboratory under Dr R. T. Grant. Drury visited him there and Wittgenstein showed him an apparatus he had designed for measuring pulse pressure.

Wittgenstein returned to Cambridge (and philosophy) in early 1944. After Drury had left that university in the early 1930s, Wittgenstein would never allow Drury to discuss with him his current work[36] but Drury retained an interest in philosophy. Thus, while in Egypt, Drury read F. H. Bradley's

---

[35] Fann, *op. cit.*, p. 67.

[36] In the 'Conversations' (first published in 1981), Drury explained: 'I think he felt that his own thinking was so much more developed than mine that there was a danger of swamping me and my becoming nothing but a pale echo of himself' (p. 97).

Essays on Truth and Reality, a book he bought in Cairo, and found it very stimulating. Drury snatched a visit in Swansea with Wittgenstein before taking up his D-Day posting in France and, on parting, Wittgenstein passed on the Beatitudinal (and Tolstoyan) advice: 'if it ever happens that you get mixed up in hand-to-hand fighting, you must just stand aside and let yourself be massacred' (C, p. 149).

After being demobbed, Drury worked as a house physician in a hospital in Taunton. He was taking time to consider his future in medicine and deliberately avoided Wittgenstein during this period, for fear of being influenced by him. Nevertheless, he eventually did as Wittgenstein had planned for him in 1933. In 1947, he took up a position as Resident Psychiatrist in St Patrick's Hospital in Dublin under Dr J. N. P. Moore. Meanwhile, Wittgenstein was also considering his future. On 27 August he wrote to Norman Malcolm, a former student now teaching Philosophy at Cornell University in Ithaca, New York, that 'my mind is rather in a turmoil these days. I am almost certain that I shall resign my professorship in the Autumn.'[37] Wittgenstein wanted to prepare his second book, *Philosophical Investigations*, for publication and to do this he needed to be free of the distraction of people. He considered going to live in either Norway (where he had done philosophical work before the First World War)

---

[37] Wittgenstein to Malcolm in Norman Malcolm, *Ludwig Wittgenstein: A Memoir, with a Biographical Sketch by G. H. von Wright*, new edition with Wittgenstein's letters to Malcolm (Oxford University Press, 1984), p. 103. Wittgenstein expressed reservations about becoming a professor: On 27 March 1939 he wrote to William Eccles: 'having got the professorship is very flattering and all that but it might have been very much better for me to have got a job opening and closing crossing gates' (Wittgenstein to Eccles in W. Eccles, 'Some Letters of Ludwig Wittgenstein', in *Hermathena* vol. 97 (1963), p. 65). Wittgenstein met Eccles, an already qualified engineer, when he was a student of aeronautical engineering at Manchester University. Eccles writes that 'Wittgenstein ... visited my Coleraine home with me before the 1914–18 war' (p. 64). It seems almost impossible now to date this (presumably first) visit to Ireland more precisely. For more on the Irish connection and related themes cf. John Hayes, 'Wittgenstein, Religion, Freud, and Ireland', in *Irish Philosophical Journal*, vol. 6 (1989), pp. 191–249.

or Ireland. Having visited Drury in Dublin in August, he returned to Cambridge clear that he should resign his professorship but still undecided about his future country of residence. He then visited his home in Vienna, a city now occupied by the Russians, and found the experience bleak beyond words. On his return, he resigned his professorship (effective 31 December 1947) and after spending a month working on the philosophy of psychology, his major philosophical preoccupation for the last period of his life, prepared to move to Dublin.

Wittgenstein arrived in Dublin at the end of November 1947, stayed at Ross's Hotel (now rebuilt as the 'Ashling') for a few days and from 9 December lodged as farmhouse guest of the Kingston family at Kilpatrick House in Red Cross (near Arklow), Co. Wicklow. At first, he seems to have found life congenial, especially the walks offered by the beautiful countryside.[38] Drury visited him there regularly. In early 1948, it was clear that all was not well with Wittgenstein. He was suffering from indigestion. In February he wrote to Malcolm that he occasionally had 'queer states of nervous instability'.[39] In April, he wrote to Rhees that he had suffered 'terrible depressions' for six to eight weeks and that this experience had been followed by a 'bad flu'.[40] He came to Dublin to see Drury and told him that he could not work; 'the continual murmur of the people in the room underneath his', talking late at night, was driving him 'crazy' (C, p. 155). Drury gave him some sleeping tablets and suggested that he

---

[38] For a good account of Wittgenstein's life with the Kingstons cf. George Hetherington, 'A Sage in Search of a Pool of Darkness', in the *Irish Times* (26 April 1989), p. 12. Maria Bagramian's article, 'Ireland in the life of Ludwig Wittgenstein', in *Hermathena*, vol. 144 (1988), pp. 69–83 is also particularly helpful on this period of Wittgenstein's life. It would appear that Wittgenstein greatly exaggerated the degree to which the Kingstons contributed to his condition.

[39] Wittgenstein to Malcolm (5 February 1948) in Norman Malcolm, *op. cit.*, p. 106.

[40] Wittgenstein to Rhees, 15 April 1948. Quoted in Hetherington's *Irish Times* article, *op. cit.*

go to Rosro – an offer which Wittgenstein promised to consider.

Although Drury did not publish the fact, it was probably at this time that he referred Wittgenstein to his chief at St Patrick's, Norman Moore, who saw him in St Patrick's on five or six occasions 'in the late 1940s'. These consultations seem to have had an informal character. They met as friends rather than as doctor and patient. According to Moore, Wittgenstein appeared a 'depressed and sad man'. He spoke 'slowly', was 'down with depressed affect', 'slowed down' and 'gloomy'.[41] From the evidence presented in his biographies and elsewhere, it is clear that this was very far from the first

---

[41] Norman Moore is quoted to this effect by the editors of this book, Michael Fitzgerald and David Berman, who interviewed him on 12 November 1993. This was in a letter to *Nature*, vol. 368 (10 March 1994), p. 92, which was in belated response to one written by J. R. Smythies (National Hospital for Neurology and Neurosurgery, Queen Square, London) in the same journal (vol. 350, 7 March 1991, p. 9). Smythies' letter was itself part of a debate begun between John C. Marshall (Neuropsychology Unit, University Department of Clinical Neurology, The Radcliffe Infirmary, Oxford) and A. J. Greenfield (Department of Biochemistry and Molecular Genetics, St Mary's Hospital Medical School, London). Marshall had written in a review of Theodore Redpath, *Ludwig Wittgenstein: A Student's Memoir* (London: Duckworth, 1990) in *Nature*, vol. 347 (4 October 1990), p. 435, that Wittgenstein had created at Trinity a 'superheated circus' – *à la* Schnitzer at the Café Griensteidl – for 'students in a strange land who would be incapable of understanding who he was and what he taught' and that 'one of the profound mysteries of the twentieth century' was 'how did a minor Viennese aphorist come to be regarded (in some circles) as a great philosopher who had twice changed the course of the discipline?'. In vol. 348 (29 November 1990), p. 384, Greenfield tried to offer a 'few remarks...[to] help towards a more balanced view of Wittgenstein's work than that allowed by Marshall's sadly vacuous "hatchet job"'. This was a futile exercise if one is to judge from Marshall's response to Greenfield in the same issue, in which he tried to quote Wittgenstein against himself: 'nothing seems to me less likely than that a scientist or mathematician who reads me should be seriously influenced in the way he works' (*Culture and Value*). It was at this point that Smythies joined the fray, claiming that Marshall had suggested an alternative view of Wittgenstein to that of 'great philosopher' viz.,

> as just one of a long line of German-speaking philosophers (such as Hegel and Heidegger) who have dazzled some innocent English-speaking philosophers by writing material whose basic nonsense is concealed by the impenetrable thickets of the German language

occasion on which Wittgenstein suffered from depression. Brian McGuinness makes some allusive statements[42] that suggest a higher than average incidence of manic depression in families with a background similar to that of the Wittgenstein family and also that Wittgenstein's mood swings might need to be described as cyclothymic or otherwise accounted for. At the same time, McGuinness also appears to suggest that Wittgenstein's early depressions were of no clinical importance. Drury does not use the terms 'manic

and that Smythies was now proposing a third hypothesis as follows:

> Russell in his autobiography (among others) draws attention to Wittgenstein's schizoid and paranoid personality. Canon C. E. Raven (who was vice-chancellor of the University of Cambridge during Wittgenstein's tenure of his chair there) told me that Wittgenstein at times actually suffered from paranoid delusions and would flee to outlying villages to escape from his imaginary enemies

and went on to inform the reader that 'certain schizoid personalities develop the ability to write in a form of speech disorder known as schizophrenese'. He gives the example of Joyce in *Finnegan's Wake* (though he was 'never overtly schizophrenic, although very schizoid') before stating that Wittgenstein's philosophical writing exhibits the same tendency to a 'singular degree'. The popular and not so popular press then took up the matter. *The Sunday Telegraph* (no. 1,554, 10 March 1991) ran a front-page story from its science correspondent headed: 'Revealed: the great philosopher was just a nutcase'. This belongs to what is now a genre of psychiatric diagnoses of various philosophers – at a distance. In respect of Wittgenstein himself, there had been the claim by Charles Hanly that in his remarks on Freud, Wittgenstein exhibited an 'unconscious need for psychoanalytic therapy' ('Wittgenstein on Psychoanalysis', in Alice Ambrose and Morris Lazerowitz (eds.), *Ludwig Wittgenstein: Philosophy and Language* (London: George Allen and Ltd, 1972), p. 941). Some other instances are mentioned in these notes. A defence of Wittgenstein against Smythies appeared in an editorial in *The Times* (Monday, 11 March 1991) entitled 'Witlessgenstein' stating that 'it has taken a lesser modern wisdom to slur with the charge of insanity the wit and wisdom of Wittgenstein' (p. 13). For a poignant aspect of Smythies' intervention, cf. note 57 *infra*.

[42] McGuinness, *op. cit.*, pp. 23 and 156–7. On p. 23, McGuinness writes:

> intermarriage has tended to produce among Jews a higher incidence of scientific and musical gifts and of the manic-depressive psychosis, so in this one instance what Karl and Poldy (Wittgenstein's parents) had inherited and transmitted ... conspired to form a generation of human beings remarkable much more for the exceptional gifts distributed among it than for its capacity to achieve harmony and happiness.

depression' nor 'cyclothymia' at all. *A fortiori*, he does not speculate about the aetiology of Wittgenstein's depression although the history of Wittgenstein's fraternal siblings and perhaps the pattern of behaviour towards his pupils that marked Wittgenstein's career as a primary school-teacher – if it were known to him or Norman Moore – might have given cause for alarm.[43]

On pp. 156–7 (regarding a typical diary entry expressing Wittgenstein's discontent), McGuinness states:

> no psychiatrist would regard it as a clinical indication of importance. [William] James suggests that those whom it [feeling discontent] oppresses to the degree that Tolstoy and Wittgenstein were oppressed have a lower 'misery threshold' than others. It does not matter here whether this linear model is adequate, whether we have to supplement it by allowing for fluctuations in the threshold – cyclothymia – or replace it by some account that allows the same nature, in some cases, to be the most easily depressed and the most easily elated.

In his review of McGuinness's biography, Stephen Toulmin (*Times Literary Supplement*, no. 4,457, 2–8 September 1988, pp. 947–8) takes McGuinness to task for being

> unwilling to recognize how far Wittgenstein's afflictions were self-generated, and might have been open to therapeutic intervention ... I have no doubt that – however much he dislikes the idea – McGuinness will see his work made a starting point for useful essays on perfectionism and the pathology of 'grandiosity'.

According to Bartley (*op. cit.*, p. 110), Wittgenstein had to undergo a psychiatric examination in 1926 as part of the investigation into the incident in the elementary school in Otterthal when Wittgenstein struck a pupil.

[43] Three of Wittgenstein's four brothers committed suicide: Hans, in 1902, in mysterious circumstances in the Chesapeake bay; Rudi in 1903 (by drinking cyanide in milk), in grief over the death of a homosexual partner, and Kurt because of a subjective feeling of loss of military honour probably arising from having lost control over his troops in a disintegrating Austrian army in 1918. Of Kurt, Wittgenstein himself wrote to Eccles on 7 May 1925 that he 'was in the army' and 'was killed' (Eccles, *op. cit.*, p. 62). In the first part of his biography, which covers only the first thirty-two years of his life, McGuinness documents Ludwig's suicidal thoughts going back as far as the age of ten or eleven (p. 48). Later, McGuinness records, Wittgenstein told his friend, David Pinsent, that he had had thoughts of committing suicide continually for nine years (p. 50). Sometimes, such thoughts arose because of difficulty with his work, sometimes because of difficulties with relationships – or grief because of the loss of a friend – and sometimes, because of a sense of futility about life itself.

On 28 April, after spending Easter with the Kingstons in Co. Wicklow, Wittgenstein went to the Drury cottage in Connemara. His needs were tended to by a family retainer, Tommy Mulkerrins, who seems to have been appraised by Drury that Wittgenstein 'had suffered a nervous breakdown'.[44] Wittgenstein preferred Mulkerrins to the Kingstons. Each day, Wittgenstein had him remove and burn large piles of rejected manuscript material – an indication that Wittgenstein was working very hard. Wittgenstein kept aloof from the local people, who formed a negative impression of him, and had few visitors. The journey was too far for Drury, who had a demanding hospital schedule to fulfil. Ben Richards, a friend, who was a medical student, and an Indian student, K. J. Shah, later Professor at Dharwar University, did visit but of Shah he wrote to Malcom that their conversation was not 'good' and he added that he was sorry to have to say that he was 'often tired and irritable now'.[45]

In August, Wittgenstein went for a few days to Dublin, thence to England, and spent most of the month of September in Vienna with his family, finishing off his trip with two weeks in Cambridge, which were spent dictating from his manuscripts what has now been published as *Remarks on the Philosophy of Psychology* (1980). He returned to Dublin

---

The vicissitudes of war helped him – an effect so common as to appear in a lowered statistical incidence of suicide during war. On at least one occasion, he himself put his condition down to the fact that he had no faith (p. 293). Of the attraction of Freud he said to Rush Rhees in 1946:

> many people have at some period, serious troubles in their lives – so serious as to lead to thoughts of suicide. This is likely to appear to one as something nasty, as a situation which is too foul to be subject of a tragedy. And it may then be an immense relief if it can be shown that one's life has the pattern rather of a tragedy – the tragic working out and repetition of a pattern which was determined by a primal scene. ('Conversations on Freud' in Barrett, *op. cit.*, p. 51).

But the '100% Hebraic' Wittgenstein would hardly have accepted such 'relief'.

[44] Joseph Mahon, 'The Great Philosopher Who Came to Ireland', in *The Irish Medical Times*, vol. 20, no. 7 (14 February 1986), p. 32.

[45] Wittgenstein to Malcolm (5 July 1948) in Malcolm, *op. cit.*, p. 112.

with the intention of returning to Rosro but Drury was apprehensive of his spending the winter in Connemara. Instead, Wittgenstein again booked into Ross's Hotel – a short walk across Kingsbridge to St Patrick's Hospital, where Drury was working. Thereafter, Drury and he met almost daily, often strolling in the Zoological Gardens in the nearby Phoenix Park, where they discussed the great philosophers. Obviously, this was not sufficient for Wittgenstein because he wrote to Malcolm about this time that 'I think I could still discuss philosophy if I had someone here to discuss with, but alone I can't concentrate on it'.[46] Drury's insufficiency in this regard is not surprising as his understanding of Wittgenstein is rooted in the *Tractatus*; and there is no evidence in his writings of an appreciation – sometimes even an awareness – of the later Wittgensteinian puzzles about private language (and the associated ones about consciousness, thought, and imagination), solipsism, rule-following, or of the debates about his relationship to logical behaviourism or therapeutic positivism.[47] However, Wittgenstein was not altogether bereft of philosophical interlocutors nor, to judge from the results, was work wholly impossible: He was visited at Ross's by

---

[46] Wittgenstein to Malcolm, 1 April 1949, *ibid.*, p. 119.

[47] In a letter to Rush Rhees (May 1966), in Lee, *op. cit.*, Drury listed a number of Wittgenstein's remarks from the 1916–18 *Notebooks* and wrote:

> when I left Cambridge it was ideas like this that I felt were for me the essence of what Wittgenstein had taught me. And these conceptions have remained central with me ever since ... Thus when the *Investigations* came out I read them with these fixed ideas in mind, and still do. But am I right? I sometimes have the feeling that I have completely misunderstood the *Investigations* ... The remarks from the *Notebooks* ... are for me more revealing than anything in the *Investigations* ... and I have tried to see the *Investigations* as more detailed exposition of just such conceptions. If philosophy is not an attempt to state the '*Wesen der Welt*' then, I feel lost. And yet I also have the feeling that such a phrase ... would be foreign to the diction of the *Investigations*. Again the thought of the self as not a part of the world but a boundary of the world is one that I keep coming to with wonder and certainty. And then once again this is not stated in the *Investigations*; am I right in thinking that it is there shown? (*Philosophical Investigations*, vol. 6, *op. cit.*, p. 174).

Elizabeth Anscombe (who stayed for two weeks) and Rush Rhees, both professional philosophers.

If Drury was worried about Wittgenstein's health, Wittgenstein, for his part, believed that Drury was too single-minded in his pursuit of hospital duties and had to help him handle a crisis when he lost his temper at an alcoholic patient whose behaviour was abusive. Wittgenstein welcomed the new methods of physical treatment for psychological illnesses; Drury was involved in the introduction to St Patrick's of lithium as a treatment for manic depression – but, true to his master's principles, tried to establish the parameters appropriate to such interventions. He was to become very interested in the treatment of phobias by hypnosis. Wittgenstein had had himself hypnotized while a student in Cambridge to enable him to concentrate better on his work on the foundations of mathematics. In the event, he could not be hypnotized 'during the session but fell into a deep trance the moment it was over'.[48] Drury wrote an unpublished treatise on hypnosis, *Introductory Lectures on Hypnosis,* which, while being thoroughly competent, does not exhibit any special originality. In a general way, Wittgenstein gave excellent advice to Drury the blossoming psychiatrist: 'let your patients feel they have time to talk to you' (C, p. 154).

There is evidence that Wittgenstein socialized with some of Drury's colleagues – Dr Tim McCracken, in particular. Dr McCracken says he introduced Wittgenstein to the Royal Irish Yacht Club in Dun Laoghaire and to Professor T. G. Moorhead of the Trinity College Medical School,[49] who gave weekly dinner parties at the club. Paddy Lynch, Emeritus Professor of Political Economy at University College, Dublin, recalls dining once with Wittgenstein as fellow guests of Moorhead. Further to an enquiry as to whether any records still existed at the RIYC that might help date this occasion, the answer was that 'the only records that might have existed

---

[48] McGuinness, *op. cit.,* p. 29.

[49] Letter of 24 January 1990 from Mrs Eileen McCracken on behalf of Dr Tim McCracken.

would have been entries to the Visitor's Book.   But these books were never preserved.'[50]   In the article, written by George Hetherington, where this information first came to light, Professor Lynch recalled driving Moorhead (who had been blinded in an accident at Euston Station, London, in 1926) to Ross's Hotel when, on one occasion in late 1948, Moorhead's dinner at the club was interrupted by a sick call. Moorhead did not disclose the identity of his patient to Prof. Lynch although Hetherington is 'almost certain'[51] it was Wittgenstein.

Ray Monk writes that Wittgenstein consulted a doctor (unnamed) in January, who diagnosed gastro-enteritis, and Professor Lynch has since written that he may have conveyed Moorhead to Ross's at the beginning of 1949 rather than the end of 1948.[52]   What we do know is that Wittgenstein felt weak and in pain in February and was unable to work after March.   In April, he visited his sister, Hermine ('Mining'), who was dying, in Vienna.   On his return, Drury advised him to consult Moorhead.   It is, however, difficult to read Drury's

[50] Private communication (29 May 1990) from Judge James J. MacMahon who kindly made this enquiry of the Commodore of the RIYC, Judge Robert Barr.

[51] George Hetherington, 'Wittgenstein in Ireland: An Account of His Various Visits from 1934–49', in *Irish University Review*, vol. 17, no. 2 (1987), p. 183.   On p. 179 of this article we read that when the poet Richard Murphy took up residence in the cottage at Rosro that had been occupied by Wittgenstein, he made a 'chance discovery of the identity of the earlier tenant of the house' in the form of a letter beginning 'Dear Wittgenstein' and signed 'Isaiah Berlin'.   Perhaps it makes no difference to the value of the sonnet 'Killary Hostel' (in *The Price of Stone*, London: Faber, 1985), which celebrates this 'discovery' but on 29 May 1990, Sir Isaiah Berlin, wrote to the present author, who was anxious to get details of this correspondence, as follows:

> I can assure you that I have never in my life written a letter to Ludwig Wittgenstein, nor received any communication from him.

On 15 July 1993, President Mary Robinson unveiled a plague commemorating Ludwig Wittgenstein at the cottage in Rosro, now the Killary Harbour Youth Hostel.   On 16 May 1988, on the initiative of George Hetherington, a plaque was unveiled at the Ashling Hotel, commemorating Wittgenstein's stay at its predecessor, Ross's Hotel.

[52] Monk, *op cit.*, p. 539; Lynch, private communication of 22 January 1990.

record of what Wittgenstein said to him when he agreed to this consultation as other than a first meeting (professionally – or even of any kind) with Moorhead: 'Yes, I will go and see this man; only I want you to tell him I am a man of intelligence who likes to be told exactly what is found wrong – to have things explained to me frankly' (*C*, p. 167). The investigation (in hospital) found 'a severe anaemia of a rather unusual kind'[53] – but the X-ray definitely showed no stomach tumour, as had been feared.

On 29 January 1949, Wittgenstein wrote that 'Drury, I think, is growing more and more unfaithful. He has found friends with whom he can live more easily.'[54] Yet, Drury saw that Wittgenstein's medical needs were attended to, ensured that he was supplied with books, and continued to converse with him about the great philosophers, whom Wittgenstein categorized as 'deep' (Kant and Berkeley) and 'shallow' (Schopenhauer) and also, more and more, about religion. Wittgenstein's time in Ireland was drawing to a close. Lured by the promise of intellectual stimulation, he decided to visit Norman Malcolm in America.

Monk recounts that on what would have been one of their last evenings together in Ireland (13 June 1949) Wittgenstein and Drury listened to a BBC Third Programme, which was a discussion between A. J. Ayer and Frederick Copleston, the Jesuit historian of philosophy. What is certain, however, from the BBC archives, is that this programme was not about 'The Existence of God', as Monk has it, but 'Logical Positivism'. Drury does indeed mention listening with Wittgenstein to a radio discussion on 'The Existence of God' between Ayer and Copleston but dates it to '1948' (*C*, p. 159). Monk, however, redates Drury's record to June 1949. There had indeed been another discussion in the series about 'The Existence of God' in 1948 (on 28 January), but while Copleston was a discussant on that occasion, Ayer was not; the other speaker was Bertrand Russell. This instance can

---

[53] Wittgenstein to Malcolm (4 June 1949) in Malcolm, *op. cit.*, p. 119.

[54] Quoted in Monk, *op. cit.*, p. 539.

only make us cautious not only about Drury's dating but, even more, his accuracy. To be fair, he warned that his dating is reliable only insofar as the entries are given in chronological order – and even that is in question here – and as to the substance of what is reported he reminds us that the 'memory, even the most recent, is deceitful' (C, p. 98).

Wittgenstein departed Ireland for what was to be the last time on or about 18 June. He left behind him half a dozen books, including (as Rhees remembers it) a second hand school edition of Livy and memories for just a few people. Wittgenstein became very ill in America. However, a definite diagnosis of cancer of the prostate was not made until after his return to England in October 1949. The diagnosis was arrived at by a former army medical colleague of Drury's, Dr Edward Bevan, on 25 November. Hormone therapy and X-ray treatment were prescribed but fourteen months later, at the beginning of February 1951, Wittgenstein accepted an offer to move into Bevan's home in Cambridge to die. Drury visited him there in April on his way home from his honeymoon in Italy; he had married Eileen Stewart, matron of St Patrick's. Wittgenstein insisted on accompanying him to the railway station. Wittgenstein's last words to Drury were: 'whatever becomes of you, don't stop thinking' (C, p. 170).

Back in Dublin a few days, Drury was recalled by Dr Bevan at Wittgenstein's request. On arrival, he found that Wittgenstein was already unconscious and dying. Other friends had assembled: Elizabeth Anscombe, Yorick Smythies and (now Dr) Ben Richards. A Dominican priest, Fr. Conrad Pepler (son of a close associate of Eric Gill), who had paid a pastoral visit in Oxford to Wittgenstein, at the latter's request, the previous year, and had instructed the converts Anscombe and Smythies in the Catholic faith, was also present. Drury recounts how the group decided on praying the Office for the Dying and having conditional absolution pronounced by Pepler on the basis of his recollection that Wittgenstein had once expressed the hope that 'his Catholic friends prayed for him' (C, p. 171). Drury also provided the information which led to the subsequently controversial decision to bury Wittgenstein according to the rites of the Roman Catholic Church.

The nature of the information was that Wittgenstein had once told Drury he approved of Tolstoy (described as a 'stern critic of the Russian Orthodox Church') (C, p. 171), having his brother interred according to the Orthodox rite. As related by Drury, this seems to be an example of Tolstoy respecting the religious affiliation of his deceased brother, despite his own reservations. Ray Monk observes that it is doubtful whether 'the story about Tolstoy quite fits the occasion'[55] since Wittgenstein had said from time to time, including to Drury, that he could not believe what Catholics believe and since, furthermore, he was not a practising Catholic. And, indeed, afterwards, Drury was troubled by what his words had facilitated.

However, in getting it wrong, the chief mourners were closer to the truth of the Tolstoy case than they, or Wittgenstein, apparently knew. In 1904, Tolstoy (by then, in fact, an excommunicate) had his brother, Sergey Nikoloyevich, buried according to the Orthodox rite even though, as Tolstoy writes in his diary (26 August), so far as he could judge, 'effective religious feeling was denied'[56] to Sergey. It seems unlikely, however, that this is the action that Wittgenstein was praising, and thus ironic that what he miscited as an exemplary act by Tolstoy, was apparently re-produced in his own case.

V

By all accounts, Drury was a very hard-working psychiatrist. From 1951, he worked not only in St Patrick's but also in a subsidiary nursing home – generally for well-off patients – St

---

[55] Monk, p. 580.

[56] *Tolstoy's Diaries*, vol. 2, 1895–1910, edited and translated by R. F. Christian (London: The Athlone Press, 1985), p. 528 (entry for 26 August 1904).

Edmundsbury's, in Lucan, Co. Dublin. He treated the wife
of the physicist Erwin Schrodinger (who was a professor at the
Dublin Institute for Advanced Studies and whose successor is
now Drury's son, Luke) for depression and also Yorick
Smythies, one of the close friends assembled around
Wittgenstein's death-bed, for schizophrenia.[57]

Drury gave lectures on psychology to medical students in
Trinity College and in the Royal College of Surgeons, in St
Stephen's Green. Apparently, his style of delivery did not
make his material especially attractive to his student audience.
One student of his (Michael Fitzgerald) has written:

> I have a sense of him in real life as an intellectual. While
> he worked very long hours and was extremely committed
> to his patients, he also had a very active intellectual life,
> especially in the area of philosophy and its relationship to
> psychiatry. In later life, this was particularly expressed in
> a very intense correspondence between Rush Rhees and
> himself. As he spoke, one was aware of quite an intellectual
> man, who was very much speaking and relating to an
> audience as an intellectual.

In 1969, Drury was promoted Consultant Psychiatrist and in
1973 published *The Danger of Words*, which was based on
his non-academic lectures to a medical club. It must be said
that, whatever the delivery, they read very well indeed. Ray
Monk describes this book as 'the most truly Wittgensteinian
work published by any of Wittgenstein's students'.[58] That is
not so easy to see in the detail of it – and Wittgenstein is not

---

[57] The source of this information is Prof. Frank Cioffi of the Department of
Philosophy, University of Essex. On 10 March 1989, he wrote:

> I have been familiar with Dr Drury's name since my undergraduate days
> through my friendship with someone who knew Drury, and like him,
> had been an intimate of Wittgenstein's – Yorick Smithies ... I didn't hear
> of Drury again until Smythies went to consult him about his (Smythies')
> schizophrenic episodes.

J. R. Smythies writes in his letter to *Nature*, *supra* that he was a 'cousin'
of Yorick Smythies.

[58] Monk, *op. cit.*, p. 264.

much quoted in the book.[59] Clearly, however, the project, indicated by the title, to get us to reflect on the place language occupies in 'our life' – the plural refers primarily to those engaged in medical practice, particularly psychiatry – is Wittgensteinian. He writes in the belief that 'a natural science which is not subjected to philosophical criticism becomes blind' (*DoW*, p. 99).

Pursuant to this belief, Drury engages the themes developed out of his favourite tractarian texts and applies them to psychiatry. The conjectural nature of scientific knowledge, the boundlessness of reality, and the corresponding necessity not to make of science – nor the scientist – a god, are discussed. Psychological science is especially tentative because the observer is also subject. Drury sees special difficulty arising from the fact that, necessarily, one is using one's mind to explore the mind. Consequently, psychology is not very advanced. Neither is neurophysiology. With regard to the latter, he rejects the view that psychological experience can be correlated in an exact way with brain activity. His understanding of the body/mind relationship is dualistic, positing a noumenal mind/soul. This clears the path for his subscription to the Lamarckian thesis that the inheritance of acquired psychological characteristics is possible. Any detailed theses, however, are proposed very tentatively. He keeps reminding his readers that mental phenomena are intractable. Such knowledge as we have is drawn from a never diminishing pool of mystery.

Drury's main method of keeping in touch with the Wittgenstein inheritance was through his voluminous correspondence with Rush Rhees, previously mentioned. Nevertheless, and although the influence is much more difficult to document, Drury said himself that 'after Wittgenstein's death I became acquainted with the writings of Simone Weil. These have had as profound an influence on my subsequent thought as Wittgenstein had had on my earlier life'

---

[59] Drury wrote a lengthy reply to a review by Ilham Dilman of *The Danger of Words* ('Fact and Hypothesis', in *The Human World*, pp. 136–9) and took the opportunity to spell out the Wittgensteinian influence more.

(*DoW*, p. 88); it is an influence that certainly surfaces in *The Danger of Words*, but complementary to Wittgenstein's intriguing references to the 'inexpressible' and 'the mystical' in the *Tractatus*. Weil wrote

> There is a reality outside the world, that is to say outside space and time, outside man's mental universe, outside any sphere whatsoever that is accessible to human faculties. Corresponding to this reality, at the centre of the human heart is the longing for an absolute good, a longing which is always there and is never appeased by any object in this world.[60]

The most interesting essay in the volume, and the one that Rush Rhees felt most strongly about, was chapter 5, on 'Madness and Religion'. Here Drury is in his specialist field, and he bases his remarks on a number of cases drawn from his clinical experience as well as his reading in the history of spirituality. This material provokes Drury's central question, viz., how to distinguish between spiritual experience and mental illness that takes a religious form. He notes that this was becoming a more urgent question when relatively effective physical treatments for depression, mania, hallucinations, and paranoia – conditions which often present themselves in guises not easily distinguishable from classical religious experience as described by saints and spiritual directors – were emerging for the first time to replace older less reliable therapies. Such treatments could be successfully administered by psychiatrists who were totally uncomprehending of the patient's subjective conviction about the religious nature of their experience. Drury raises an important issue and handles it with considerable finesse, eschewing extreme or facile solutions.

He rejects, in particular, the extremes of Freud and Jung. He will accept neither Freud's view that all religion is collective neurosis nor Jung's contrary contention that mental

---

[60] 'Notes', p. 83; also, 'Facts and Hypotheses', *op cit.*, p. 139. The quotation is from *Draft for a Statement of Human Obligations* (1943). Given as *Écrits de Londres et dernières lettres* (Paris, 1957), p. 74 by Rhees.

health is almost impossible in a non-religious mode. His rejection of Freud does not engage Freud's theory of religion as such. Drury adduces instead the distinct phenomenon of inconsistency between the theory of ethics (admittedly sharing the same root as the theory of religion) and Freud's own sense of duty. His point is apparently that Freudian determinism is belied by Freud's practice. His mode of life proclaimed the reality and value of ethical action. It is not clear how this argument establishes the parallel reality and autonomy of the religious sphere. Drury finds Jung's view more appealing than Freud's but impractical. His clinical experience was that drugs, not words, were called for in the cases under discussion. At the same time, although 'our sanity is at the mercy of a molecule' (*DoW*, p. 134), the story is not entirely physical and this Drury held not only because of his philosophical dualism but also because physical disturbances do not invariably accompany mental illness. Perhaps we can make some progress if we base our judgements on what a person does with their religious experiences ie. on what they have 'achieved' (*DoW*, p. 131)? This apparently was Wittgenstein's position, as noted earlier. But this simply raises the further question as to what is to be accounted success and what failure.

In the final analysis, therefore, and consistent with his profound sense of the mystery of mental health, Drury accepts that he has no clear criteria to hand to judge whether a person is saint or simply ill. He declares that the distinction between religion and madness 'we spent so much time looking for was nothing but a will-o'-the wisp' (*DoW*, p. 136). Great spiritual achievement may be preceded or accompanied by episodes of mental illness, as instanced in the lives of Tolstoy, George Fox, and Joan of Arc – and perhaps, we might add, Wittgenstein in the philosophical sphere. Drury accepts that the doctor should follow his vocation in trying to alleviate suffering by whatever means are at his disposal. He is, however, prepared to at least entertain the idea that it may not be ethical to administer drugs to someone suffering from what one considers a genuine religious experience. He goes even further and expresses his belief that, in any case, madness is not a loss of what is ultimately valuable because religious salvation, and the Christian virtues that accompany it, are of higher worth. Consistent with this, Drury suggests that the ancient pagan belief, that sometimes those whom God intends to destroy he first has to make mad, should be baptized as 'sometimes those whom God intends to save he first has to make mad'.[61] The battle with a mental illness may curb pride, self-sufficiency and smugness and teach humility through suffering. This robust attitude Drury found also in Kierkegaard and Weil.

The therapist too must learn humility. Wittgenstein had stressed this to Drury: 'You should never cease to be amazed at symptoms mental patients show. If I became mad the thing I would fear most would be your common-sense attitude. That you would take it all as a matter of course that I should be suffering from delusions.'[62] And the reader of *The Danger of Words* and of the other material printed here can judge for herself or himself whether Wittgenstein's 'pupil' (*DoW*, p. xi), as Drury called himself, had not learnt that lesson well when he wrote:

> there is, and always will be, a mystery regarding mental ill-health which makes it different from any disease of the body. Every mentally ill patient is an individual enigma, and we should always think of him as such. There is something more disturbing and puzzling in the dissolution of the personality than in any bodily disease. (*DoW*, p. 89)

Dr John Hayes
Mary Immaculate College, Limerick, 1996

---

[61] *Ibid.*, pp. 133–6. Particularly germane is the quotation from Kierkegaard's *Journal*:

> To lead a really spiritual life while physically and psychologically healthy is altogether impossible. One's sense of well-being runs away with one. If one suffers every day, if one is so frail that the thought of death is quite naturally and immediately to hand, then it is just possible to succeed a little; to be conscious that one needs God. (p. 135)

[62] Quoted by Drury in Fann, *op. cit.*, p. 67.

THE DANGER OF WORDS

THE DANGER OF WORDS

by

H. O'C. DRURY

CONTENTS

PREFACE

The title of this book will at least indicate the hesitation I have long felt in putting forward these fragments for publication. They were written to be spoken
aloud; hence the colloquial style, in many ways un-
suitable for reading in the study. They were written
for special occasions and with a specific audience in
mind; hence the assumption of technical terms which
are not otherwise defined. They were written to
inaugurate a discussion; hence the incomplete manner
in which every topic is left. For I have long held that
discussion face to face is the proper medium for
philosophy. Wittgenstein used to say that a philosopher who did not join in discussions was like to a
boxer who never went into the ring.

Why then do I now bring these papers together?
For one reason only. The author of these writings was
at one time a pupil of Ludwig Wittgenstein. Now it
is well known that Wittgenstein encouraged his pupils
(those at least whom he considered had no great
originality in philosophical ability) to turn from
academic philosophy to the active study and practice
of some particular avocation. In my own case he
urged me to turn to the study of medicine, not that

I should make no use of what he had taught me, but rather that on no account should I 'give up thinking'. I therefore hesitatingly put these essays forward as an illustration of the influence that Wittgenstein had on the thought of one who was confronted by problems which had both an immediate practical difficulty to contend with, as well as a deeper philosophical perplexity to ponder over. I do not of course claim Wittgenstein's authority for a single idea expressed in these papers. So far as I can remember I never discussed any of the topics touched on with him. They were all written in the last few years, that is to say well over a decade after his death. For what is written here I take full responsibility, and write only what seems to me to be the truth, and which I would be prepared to defend in discussion. But that it was the profound influence that Wittgenstein had on me as a student that has developed into these reflections, of that also I am certain. So perhaps then I can bring some unity into what must otherwise appear very fragmentary, if in this Preface I say something concerning the orientation that Wittgenstein gave to my outlook.

For me from the very first, and ever since, and still now, certain sentences from the *Tractatus Logico-Philosophicus* stuck in my mind like arrows, and have determined the direction of my thinking. They are these:

Everything that can be put into words can be put clearly.

Philosophy will signify what cannot be said by presenting clearly what can be said.

> There are, indeed, things which cannot be put into
> words. They make themselves manifest. They are
> what is mystical.

This would not be the place, nor would I have the
ability, to discuss the differences and developments
which can be found between the *Tractatus Logico-
Philosophicus* and the *Philosophical Investigations.*
But this I must place on record. When Wittgenstein
was living in Dublin and I was seeing him constantly
he was at that time hard at work on the manuscript
of the *Investigations.* One day we discussed the
development of his thought and he said to me (I can
vouch for the accuracy of the words): 'My fundamental ideas came to me very early in life.' Now
among these fundamental ideas I would place the
sentences I quoted above. I think perhaps the remark
that Wittgenstein made, that after his conversations
with Sraffa he felt like a tree with all its branches
lopped off, has been misinterpreted. Wittgenstein
chose his metaphors with great care, and here he says
nothing about the roots or the main trunk of the tree,
these – his fundamental ideas – remain I believe
unchanged.

So now I want to say something about the word
'clarity' as it was understood by Wittgenstein. I owe
it to Mr Rush Rhees that he drew my attention to,
and translated for me, a remark that Wittgenstein
wrote in his notebook in 1930:

> Our civilisation is characterised by the word progress.
> Progress is its form: it is not one of its properties that
> it progresses. It is typical of it that it is building, con-
> structing. Its activity is one of constructing more

and more complex structures. And even clarity serves
only this end, and is not sought on its own account.
For me on the other hand clarity, lucidity, is the goal
sought.

In this distinction between the two uses of clarity I
see a difference of the very greatest importance. Let
me make the point clear by a reminiscence. At one
time for a short period Wittgenstein got me to read
aloud to him the opening chapters of Frazer's *Golden
Bough*. Frazer thinks he can make *clear* the origin of
the rites and ceremonies he describes by regarding
them as primitive and erroneous scientific beliefs. The
words he uses are, 'We shall do well to look with
leniency upon the errors as inevitable slips made in
the search for truth.' Now Wittgenstein made it clear
to me that on the contrary the people who practised
these rites already possessed a considerable scientific
achievement: agriculture, metalworking, building,
etc., etc.; and the ceremonies existed alongside these
sober techniques. They were not mistaken beliefs
that produced the rites but the need to *express* something; the ceremonies were a form of language, a form
of life. Thus today if we are introduced to someone
we shake hands; if we enter a church we take off our
hats and speak in a low voice; at Christmas perhaps
we decorate a tree. These are expressions of friendliness, reverence, and of celebration. We do not believe
that shaking hands has any mysterious efficacy, or
that to keep one's hat on in church is dangerous!
     Now this I regard as a good illustration of how I
understand clarity as something to be desired as a
goal, as distinct from clarity as something to serve a

further elaboration. For seeing these rites as a form of language immediately puts an end to all the elaborate theorising concerning 'primitive mentality'. The clarity prevents a condescending misunderstanding, and puts a full-stop to a lot of idle speculation.

I would dwell a little longer on the distinction between these two kinds of clarity, for it is a distinction that I hope will make my subsequent papers a little clearer in their intention.

At one time I told Wittgenstein of an incident that seemed to interest and please him. It was when I was having my oral examination in physiology. The examiner said to me: 'Sir Arthur Keith once remarked to me that the reason why the spleen drained into the portal system was of the greatest importance; but he never told me what that importance was, now can you tell me?' I had to confess that I couldn't see any anatomical or physiological significance in this fact. The examiner then went on to say: 'Do you think there *must* be a significance, an explanation? As I see it there are two sorts of people: one man sees a bird sitting on a telegraph wire and says to himself "Why is that bird sitting just there?", the other man replies "Damn it all, the bird has to sit somewhere".'

The reason why this story pleased Wittgenstein was that it made clear the distinction between scientific clarity, and philosophical clarity. Let me explain this by an example of my own. Astronomers are rightly interested in finding an explanation for the remarkable 'red shift' in the spectral lines of the very distant nebulae. The generally accepted explanation is that it is a manifestation of the Doppler effect (which is familiar enough to us in the way the pitch of a rapidly moving whistle of a train changes as the train either approaches or recedes from us). So it is thought that these nebulae are receding from us at prodigious speeds. Now this is a possible scientific explanation, and in one sense it makes the phenomena clear. But then we at once want to ask, 'Why are all these nebulae receding at such speeds?' And this shows us that ultimately we will have to accept some facts as unexplained, and say, 'Well that is just how it is'. So then there would be nothing illogical in saying of the shift in the spectral lines, 'That is just how the spectra of distant nebulae are', and we are not *forced* to give any explanation. Philosophical clarity then arises when we see that behind every scientific construction there lies the inexplicable.

> The whole modern conception of the world is founded on the illusion that the so-called laws of nature are the explanation of natural phenomena.

Scientific explanations lead us on indefinitely from one inexplicable to another, so that the building grows and grows and grows, and we never find a real resting place. Philosophical clarity puts a full-stop to our enquiry and restlessness by showing that our quest is in one sense mistaken.

I would just give a few instances of reminiscences of conversations with Wittgenstein where a remark of his introduced sudden philosophical clarity by means of a full-stop.

> I told him I was reading a book about the 'Desert Fathers', those heroic ascetics of the Egyptian Thebaid. And, in the shallowness of those days, said

something to the effect that I thought they might have made better use of their lives. Wittgenstein turned on me angrily and said, 'That's just the sort of stupid remark an English parson would make; how can you know what their problems were in those days and what they had to do about them?'

He told me that he had just finished reading a book in which the author blamed Calvin for the rise of our present bourgeois capitalist culture. He said that he realised how attractive such a thesis could seem, but he for his part 'wouldn't dare to criticise a man such as Calvin was'.

Someone was inclined to defend Russell's writings on marriage, sex, and 'free love': Wittgenstein interposed by saying: 'If a person tells me he has been to the worst of places I have no right to judge him, but if he tells me it was his superior wisdom that enabled him to go there, then I know that he is a fraud.' He went on to say how absurd it was to deprive Russell of his Professorship on 'moral grounds'. 'If ever there was such a thing as an an-aphrodisiac it is Russell writing about sex!'

We had a discussion about the difficulty of reconciling the discourses and history in the fourth Gospel with the other three. Then he suddenly said: 'But if you can accept the miracle that God became man all these difficulties are as nothing, for then I couldn't possibly say what form the record of such an event would take.'

I have been trying to draw from my memories incidents which illustrate the conception of saying something clearly; bringing what looked like being a long and controversial discussion to a full-stop. It would be a contradiction to go on and say anything about

'There are indeed things which cannot be put into words'. But I would draw attention to this. In a letter written when he wanted to get the *Tractatus* published he said that 'it was really a book about ethics', and that the most important part is what is not said in it. I find myself thinking about this remark when reading all that he subsequently wrote. When he was hard at work at the manuscript of the *Philosophical Investigations* he said to me: 'I am not a religious man, but I can't help seeing every thing from a religious point of view.' And on another occasion: 'It is impossible for me to say one word in my book about all that music has meant in my life; how then can I possibly make myself understood?' And with regard to music this, which I have mentioned on another occasion: 'Bach put at the head of his Orgelbuchlein, "To the glory of the most high God, and that my neighbour may be benefited thereby". I would have liked to be able to say this of my work.'

I fear that these papers may be too metaphysical to be of interest to my colleagues occupied with the day-to-day problems of mental illness; and their topic too circumscribed and limited to interest philosophers. They are certainly not intended as in any sense a commentary on Wittgenstein's philosophy, but with the increasing importance that is now being given to his writings, they may possess a peripheral interest, as an illustration of his influence on one particular pupil. But then it must be added that all his life Wittgenstein was very dubious as to whether his influence on others (and on contemporary philosophy) was not more harmful than beneficial.

ACKNOWLEDGMENTS

The translations of Lichtenberg's Aphorisms which appear in this book are taken from Dr J. P. Stern's *Lichtenberg, a Doctrine of Scattered Occasions*. I wish to thank Dr Stern and his publishers, Thames and Hudson, and Indiana University Press, for permission to use these translations.

In the chapter on 'Hypotheses and Philosophy' the material for criticising the mutation-selection theory of evolution is deeply indebted to Professor C. P. Martin's important book entitled *Psychology, Evolution and Sex*. I am grateful to Professor Martin and to his publisher Charles C. Thomas, Springfield, Illinois, for allowing me to use this material and to quote from the book itself. I would like to thank Professor J. C. Eccles and his publishers, the Clarendon Press, for permission to quote from his book *The Neuro-Physiological Basis of Mind*, and Gallimard for permission to quote Simone Weil's 'Lettre à une élève' from *La Condition Ouvvrière*.

In conclusion I would like to express my gratitude to Professor R. F. Holland for all his valuable help in preparing my manuscript for publication.

Nous savons au moyen de l'intelligence que ce que l'intelligence n'apprehende pas est plus réel que ce qu'elle apprehende.

SIMONE WEIL

CHAPTER 1

WORDS AND TRANSGRESSIONS

I WOULD counsel all young people to put all new words in careful order and arrange them like minerals, in their various class, so that they can be found when asked for or when required for one's own use. This is called word economy, and is as lucrative to the mind as money economy is to the purse.

LICHTENBERG

In the Proverbs 10:19 it is written: 'With a multitude of words transgressions are increased.' And I will make this text an excuse for the substance of this paper. For I want to speak to you about the way words can lead us into confusion, misunderstandings, error. Confusion when we are talking to patients, misunderstandings when we discuss mutual problems with our colleagues, error when in solitude we try to clarify our own thinking.

For the purpose of classification I have divided these fallacies under five separate headings. The first I call the fallacy of the alchemists; the second the fallacy of Molière's physician; the third the fallacy of Van Helmont's tree; and the fourth the fallacy of the missing hippopotamus; finally, for the fifth, I have chosen the unoriginal title of the fallacy of Pickwickian senses.

BDW

First then the fallacy of the alchemists. I have chosen this name because of what Lavoisier says in the Introduction to his *Treatise on Chemistry*. Lavoisier, you will remember, was the first chemist to introduce our modern system of nomenclature into chemistry; a system whereby different substances are named in terms of the elements which go to form them. Sodium chloride, potassium permanganate, calcium carbonate, etc., etc. Prior to this book many of these substances, though well known, had bizarre names which in no way indicated their relationship to each other. These names often going back to the days of the alchemists; sometimes indicative of their original discoverer, sometimes from their place of origin, sometimes to some irrelevant outward appearance. Thus we had 'Glauber's salts', 'Fuming liquor of Libavius', 'Butter of arsenic', 'Vitriol of Venus', and so on. In his Introduction Lavoisier says that he is now introducing a *method of naming* as distinct from a *nomenclature*, and he adds the following wise remark about the importance of what he is now doing:

> If languages really are instruments fashioned by men to make thinking easier, they should be of the best possible kind, and to strive to perfect them is indeed to work for the advancement of science. For those who are beginning the study of a science the perfecting of its language is of high importance.

And later on in the same Preface he writes:

> It is therefore not surprising that in the early childhood of chemistry, suppositions instead of conclusions were drawn; that these suppositions transmitted from age to age were changed into presumptions, and

that these presumptions were then regarded as fundamental truths by even the ablest minds.

Now I think if we are to be honest with ourselves
we must admit that the vocabulary of psychiatry
today is only too comparable with what Lavoisier has
to say about the nomenclature of chemistry in its
childhood. We have indeed a *nomenclature*, but we
have no *system of naming*. Some diseases are named
after those famous physicians who first described
them; thus we have Korsakov's psychosis, Alzheimer's
disease, Ganser's syndrome; some are named in terms
of a long discarded pathology, hysteria for example
and schizophrenia. Some are named in terms of the
most prominent symptom; the word 'depression' is
used both for a complaint of the patient and the
diagnosis of the attending physician; similarly with
the words 'anxiety state'.

I would have to agree that having no better terminology at hand we must for the present do the best with
what we have. But let us be on our guard against those
dangers that Lavoisier warned us against. Let us
beware lest from this unsystematic nomenclature
suppositions are drawn, which then become presumptions and only too easily pass over into established truths.

I would say that the chief danger of an unsystematic
nomenclature is the danger of regarding its classifica-
tions as mutually exclusive and completely exhaustive.
For example it is only too easy to get involved in a
controversy as to whether this patient is a schizophrenic or a case of endogenous depression, when for
all we know he might be both at the same time; or

neither, but some other disease for which we have at present no convenient name.

There is a story told of a candidate up for the membership examination who in answer to one of the more difficult questions on the paper could only reply indignantly, 'This is not mentioned in Tidy's *Synopsis of Medicine*.' It is important for us to bear in mind that there are still many diseases both of mind and body which are not only not mentioned in Tidy's *Synopsis*, but are not in *any* text-book or encyclopaedia of medicine. The science of medicine, and particularly psychiatry, is not yet complete.

Janet wrote an interesting essay on the history of the word 'neurosis'. He showed that in spite of various attempts to define the limits of this term, in practice the word has been used to cover all those clinical condicions which at the time of writing could not be accounted for by any known pathology. Thus the famous Pinel, in whose days the ophthalmoscope had not been invented, classified all cases of blindness in which there was no manifest disease of the external eye, cornea, or lens, as hysterical amaurosis. Trousseau, that prince of clinicians, after giving a masterly description of the symptoms and signs of *tabes dorsalis*, classifies it as a form of neurosis. For in his day there was no known method of staining nervous tissue and demonstrating the degeneration of the posterior columns of the spinal cord. Other equally able writers have in their time classified Parkinson's disease, Grave's disease, hydrophobia, tetanus, eclampsia, as psychogenic in origin.

Now these things were written for our learning. We are certainly making similar mistakes today. Considering the immense complexity of the anatomy, physiology, and bio-chemistry of the human body, it is certain that there are probably more diseases still to be described than have so far been given a precise description and a name. For example the estimation of the blood sugar is a comparatively recent achievement. In the past, spontaneous hypo-glycaemia certainly occurred, and the mental and behavioural disorder so produced was described as neurotic, psychotic or epileptic, according to the degree and rapidity of the hypo-glycaemia involved. Wisdom demands that we remember constantly our ignorance.

This then brings me on to the second danger of words, that which I have called the fallacy of Molière's physician.

In one of his plays Molière has a physician asked this question: 'How is it that opium is able to put people to sleep?' The physician replies with great profundity that it is because opium has 'dormitive properties', and this answer is found entirely satisfactory by his interlocutors. I think we all have a tendency to deceive ourselves in this way. To use obscure and learned phrases, thinking thereby that we have obtained a deeper insight. I remember as a medical student reading the chapter on fractures in a manual of surgery; it began by stating that by a fracture is meant 'the dissolution of continuity in a bone'. This struck me as quite as funny as Molière's joke. It is a wise rule from time to time to force oneself to write down in simple language the precise meaning of any involved circumlocution we have become in the habit of using. If we did this we would find, I think, that such words as 'hysteria', 'psychopathic personality', 'character neurosis', are symbols of our ignorance rather than of any understanding.

Let me for a moment give you an example of a more serious error of this type. It was for a time fashionable, and still is, I am told, to produce a dramatic emotional reaction in a patient by getting him or her to inhale a mixture of carbon dioxide and oxygen; and other chemical means either by inhalation or injection were also used. Such a reaction was given the profound sounding name of 'abreaction', and this technical term led people to believe that they understood what was happening; that the patient undergoing this treatment was releasing forces and tendencies which in his previous state were repressed and causing his symptoms, and therefore that such abreaction was certain to be both informative to the psychiatrist and beneficial to the patient. One of my colleagues told me that he saw this treatment being administered to a rather timid little man who was a victim of alcoholism. When the mask through which the carbon-dioxide mixture was administered was firmly held over his face, this little fellow fought back with surprising fury. Ah! said the psychiatrist, now you see that the cause of his addiction is this deeply repressed aggressiveness. On hearing this story I was reminded of Voltaire's remark: 'This animal is very dangerous, when it is attacked it defends itself.'

You might reply to me that unless we experiment in this way research in psychiatry and in medicine generally will come to a standstill. And so I must now speak about that most dangerous word in our present medical vocabulary, 'research'. I am informed that something in the region of a million new scientific papers are published in the journals every year, and that these if they were all to be bound in one volume would be equivalent to three complete editions of the *Encyclopaedia Britannica*. Gentlemen, I do not believe we are living in an age of such colossal originality. Let this be clearly said: research in the proper meaning of the much abused word does not mean *collecting facts*; there is much too much fact collecting going on. Research means new ideas; new concepts, new ways of looking at old and familiar facts. The important part of research is the thinking done *before* the experimental verification gets under way.

The ability to think in this particular way is, I believe, a comparatively rare talent. A gift for research is not the automatic accompaniment of a grant for research. There is, I suppose, no more honoured name in the history of physiology than that of Claude Bernard. At one time when a prolonged illness prevented him continuing his experiments in the laboratory, Bernard composed a short treatise setting out the principles which had guided him in making his discoveries. This volume, though now over a hundred years old, contains much that needs repeating today. If I may just quote a few short passages from it you will perceive how apposite it is.

Bernard writes:

Two operations must therefore be considered in any experiment. The first consists in *premeditating* and bringing to pass the conditions of the experiment; the second consists in noting the results of the experiment. It is impossible to devise an experiment without a pre-conceived idea; devising an experiment, we said, is putting a question; we never conceive a question without an idea which invites an answer. I consider it therefore an absolute principle that experiments must always be devised in view of a preconceived idea, no matter if the idea be not very clear or well defined. As for noting the results of the experiment, which is itself only an induced observation, I posit it similarly as a principle that we must here, as always *observe* without a preconceived idea.

Once in conversation with a friend Bernard put the same important principle in a more aphoristic form. 'When you go into the laboratory do not forget to leave your imagination in the ante-room with your overcoat; on the other hand never forget to take it away with you when you go home.'

There are two further points I would just touch on concerning which Bernard's teaching is much needed as a corrective to what often passes under the name of research today.

He writes:

Misconceived erudition has been, and still is, one of the greatest *obstacles* to the advancement of experimental science.

Now if you pick up any modern scientific journal it seems almost a standard practice for the author to start with a review of the previous literature. Thus often such articles have a hundred or more references at the end, and it is even worse when it comes to the bibliography at the end of some books. I am inclined when I see such a display of erudition to pass on to something more profitable. For I fear that such an author will have his mind so constipated with facts as to be incapable of producing anything but wind. If an author really has a contribution of value to make, then let him get on with it at once, there is no need for him to give a display of his homework.

The second point that Bernard emphasises is in my opinion even more important for what goes by the name of research in the behavioural sciences today. He writes:

> In every science we must recognise two classes of phenomena, those whose cause is already defined; next those whose cause is still undefined. With phenomena whose cause is defined statistics have nothing to do; they would even be absurd. As soon as the circumstances of an experiment are well known we stop gathering statistics . . . Only when a phenomenon includes conditions as yet undefined, can we compile statistics; we must learn therefore that we compile statistics *only when we cannot possibly help it*; for in my opinion statistics can never yield scientific truth, and therefore cannot establish any final scientific method.
>
> Statistics can bring to birth only conjectural sciences; they can never produce active experimental sciences, i.e. sciences which regulate phenomena according to definite laws. By statistics we get a conjecture of greater or less probability about a given case, but never any certainty, never any absolute determinism. Of course statistics may guide a physician's prognosis; to that extent they may be useful. I do not therefore reject the use of statistics in medicine, but I condemn *not trying to get beyond them* and believing in statistics as the foundation of medical science.

I do not think that those wise words need any further

comment from me. But perhaps you would bear them in mind next time you find yet one more mass of statistical information in the *British Journal of Psychiatry.*

This gives me the cue to introduce the next fallacy I mentioned, the one I called the fallacy of Van Helmont's tree.

Van Helmont, as you know, was one of the great founders of chemistry. He was the first chemist to realise the importance of the chemical balance; of carefully weighing everything both before and after a chemical reaction. Indeed, it was largely due to his work that the principle of the conservation of matter became an established axiom. Now Van Helmont performed a certain experiment with great care and accuracy, whose result seemed irrefutable and yet at the same time absurd. It was this.

He weighed accurately a certain quantity of earth and placing it in a large pot, planted a small ash sapling. Every day he watered the plant with pure distilled water, and in between these waterings he kept the surface of the soil covered so that no foreign extraneous matter should fall on it. In due time the sapling grew to such a size that its weight had increased more than a hundredfold, in fact it had become too big for the pot to hold it. Van Helmont weighed it carefully, and then weighed the original soil he had filled the pot with, finding that this latter had lost nothing. He argued therefore that as the only additions made were those of pure water all the materials in the tree, bark, pith, leaves, etc., were in some way composed of nothing but water. This certainly seemed paradoxical both to him and his contemporaries, but the evidence of the experiment seemed irrefutable. Where did they go wrong? Well of course they did not know that a plant is able to extract carbon from the carbon dioxide of the air by the process of photosynthesis; the very existence of such a substance as carbon dioxide or such a process as photosynthesis was then undreamed of. Similarly how could they have guessed that there were minute organisms in the soil that could extract nitrogen from the air and transmit it to the plant?

Now the motto of this is that in the early stages of any science when there are still a host of unknown factors at work it can be most misleading to draw conclusions from experiments however accurately performed. The methods employed may be too precise for the data on which they have to work. I am told that today if you wish to get any report on the use of a new method of treatment it is essential that the investigation be carried out on the basis of what is known as a 'double blind trial'. When I hear this I murmur to myself, 'Remember Van Helmont's tree.' For it seems clear to me that psychiatry is still dealing with too many unknowns for the method of the double blind trial to be either safe or applicable. I speak here only of the logic involved, and say nothing of the ethical aspect of doctors deliberately allowing themselves to be in ignorance of the treatment their patients are receiving.

The logical essential for the double blind trial to be in any way convincing is that the experimental group and the control group should be evenly matched. This today means matched as to age, sex, duration of illness, nature of symptoms, previous treatments given. But it may well be that these are not the necessary factors alone. May it not be that there are a host of genetic, bio-chemical, histological factors that also need to be taken into account and of which we are at present totally unaware?

Perhaps I can make this point clearer by an imaginary example. In the seventeenth century 'being sick of a fever' was a respectable diagnosis for a physician to make. It was not known nor even guessed that the important factor was the micro-organism causing the fever. Quinine had recently been introduced into Europe, and malaria being more common in these parts than it is now, quinine soon proved its usefulness. Now suppose some physicians had in those days said: we must now have a double blind trial to make sure that quinine is not just a placebo. Those whose trial contained many cases of malaria would have statistical proof of its efficiency. Whilst in another group there might be more cases of Relapsing fever on which quinine would show no therapeutic benefit. Thus we would get two properly carried out double blind trials and contradictory results. This seems to me to be happening in the trial of new psycho-tropic drugs today. Statistically adequate trials, but contradictory results. Our psychopathology is not yet adequate to make such elaborate experiments justified. For as Osler said long ago: 'As is our pathology, so is our therapeutics.' The example I have given is of course only an imaginary one. So let me further emphasise the possibility of such fallacious argument from apparently irrefutable data by a real example from the history of psychiatry. That disease which we now call G.P.I. was first described and clearly differentiated as a clinical entity by French clinicians in the decade 1820 to 1830. Nearly all the cases first described were old soldiers from Napoleon's Grand Army. We know only too well why *that* should have been the case. But to those clinicians it seemed statistically self-evident that the cause of G.P I. was the undermining of the nervous constitution of those who had endured the privations and the horrors of the retreat from Moscow. They knew nothing of a minute spirochaete; but the battle of Borodino and the crossing of the Beresina were still vivid memories.

So I would sum up the fallacy which I have entitled 'the fallacy of Van Helmont's tree' in these terms. Carefully planned and well executed investigations in the early stages of a science may be completely misleading, just because of our ignorance of the possible factors involved.

But what then are we to do? We are daily inundated with information concerning new drugs by those who with the best intentions are yet financially interested in their sale. Surely we must adopt some scientific procedure to sift out the good from the mediocre or even the useless. Yes, indeed, it is necessary that this should be done. But I do not believe the double blind trial is in the present state of our knowledge either scientific or helpful. During the twenty years or so that I have been working in psychiatry I have seen and used many forms of treatment; some I still use, others I have almost forgotten about until looking through some old notes I am reminded that for a short period they seemed to be worth trying. (For instance, a few days ago I had occasion to look up the notes of a patient whom I had not seen for many years, and I saw that when I last treated her I used a drug called 'Cavo-dil'; I had to think twice before I remembered that it was one of the M.A.O. group that enjoyed consider-able popularity for a year or so.) My experience has been that there is a process of *natural selection* at work in all forms of treatment, and that there is the survival of the fittest. And that this process of selection takes place without any one person or any particular investigation deciding the matter once and for all. Let me give you an example. When I came into psychiatry 'insulin coma therapy' was the best and only treat-ment we had for schizophrenia. Having worked for three years in an insulin coma clinic I am certain that it was worth doing, that it was better than doing nothing. With the introduction of chlorpromazine the number of cases coming for insulin coma gradually decreased until it became certain that we could dis-pense with insulin coma altogether. Now this was not *one* person's decision, nor was it one deliberately made on a *particular* occasion; it just happened. If we as clinicians continue to do our work with attention, with courage when it is needed, and with the necessary amount of scepticism, then this natural selection will continue to work for us. I am impressed when I read the works of some of the great clinicians of the last century, by their style of description. They do not hesitate to use such expressions as 'my experience has been', 'I have often noticed', 'the following case impressed me', etc. This would now be rejected by some as 'merely anecdotal evidence'. At the risk of appearing very old-fashioned I am going to claim that this keen attention to *anecdotes* is of the first impor-tance. I do not of course mean that we should publish

these anecdotes; that would merely add to the confusion. But we should have our eyes and ears open,
and our pens ready to note down in our case-books,
every incident or remark that seems in any way novel
or strikes our attention. I know for myself the danger
for my case history taking to become stereotyped. I
wish we all had more time to listen. Again if I can refer
back to Claude Bernard's account of his own discoveries, he describes in detail many particular and
unsought-for observations, which after reflection and
speculation led him to a new hypothesis to be tested
by a planned and crucial experiment. One of his
pupils describes how during an experiment Claude
Bernard seemed to have eyes all round his head, he
would point out quite evident phenomena which no
one else had noticed. Of course such a great hypothesis
as 'the preservation of the constancy of the internal
milieu' was the result of imagination and not of any
one particular observation. But it was the ability by
means of which this imagination was stirred into
speculation by some one particular observation, that
constituted him the great scientist that he was. Such
minds are rare; it is probable that there are few in
any one generation, but then the real contributions to
the permanent advancement of science are equally
rare.

I sometimes wish it was a law that every scientific
paper had to be allowed to mature for ten years in
bond, like good whisky, before being allowed in
print.

These reflections bring me directly to a considera-
tion of the fourth type of verbal fallacy, the one I
have called 'the fallacy of the missing hippopotamus'.

I chose this rather bizarre name from a discussion which once took place between the two philosophers, Bertrand Russell and Ludwig Wittgenstein. Wittgenstein illustrated the point he wished to make by the following example. Suppose I state 'There is an hippopotamus in this room at this minute, but no one can see it, no one can hear it, no one can smell it, no one can touch it; have I now with all these added provisos said anything meaningful at all?' Surely not, for a proposition that can neither be verified nor refuted has no useful place in scientific language.

But I think you would be surprised to find how easy it is to make just this sort of logical error. Modern science is full of missing hippopotami. We are inclined to fall in love with an hypothesis, and so when facts begin to tell against it, we invent a subsidiary hypothesis to save the face of the first, and this process continues until without realising it our first hypothesis has become so secure as to be irrefutable. But alas, in doing just this we have at the same time deprived it of all significance.

Two examples from our own sphere of science will make my point clearer. Freud had the original and suggestive idea that dreams were really wish fulfilments, and not only that but always sexual with fulfilments. Some dreams obviously are. But others on the face of it were not. So in order to save his beloved hypothesis he had to invent a great many subsidiary hypotheses, those that he described under the name of the dream mechanisms: condensation, displacement of affect, symbolism, etc., etc. He does not seem to me to have observed that in so introducing all these extra hypotheses he has emasculated his original idea of all significance. Let me make this clearer by an incident which Janet relates. Janet was talking to an enthusiastic pupil of Freud: 'Last night,' said Janet, 'I dreamt that I was standing on a railway station: surely that has no sexual significance.' 'Oh! indeed it has,' said the Freudian; 'a railway station is a place where trains go to and fro, to and fro, and all to and fro movements are highly suggestive. And what about a railway signal; it can be either up or down, need I say more?' Now as Janet rightly went on to point out, if you allow yourself such a freedom in symbolism, every possible content of any dream whatsoever can be forced into this type of interpretation. The theory has become 'fact proof'; it just can't be refuted. But that which cannot be proved wrong by any conceivable experience is without meaning. The object of a statement, of an hypothesis, is to state which of two possible alternatives is in fact the case. If *no* alternative is allowed, the statement decides nothing about a possible state of affairs.

One further example of the same verbal fallacy, one more missing hippopotamus. Wolpe put forward the interesting hypothesis that all neurotic behaviour was learnt behaviour, and that therefore such maladaptive behaviour could be 'cured' by the application of what certain psychologists have called 'learning theory'. Now for Wolpe and those who have taken up behaviour therapy with enthusiasm, learning is always a matter of establishing a stimulus-response connection. Therefore the first task of the behaviour therapist must be to ascertain the stimuli which have become unnecessarily linked with anxiety. But then,

CDW

as Wolpe has to admit, this is not always easy. It is easy enough with a straightforward mono-symptomatic phobia such for example as a phobia for cats. Such mono-symptomatic phobias are not common, and when they do occur, such an aetiology and therapy as Wolpe suggests is probably correct. But what about that much more common syndrome which Freud described under the very suitable name of 'free floating anxiety'? Here the specific stimulus linked with the anxiety reaction is hard to discern. But Wolpe has become too attached to his all-embracing explanation of anxiety states. Free floating anxiety, he claims, is anxiety linked with such ever present stimuli as Space, Time, and the idea of Self! Now if the word 'stimulus' is to be applied to such concepts as these then the whole stimulus-response theory of learning becomes irrefutable and at the same time meaningless. The theory, as is well known, depends on the experimental work with animals carried out originally by Pavlov, Thorndike, Hull, Skinner, and their followers. One only has to ask oneself to imagine these experimenters using Space, Time, or the idea of Self, as a stimulus in any of their experiments to see the enormous extrapolation that Wolpe has here made. It is not possible to refute him because he has said nothing. I cannot refrain from quoting Janet once again. Janet built up a most interesting psychology based on the twin concepts of 'psychic energy' and 'psychic tension'. In the Introduction to one of his books he makes the profound remark that one great advantage of his theory is that time may prove him to be completely wrong. As a matter of fact I think Janet's hypothesis has not been substantiated, and if he was still alive he would perhaps have replied, 'Well, what did I tell you'. I think we must all be on the watch that in psychology and psychiatry we take care to formulate hypotheses which are capable of being refuted. No more missing hippopotami please.

I come then, finally, to that fallacy which has now the name of the fallacy of 'Pickwickian senses'. The name was taken from a famous scene which took place one evening at the Pickwick Club. Mr Blotton had the termerity to call Mr Pickwick a humbug. This was the occasion for some heated words between various members, and order was only restored to the meeting when the chairman suggested to Mr Blotton that he had only used the term 'humbug' in a purely *Pickwickian* sense, and not with its usual connotation. Mr Blotton agreed that he had the highest regard for the honourable member Mr Pickwick and only described him as a humbug in a purely Pickwickian sense. After this explanation Mr Pickwick said he was completely satisfied with his friend's explanation and that he had used certain terms of abuse during the incident in a purely Pickwickian sense also. Peace was restored once more to the meeting.

Now I think that in psychiatry today we are inclined to use certain words in 'a purely Pickwickian sense' – words which to our patients sound as a reflection on their personality although we mean no such moral criticism. I have for many years tried to get the word 'alcoholic' dropped. For if we ask a patient to accept this description of himself he thinks of the familiar drunkard of literature and stage. One who is never quite sober, smelling of drink, a large red nose

and blood-shot eyes, etc., etc. Now of course we don't
mean this description at all when we diagnose the
disease alcoholism. We know that a patient may be
addicted to alcohol without ever having been intoxi-
cated, who has had long periods of contented sobriety,
who does not experience a constant craving for alcohol, who on examination may show no outward and
visible signs of his illness. We mean by an alcoholic
one whose pattern of drinking has developed certain
sinister signs with which you are all familiar and
which I therefore need not elaborate here. But to the
patient we are using a term which reflects on his
personal integrity. He or she does not realise that
psychiatrists today use the term 'alcoholic' in a purely
Pickwickian sense. We mean a person who either for
metabolic or temperamental reasons (it is not yet
known exactly which; or possibly both of these
explanations apply) should be advised by his doctor to
abstain from alcohol entirely. Surely it would be possible for us to find a name for this medical condition
which would obviate so many unnecessary arguments.
My own experience has been, when I tell a patient
that alcoholism is not a scientific term, that therefore
I am not calling him an alcoholic but I am advising
him that he has shown signs which clearly prognosti-
cate the need for total abstinence in the future, that
such an explanation is more readily agreed to, or at
least open to an intelligent discussion.

A similar state of affairs exists, I believe, with
regard to the use of the word 'hysteria'. If we tell a
patient that her symptoms are hysterical in origin, or
even if we use this term in writing to her general
practitioner, we will be taken to mean that the

patient's condition need not be taken seriously, and that a dose of cold water either literally or metaphorically is all that is required. It is a word that should be dropped from a scientific vocabulary. I know that the word is often used by competent psychiatrists in a purely Pickwickian sense and without meaning to minimise the need for help and therapy. But I am also well aware in my own case of a strong temptation to label as hysterical all those symptoms for which I can find no good cause and where my therapeutic attempts have not met with success. It has been suggested, I know, that the word 'functional' should be used instead of 'hysterical'. This avoids the fallacy of 'Pickwickian senses' in that it will not offend the patient; but it is an example of the fallacy of Molière's physician in that it pretends to explain by a learned circumlocution a condition which to date neither doctors nor patients understand. I am not convinced that in psychiatry an air of omniscience and omnipotence is appreciated by the patient; more often all that is required is a concerned listening and an obvious attempt to do something helpful.

I am not sure, but I feel that the word 'depression' is beginning to be used in a Pickwickian sense, a sense in which the psychiatrist means one thing and the patient understands another. The development of effective treatment for the old-fashioned melancholia or manic-depressive psychosis has contributed to this state of affairs. For we now find that these treatments are effective in some conditions where 'depression' or 'melancholy' are not complained of by the patient. Hence if we tell him that he is 'depressed' he may well come to the conclusion that we are confused about his condition. There is a danger too that if we begin to talk about 'atypical depression', or 'masked depression', we may be committing that fallacy which I called the fallacy of the alchemists. There is a danger that this nomenclature may lead us into accepting as an established truth what at best is only a conjecture. In our present state of knowlege two conjectures are possible. One is that the illnesses which respond to the same treatment are all manifestations of one and the same underlying pathology. The other is that the new forms of chemotherapy are potent against a variety of different diseases. Penicillin can cure both a carbuncle and lobar pneumonia. It may be that the mental conditions which respond to the tri-cyclic thymoleptics are equally disparate. It is important that for future understanding we keep the choice between these two alternatives open.

One word more about the confusion that the word 'depression' can cause. Patients cannot be expected to understand that by the word 'depression' the psychiatrist understands a very different condition from that denoted by the word 'unhappiness'. It will inevitably happen from time to time that we will be asked and expected to remedy the normal discontents and disappointments that are part of our common human life. Freud showed real profundity when he stated that the aim of psycho-analysis was to replace neurotic unhappiness by normal unhappiness. A psychiatry based on a purely hedonistic ethics, a psychiatry that does not recognise that periods of anxiety and periods of melancholy are a necessary part of every human life, such a psychiatry will never be

more than a superficial affair. Our task must be not
only to relieve but also to interpret.

Another source of considerable confusion between
doctors and patients today is in the use of the word
drugs. In strict etymology the word 'drug' means any
measured quantity of medicine. So that a patient who
is taking iron for anaemia. Vitamin B for neuritis, or
insulin for diabetes, is receiving drug treatment. But
of course in the popular mind the word 'drugs' has
many frightening associations: drug addiction, being
under the influence of drugs, the drug traffic, etc. In
the popular mind a drug is something that is taken
for its immediate soporific or stimulating effect. Now
it is one of the happier features of this present age
that chemical substances have been discovered which
have a profound psycho-tropic effect. Both 'endogenous depression' and 'schizophrenia' can be treated
by the prolonged administration of certain 'drugs'.
But we must explain to our patients that these substances are not given for purely immediate sedative
or stimulating effects; they are given over a prolonged
time and only show their benefits after several weeks.
My own belief is that these substances are more in the
nature of replacement therapies, like the iron, the
vitamin, the insulin I mentioned above. Hence when
we tell a patient that we propose to treat him with
drug therapy we must beware of the fallacy of 'Pickwickian senses', and explain to him the difference
between a necessary chemical and a temporary ano-
dyne. There is much talk nowadays about the spread
of drug addiction, and I have known some patients
who have given up their necessary medication
because of what they have read in the popular press.

Of course it is best of all when a patient no longer needs a doctor or his prescriptions, but this is not always possible to achieve.

It is written in the Book of Proverbs that 'with a multitude of words transgressions are increased.' What an excellent motto that would be for our new Royal College of Psychiatry.

CHAPTER 2

SCIENCE AND PSYCHOLOGY

PEOPLE do not readily give up false opinions about man once they feel justified in claiming that they derive them from a subtle knowledge of humanity, and that only certain initiates are capable of such insights into the hearts of their fellow men. Consequently there are few branches of human knowledge where a little learning is more harmful than in this.

LICHTENBERG

Ladies and gentlemen,

I think I can best introduce the subject of my paper tonight by a series of quotations. Quotations taken from the writings of psychologists, who either in their own day, or at the present time, were and are recognised as authorities in the faculty of psychology.

My first quotation is from the justly famous American psychologist William James; the author of the *Principles of Psychology*, a book which is still well worth reading. But my quotation is this:

Psychology is not yet a science but only the hope of a science.

That was written in 1890. Thirty years later the

eminent French psychologist, Pierre Janet, concluded his two large volumes on psychological healing with the remark:

> Medical practitioners have suddenly turned to psychology, and have demanded of this science a service which the psychologists were far from being prepared to render. Psychology has not proved equal to the occasion and the failure of the science has thrown discredit upon psychotherapy itself. But this very failure has necessitated entirely new psychological studies, whereby the science of psychology has been regenerated.... Some day we may hope that there will be enough knowledge to make it possible to budget the income and expenditure of a mind, just as today we budget the income and expenditure of a commercial concern.

Thirty years later again Hebb published his book called *The Organisation of Behaviour*. This book had no small influence on future psychological thinking, and is still often quoted in the literature. In the Introduction to his book Hebb commences with this statement.

> It might be argued that the task of the psychologist, the task of understanding behaviour and reducing the vagaries of human thought to a mechanical process of cause and effect, is a more difficult one than that of any other scientist. Certainly the problem is enormously complex; and although it could be argued that the progress made by psychology in the century following the death of James Mill, with his crude theory of association, is an achievement scarcely less than that of the physical sciences in the same period, it is never the less true that psychological

theory is still in its infancy. There is a long way to go before we can speak of understanding the principles of behaviour to the degree that we understand the principles of chemical reaction.

Ten years later O. L. Zangwill in an article on psychology written for the 1950 edition of *Chambers' Encyclopaedia* stated:

At the present time it must be admitted that psychology falls sadly short of its aim. In view of the complexity of its data and the difficulties confronting crucial experiments in the psychological sphere, the explanations offered by mental science remain at the descriptive level. Hypotheses intending to co-ordinate large bodies of fact, such as the psycho-analytic or the gestalt theory, fall short of the necessary requirements for truly scientific precision. But the prevailing uncertainty of psychological explanation need imply no fault more severe than scientific immaturity. Indeed the contemporary situation in psychology is strikingly parallel to that of physiology in the sixteenth century. The notable development of modern experimental physiology leads one confidently to expect that a coherent science of mind will slowly take shape in the general frame work of the sciences of life.

Ten years later again H. J. Eysenck in the Introduction to his big book on *Abnormal Psychology* writes as follows:

Originally I conceived the writing of a book such as this fifteen years ago when the exigencies of war threw me into contact with psychoneurotic patients at the Mill Hill Emergency hospital. Having little knowledge of the field, I naturally turned to the textbooks available on psychiatry and abnormal clinical psychology. The perusal of some fifty of these left me in a state of profound depression, as none of them contained any evidence of properly planned or executed experimental investigations, or even the realisation of the necessity for such. Nor did I find that concise and consistent frame work of theories and hypotheses which usually precede experimental investigations; all was speculation and surmise, laced with reference to clinical experience. Michael Faraday's words seemed only too apposite: 'They reason theoretically without demonstrating experimentally, and errors are the result'. . . . It is for this reason that the dedication is to E. Kraepelin, the first person to be trained in the psychological laboratory, and to apply experimental methods to abnormal psychology. It is sobering to consider, if only his outlook had prevailed in psychiatry how much further advanced our knowledge would now be.

You will see, I think, from these quotations that there has been over the last eighty years or so a general agreement among psychologists that the really important work, the really significant discoveries, in the science of psychology, belong to the future. Psychology, they seem to agree, is still a very young science, but one that once it adopts the rigour of experimental science, will bear great fruit. When Galileo performed his first experiments in rolling marbles down an inclined plane, and measured mass, time, and velocity, he made the remark: 'This is the beginning of a great science.' And so indeed it was. It was the beginning of physics. And I need not remind you how today the science of physics has changed the whole manner of human life, and of our way of thinking about the nature of the universe we live in.

Unless I misunderstand them, the psychologists I have just quoted are encouraged by the hope that their rudimentary experiments – dogs salivating at the sound of a bell, rats learning to run a maze, pigeons learning to do strange tricks in Professor Skinner's box, human beings day-dreaming over ink-blots – that these experiments are the harbinger of a new science. A science which will place on a sound scientific basis such important subjects as psychiatry, education, sociology, criminology and penology, and even international politics. The hope is that in the future a truly scientific psychology will enable us to control the vagaries of the human mind to the same extent that the physical sciences have given us such power over our material environment. I remember as an undergraduate Dr Tennant stating that the mental sciences still awaited their Sir Isaac Newton.

The object of my paper is to show that on purely theoretical grounds this hope is vain. There is indeed a science of experimental psychology, this science will continue to grow. But as to the great expectations that the very word psychology arouses in some minds, these hopes will always remain unfulfilled. The psychological and social sciences will not transform either by power or understanding the great and terrible problems of our present discontents. For here we have to do not merely with ignorance but with the power of evil.

Before I proceed to the main arguments in support of my thesis, I would like to call to my support two eminent thinkers. I do not of course claim their authority for what I will try to prove later, but the two following quotations will perhaps not only make my thesis clearer, but also recommend it as not entirely heretical and idiosyncratic.

The first quotation is from an eighteenth-century scientist and philosopher, G. C. Lichtenberg. In one of his aphorisms he writes:

> We must not believe when we make a few discoveries in this field or that, that this process will just go on for ever. The high jumper jumps better than the farm boy, and one high jumper better than another but the height that no human can jump over is very small. Just as people find water wherever they dig, man finds the incomprehensible sooner or later.

The second quotation comes from one who can justly be regarded as the most influential thinker of my generation, Wittgenstein. Towards the end of his *Philosophical Investigations*, Wittgenstein makes this remark:

> The confusion and barrenness of psychology is not to be explained by calling it a young science; its state is not comparable with that of physics, for instance, in its beginning. (Rather with certain branches of mathematics, Set Theory.) For in psychology there are experimental methods and conceptual confusion. (As in the other case conceptual confusion and methods of proof.)
>
> The existence of experimental methods makes us think we have means of solving problems which trouble us; though problems and methods pass one another by.

I would like, indeed, to define my thesis as a logical exposition of the fact that in psychology the real problems that confront us, and the experimental methods which are being increasingly elaborated, pass each other by. And that although experimental psychology can show us new facts and confirm new hypotheses, yet in this discipline we very soon come up against the incomprehensible.

It is true enough that Hebb can 'jump' higher than James Mill. But it doesn't follow from this that a psychologist of the future will be able to jump to infinity! That he will be able, to use Hebb's own words, 'Reduce the vagaries of human thought to a mechanical process of cause and effect.'

But now it is high time that we engaged in battle in real earnest. And first a preliminary skirmish before the main thrust at the centre. I am puzzled to find one psychologist after another repeating that psychology is still a young science. For myself I find the psychological concepts which are discussed and defined in Plato's dialogues, and even more so the myths he devises to bring home to us his fundamental themes, to be a constant source of instruction. I would claim Aristotle's 'De Anima' as the first treatise to deal specifically with psychology as a separate subject. (Only a short time ago I heard a Professor of Psychology in one of our senior Universities describe Plato and Aristotle as 'superstitious blighters'; and he a believer in the Rorschach test!) Aristotle's pupil Theophrastus wrote a treatise on 'Characters', and his delineation is such that we can still recognise the types he describes among our own contemporaries. But to come to something on a more serious level. I would describe St Augustine's Confessions as perhaps the most profound psychological analysis ever carried out.

If it be true, as indeed it is, that 'Fecisti nos ad Te,

et inquietum est cor nostrum donec requiescat in Te', then any psychology which ignores the persistent inquietude of the human soul is a shallow and superficial affair.

Then coming to more recent times. We have Descartes's *Treatise on the Passions of the Soul*. The psychological discriminations in Spinoza's *Ethics*; Locke's *Essay Concerning Human Understanding*; Berkeley's *New Theory of Vision*; Hume's *Treatise on Human Nature*; Reid's *Powers of the Human Mind*; I could continue the list but there is surely no need to labour the point. What in heaven's name possessed Hebb to take as his origin such an unimportant figure in the history of psychology as James Mill!

The psychologists I quoted at the commencement of this paper would, I imagine, reply that they were talking of experimental psychology, and in particular the introduction of measurement and mathematical statistics into the study. They would once again refer me to the undoubted fact that physics only got under way when Galileo made it a matter of accurate measurement and the construction of mathematical formulae to explain the phenomena. Similarly chemistry as a precise science owed its beginning to the demonstration of Robert Boyle that the volume and pressure of a gas could be measured and related by a mathematical law.

Now (says the modern exponent of experimental psychology) that we have begun to introduce *measurement* and *mathematics* into the science of psychology, we can indeed speak of a new science with a triumphant future. It began with Binet introducing the conception of an Intelligence Quotient which could be expressed numerically. Then Pavlov was able to measure the strength of a conditioned reflex in terms of the quantity of saliva secreted. Similarly the maze learning of rats could be quantified in terms of errors made, time taken to learn, time taken to run. And motivation could be expressed in terms of the extent of deprivation of food or water. Certainly psychology has in the last seventy years become increasingly mathematical, often requiring an advanced knowledge of statistics to be even understood.

It is a big assumption though to assume without discussion that precisely the same method which has proved so powerful in the physical sciences will be applicable to every other investigation. Aristotle, at the commencement of the treatise I referred to a moment ago, makes precisely this point. He warns us: 'If there is no single common method by which we may discover what a thing is, the treatment of the subject becomes still more difficult; for we will have to find the appropriate method for each subject.' I believe we should take this warning of Aristotle's seriously (and not dismiss him as a superstitious blighter). We should ask ourselves first, can psychology make use profitably of the same methods that have been so advantageous in the physical sciences? I emphasise the word 'profitably', for I am not calling in question the accuracy of the measurements made, but only questioning their present importance and future promise.

Let me put it this way. I have here in my hand a piece of chalk. What interests the physicist and the chemist are the properties that this piece of chalk has in common with every other piece of chalk. Its density,

DDW

its specific heat, its molecular composition, etc. No doubt this piece of chalk is in some sense unique; no other piece of chalk in the world has exactly the same markings, the same shape, the same size, but these peculiarities are of no interest to science.

But what about an individual human being? He no doubt has many properties which he shares with every other human being, and some he shares with a particular group of human beings. But to me, at any rate, what is of supreme interest is just the uniqueness of this very person, the way in which he differs from any that ever came before him or will come after. His individuality, his unpredictability, his uniqueness. In a popular work entitled *Sense and Nonsense in Psychology*, Eysenck gives a list of people whom he would classify as typical introverts, and a similar list for extroverts. His list of extroverts includes Boswell, Pepys, and Cicero. I don't imagine Eysenck intended this list as more than a rough indication of what he was wishing to describe, but it will do very well for the point I am trying to bring home. It may be true that Boswell, Pepys, and Cicero all have some common abstract trait in common, but that is not what is psychologically interesting or important. What interests me is that Boswell, in spite of his ludicrous vanity, his gross licentiousness, his petty mindedness, was able to write the greatest biography in literature. As Macaulay well puts it: 'Many great men have written biographies, Boswell was one of the smallest of men and has beaten them all.' Then again take the picture that Boswell has given us of Dr Johnson; it tells us little to hear that Johnson was a high church Tory, a great Latin scholar, and a learned lexicographer. What does tell us a lot are the details Boswell gives us of his conversation and repartee. Even more psychologically interesting is the deep and lasting friendship that sprang up and endured between these two very diverse characters. I am reminded here of a wonderful remark that Montaigne made when asked for a definition of friendship, 'Parce que c'est lui, parce que c'est moi.' Now do I make myself clear? In psychology what interests us, what is of deep significance, are particulars not universals. The physical sciences are interested in the universals and the mathematical relations between them. The two subjects are not comparable.

I said a moment ago that I did not question the measurements made by experimental psychologists, I did question their significance. Take for a moment the ascertainment of the Intelligence Quotient by means of one of the properly standardised tests. I do not deny that these measurements do measure some abstract ability of the individual tested, call it intelligence if you wish. But remember a remark of Janet's: he said that the most important book every written on psychology was a dictionary. Why a dictionary? Well, because a dictionary reminds us of the enormous vocabulary that mankind has found necessary to express all the different facets of personality. Just consider the word 'intelligence' and consider all the cognate words that cluster round it. Wisdom, cleverness, depth, originality, genius, clarity, docility, perseverance, and I could add more. And remember that although these are all separate words in the dictionary they are intimately blended together in the person. If I may quote Lichtenberg again:

The qualities we observe in our souls are connected in such a way that it is not easy to establish a boundary between any two of them, but the words by which we express them are not so constituted; and two successive related qualities are expressed by signs which do not reflect this relationship.

Let me then give an example from my own experience of taking the Intelligence Quotient too seriously. When I was a regimental medical officer during the war we found that one of our new recruits could neither read nor write. He was sent to the area psychiatrist for an opinion and was returned with the report that his mental age was that of a boy of twelve and a half; he was recommended for discharge. He didn't want to be discharged and it turned out that he was an expert in handling dogs and ferrets, and as we were at that time plagued with rats he was appointed official 'rodent operator' to the unit. But I needn't labour the point for I think that we are all becoming aware of the limitations of intelligence testing. I would, however, use this story for a brief digression concerning 'animal psychology'. I have for many years been an avid reader of books describing animal behaviour both in laboratory experiments in learning, and more especially the field observations made by 'ethologists'. Such a book as Thorpe's *Instinct and Learning in Animals* is one I turn to with interest from time to time. But in all these writings I find missing that which for me is the most important fact about animal behaviour; it is that all living creatures from the simplest to the nearest human are just about the most un-understandable things in the world. It is this 'un-understandability' that makes the patient watching of them such a fascination. The increasing mechanisation and urbanisation of modern times is depriving us of any close contact with the wild things of nature. This is a great psychological impoverishment. There is an aphorism of Wittgenstein's; 'That if a lion could speak we would not be able to understand him.' This one sentence says more to me than all the books that pretend to *explain* animal behaviour.

But it is time to come back to my main thesis. I want to say that the word 'psychology' is a Janus-faced word, a word that faces in two opposite directions. And that it is the fact that these are two *opposite* directions that is of the greatest importance. The first direction, and which I would claim is the original meaning of the word, occurs in phrases such as this. We might say of a great novelist such as Tolstoy, or our own George Eliot, that they show profound psychological insight into the characters they depict. Or again we would say of a historian such as Burckhart that he had great psychological acumen in penetrating the motives behind the facts of history. In general, then, it is the great novelists, dramatists, biographers, historians, that are the real psychologists. For the sake of future clarity I am going to refer to this meaning of the word psychology as 'psychology *A*'.

Now the other meaning of the word psychology I shall call 'psychology *B*'. By psychology *B*, I refer to those subjects that are studied in a university faculty of psychology and are necessary to obtain a degree in that subject. The copious literature on perception in all its modalities. The numerous experiments and very diverse theories that are subsumed under the name of 'learning theory'. The various and conflicting schools of 'abnormal psychology'. Personality testing, vocational guidance, statistical method, and so on. Quite an undertaking.

But here I seem to hear the voice of my former teacher, Wittgenstein, thundering at me. 'Give examples, give examples, don't just talk in abstract terms, that is what all these present-day philosophers are doing.' So now I want to give an example of what I mean by 'psychology A'. It is a letter written to one of her pupils by Simone Weil. Notice that it contains nothing that one could call learning or cleverness, no attempt to be scientific or dictatorial. Yet it does contain profound psychological insight and not only for the particular individual and her immediate state, but also and perhaps even more so, for us living at the present time thirty-five years after it was written. (I only include that part of the letter which serves to illustrate my conception of psychology A.)

I have talked enough about myself, let's talk about you. Your letter alarms me. If you persist in your intention of experiencing all possible sensations – although as a transitory state of mind that is quite normal at your age – you will never attain to much. I was much happier when you said that you wished to be in contact with all that was real in life. You may think that they both amount to the same thing, on the contrary they are diametrically opposed. There are people who live only for sensations and by means of sensations; André Gide for example. Such people are in reality deceived by life, and as they come to feel this in a confused manner, they have only one refuge, to conceal the truth from themselves by miserable lies. The life which is truly real is not one that consists in experiencing sensations, but in activity, I mean activity both in thought and in deed. Those who live for sensations are parasites in the material and moral sense of the word compared with the those who labour and create; these are the true human beings. I would add too that those who do not run after sensations are rewarded in the end by much that is more alive, deeper, truer, less artificial, than anything the sensation seekers experience. To sum up, to seek after sensations implies a selfishness that revolts me, that is my considered opinion. It obviously does not prevent love, but it does imply that those whom one loves are no more than objects of one's own pleasure or pain, it overlooks completely that they exist as people in their own right. Such a person passes his life among shadows. He is a dreamer, not one who is fully alive.

About love itself I have no wisdom to give you, but I have at least a warning to make. Love is such a serious affair, it often means involving for ever your own life and that of another. Indeed it must always involve this, unless one of the two lovers treats the other as a plaything; in that case, one that is only too common, love has changed into something odious. You see, the essential thing about love is that it consists in a vital need that one human being feels for another, a need which may be reciprocated or not, enduring or not, as the case may be. Because of this the problem is to reconcile this need with the equally imperious need for freedom; this is a problem that men have wrestled with since time immemorial. Thus it is that the idea of seeking after love in order to find out what it is like, just to bring a little excitement into a life which was becoming tedious, etc., this seems to me dangerous, and more than that, puerile. I can tell you that when I was your age, and again when I was older, I too felt the temptation to find out what love was like, I turned it aside by telling myself that it was of greater importance for me not to risk involving myself in a way whose eventual outcome I could not possibly foresee, and before too I had attained to any mature idea of what I wanted my life to be and what I hoped for from it. I am not saying all this as a piece of instruction; each one of us has to develop in our own way. But you may find something here to ponder over. I will add that love seems to me to carry with it an even more serious risk than just a blind pledging of one's own being; it is the risk of becoming the destiny of another person's life, for that is what happens if the other comes to love you deeply. My conclusion (and I give you this solely as a piece of information) is not that one should shun love, but that on should not go out of one's way to try and find it, and especially so when you are very young. I believe at that age it is much better not to meet with it. . . .

I think you are the sort of person who will have to suffer all through your life. Indeed I am sure of it. You have so much enthusiasm, you are so impetuous, that you will never be able to fit into the social life of our times. But you are not alone in that respect. As to suffering, that is not too serious a matter so long as you also experience the intense joy of being alive. What is important is that you don't let your life be a waste of time. That means you must exercise self-discipline.

I am so sorry that you are not allowed to take part in sports: that is exactly what you need. Try once more to persuade your parents to let you do this. I hope at least that happy days hiking in the mountains is not forbidden. Give those mountains of yours my greetings.

I regard this letter with its deep personal and individual message, yet also one that has a much wider implication, as a perfect example of what I have called psychology *A*. You will see that it has nothing whatever to do with the sort of studies that a degree course in academic and experimental psychology provides. So I distinguish this latter by calling it psychology *B*. Now you may say to me that there is nothing new in this distinction between a psychology which has insight into individual characters, and a psychology which is concerned with the scientific study of universal types. It is a distinction that many competent writers on the subject refer to in the Introduction to their books. I know no better account of just this distinction than what Eysenck has to say in the Introduction to his book on *Abnormal Psychology*. But my object is not just to refer to the two different meanings of the word psychology, I want to draw attention to what I have called their two different *directions*. I have the impression that most psychologists think that in time what I have called psychology *B* will enable them to be much more efficient and scientific in dealing with problems in psychology *A*. That at least is what I make of all this talk of a young science and its unlimited promise for the future. When Hebb talks of 'understanding behaviour and reducing the vagaries of human thought to a mechanical process of cause and effect', or when Eysenck states that the same laws of learning apply 'to neurotics, college students and rats', I take them to imply that the day will come when clinical insight and intuitive personal understanding will no longer be necessary, for the science of psychology will replace this primitive way of coping with problems.

It certainly has happened in the history of science that a particular and difficult skill has been replaced by a new and more accurate scientific technique. The old physicians used to pride themselves on what they called the 'tactus eruditus', the ability to gauge the patient's temperature by laying their hand on the forehead; nowadays any probationer nurse can make a more accurate reading by the use of the clinical thermometer. Similarly it used to be customary to judge the degree of anaemia by the pallor of the palpebral conjunctiva; now it is possible to estimate the percentage of iron in the blood with accuracy.

So why shouldn't a further progress in the science of psychological testing improve by means of psychology *B* the rough intuitive guesses of psychology *A*? Well, I would say tha analogy is all wrong. For it is always measurement that is improved by new technique, and the importance of psychology *A* is that it deals with the *immeasurable*. It would only be a superficial and puerile estimation of personality that (say) took as its measure the Intelligence Quotient, the amount of dollars earned, the rank held in society, the position held in Eysenck's normal-neurotic and introversion-extroversion dimension. These are capable of being expressed numerically. But remember that most important book the dictionary, and think of all the numerous words that we need to describe all the facets of personality. What are they? Well, here is a venerable list that will do as well as any: Love, joy, peace, longsuffering, gentleness, goodness, faith, meekness, temperance – and if any psychologist thinks these are measurable he only shows that he does not understand the qualities the words refer to. It is hidden inwardness that is the rock over which a scientific and objective psychology will always come to grief. The truth is that we human beings are not meant to study each other as objects of scientific scrutiny, but to see each one as an individual subject that evolves according to its own laws.

So I wish to state emphatically that Psychology *B*, whatever progress it makes (and I intend to discuss the proper direction of that progress later) will never replace Psychology *A*, as a more accurate, a more scientific, a more efficient discipline.

I would not have considered this paper necessary if the belief that Psychology *B* would one day take over the work of Psychology *A* had merely been a pious hope. What does seem to me to be serious is that in some places I find the belief that the dawn has already broken. I will begin by some rather trivial examples and then go on to what I regard as more dangerous errors.

If you go into a bookshop today you will find books with some such titles as: *How to Win Friends and Influence People*, or *The Power of Positive Thinking*, or one that amused me the other day, *How to Help your Husband to be a Success*. Well, we all know that such books never helped anyone who was in serious emotional difficulties, still less anyone who was mentally ill. These books are full of harmless platitudes, but the fact that they attract a public to buy them is far from harmless; it shows a thoughtless attitude to the deeper problems of human life. It reflects a widespread error which extends even to educated people, that for every problem there is some particular *science* and some particular *expert* who can provide the necessary answer in a book.

Not so long ago an intelligent medical student came to see me. He had decided to change from the study of medicine to the faculty of psychology, for he felt that this latter study would not only enable him to cope more efficiently with his own personal problems, but also make him able to advise on the problems that other people had to contend with. I had some difficulty in persuading him that this would be a serious error to make, that he would find academic psychology a barren subject as compared with a knowledge of general medicine.

Then again a good many years ago now I was asked to give a course of lectures on 'normal psychology' to a class of students in the School of Physiotherapy. I imagine that the idea behind this request was that physiotherapists would in the course of their work have to cope with patients who needed tact and understanding in their handling. Now of course it is important that physiotherapists should have such tact and understanding, but this they will only acquire by experience and by working under one who already has achieved such wisdom. They could learn nothing from a course of lectures on 'normal psychology'. The lectures were not given.

In the medical curriculum today it is obligatory for students to attend and pass an examination in normal psychology. These lectures are usually given just after the student has completed his course in anatomy and physiology. The idea I imagine is that just as a grounding in anatomy and physiology is a necessary prolegomenon to the study of pathology and materia medica, so a course on normal psychology will be the groundwork by means of which the future instruction on psychiatry will be built. But the analogy is all wrong. Normal and abnormal psychology do not stand in this relation to each other. After a time I gave up giving these lectures for I felt they were an unnecessary burden on an already overcrowded curriculum.

We all from time to time in the course of our clinical work come up against personality problems where we feel out of our depth. (Perhaps we would be better psychiatrists if we felt this more often.) I notice a temptation both in my own case and that of some of my colleagues to think that such problems could be solved for me by resource to a 'clinical psychologist'. That he by means of some superior science, some highly sophisticated tests, will come up with the right answer. The analogy that one has in mind is the way the clinical pathologist can help with a specialised blood examination, the radiologist with his experience in interpreting the skiagram, or now the extremely specialised interpretation of the electro-encephalogram. But if one looks more closely the analogy breaks down completely. For these last mentioned specialities all employ a standard technique, the facts of which I am acquainted with but lack the necessary daily practice of. But if I send a patient to a clinical psychologist I do not know what he may be subjected to. Will he be asked to interpret certain standard formless ink-blots? Will he be subjected to a series of behavioural tests? I would myself have to have enough knowledge of personality testing to know whom to trust. And maybe when I have read some of the literature on these tests and been presented with some of the clinical psychologists' reports, I will wish no longer to have recourse to this very dubious help. The clinical psychologist may assess a personality in terms of the Intelligence Quotient, the degree of introversion, the adjustment to 'reality' (though here I would want to ask what 'reality' means). I have even seen the annual earning in dollars used as a measure of 'success', but all those aspects of personality which are of deep importance escape out of the net of knowledge.

I must add a warning here though. It may well be that a particular clinical psychologist is gifted with that form of insight that I have called Psychology *A*, and be able to help just because of this gift. All I am protesting against is the supposition that there exists already, or will soon be perfected, a scientific technique which will render the clinical insight gained by long experience an unnecessary acquirement. Here, now, and always, the old rule holds: 'Cor ad cor loquitur.'

There is, however, one point at the present time where 'psychology *A*' and 'psychology *B*' have already come into conflict. And this I must now discuss. There has grown up in 'psychology *B*' an immense literature concerned with what is called 'learning theory'. And some psychologists are claiming that the application of 'the laws of learning' can provide a scientific treatment for all forms of 'neurosis' and possibly some forms of psychotic behaviour as well. Thus remember Eysenck's statement:

> The laws of learning theory, to take but one example, apply no less to neurotics than to rats and college students.

Hilgard has written a comprehensive book of which the title is: *Theories of Learning* – notice the plural. For in this book he describes no less than ten different theories of learning. Osgood, in his *Theory and Method in Experimental Psychology,* has shown that many of the differences between these diverse theories are largely semantic, but in spite of this there is all the difference in the world between classical Pavlovian conditioning, Skinner's operant conditioning and the field theories of the Gestalt school. So if we are to make use of 'learning theory' in therapeutics it would be necessary to say which school of thought we support and why. As a matter of fact the Behaviour therapists seem to accept some form of 'stimulus-response' theory of learning entirely, without as far as I have been able to discover any reply to the cogent arguments and experimental facts produced by the Gestalt theorists. Still less have they paid any attention to what Freud called 'Instincts and their Viscissitudes', for it is a dogma of the behaviour therapist that all neurotic symptoms are learnt in their origin, and can be cured by the application of 'learning theory'.

But it would lead us too far astray to go into the complications involved in the different theories of learning or the place to be attributed to disturbed instincts in neurotic behaviour. I would avoid such a digression by coming right away to what I regard as the central error in the whole attempt of psychology *B* to establish one unified theory of learning. For the truth is that the word learning has a great many *different* meanings and there is not one special characteristic common to all forms of learning. It may be

true that we human beings sometimes form conditioned reflexes, sometimes make use of the mechanism
called operant conditioning: these may lie at the basis
of some fundamental habits. But that we learn in
many more important ways seems to me obvious.
Consider a child learning its native language at the
age of three, what an inexplicable wonder is there.
Skinner taught his pigeons to do many strange and
unexpected things, but he never was rash enough to
try to teach them to talk to him. Then later a child
begins to think for himself, as the phrase goes, and it
is the function of a good teacher to stimulate interest
in new subjects and in a general desire for clarity and
truth. These become ends in themselves. All the
experiments in animal learning depend on primary or
secondary reinforcement of the basic animal needs.
No animal desires truth for its own sake, and yet
surely that is the prime object of human education.
I cannot understand how such a clear thinker as
Eysenck shows himself to be, could allow himself to
state that 'the laws of learning apply equally to
neurotics, college students, and rats.' Eysenck, I
believe, when teaching his students, wants to arouse
an interest in psychology for its own sake, and for
truth as an end in itself.

This enormous difference between what we mean
when we talk about human learning and when the
experimental psychologist talks about animal learning, becomes very manifest when we consider the great
difficulty that all behaviour therapy comes up against
when it tries to employ the language of animal learning to the correction of human behaviour. What is
reinforcement for a human being? The rat wants its

food at the end of the maze; the pigeon gets its grain when it has discovered the necessary lever to peck at; and Köhler's chimpanzee reaches his banana when he discovers how to join two sticks together. But human beings in the throes of emotional conflict are not rewarded by toys such as these. Punishment is easier, but I find, and agree with the more critical behaviour therapists, that 'avoidance therapy' is ethically unpleasant and therapeutically inefficient.

Perhaps I can clinch the matter by introducing here a little fragment of 'psychology *A*'. Just two lines from the poet Aeschylus:

Zeus has opened to mortal man a way of knowledge; he has ordained a sovereign decree – through suffering comes understanding.

The knowledge that Aeschylus speaks of here, the understanding that comes from having suffered oneself, what has this to do with the theories of learning that the experimental psychologist writes about? And yet surely it is such an understanding that is needed in psychiatry.

When I commenced the study of psychology forty-five years ago it was considered then advisable that the student should combine this subject with the study of logic, ethics, and metaphysics. But today there is a tendency to break away from this tradition and for psychology 'to go it alone'. It is considered desirable for psychology to become one of the experimental sciences and be no more dependent on a general philosophical education than, say, physics or chemistry. Now certainly the physical sciences have progressed and continue to make progress without

EDW

any need of becoming involved in disputes about first principles or ultimate objectives. But it is my belief that psychology is in a very different position, and that the more ancient tradition rested on a wise understanding. For the great difference between psychology and any other science is that the psychologist is himself part, and a very important part, of the subject matter itself. I do not see how an intelligent student of psychology could help becoming involved in all the logical problems that surround the concept of 'self'. What gives unity and continuity to his own personality. The 'I' which is always subject and never object. The logical difficulties involved in the concepts of 'inner' and 'outer experience'. These puzzlements cannot be resolved by any experimental investigations, they are prior to all experiments, they are the subject matter of logic.

If then the student of psychology must become involved in problems of logic, still more so will he come face to face with the great problems of ethics. For the psychologist like any other human being must recognise that a sense of 'oughtness', of obligation, forms a fundamental part of what being a person means. The question of what is good in itself as distinct from mere means, what is the ultimate meaning of life, the realm of ends – a psychology which excluded the enormous part that these questions have played and continue to play in the life of the mind would be put a pale abstraction from the real life of the individual. I am not of course saying that it is the function of psychology to answer such questions, I am saying that a student of psychology who does not find his chosen subject leading him away from experimen-

tal procedures to thinking about ethics is to me a
strangely absent-minded thinker. For whatever we
may learn from observing the behaviour of animals,
whatever we may learn from experiments on perception, whatever we may learn from the study of 'individual differences', the great questions still stand over
us, whence? whither? how? If you go back to a
previous generation of psychologists (that is to say
before behaviourism had come to dominate the scene)
you will find that they realised the necessity of a
comprehensive psychology saying something about
this important aspect of human life. Thus William
James came to write his *Varieties of Religious Experience*; Freud could not rest until he had written *Totem
and Taboo, The Future of an Illusion,* and *Moses and
Monotheism*; Janet too, in his two big volumes *De
l'Angoisse à l'Extase,* is concerned to give an account
of the ethical and religious experiences which have
played and will continue to play a dominant role in
human behaviour.

It is curious to say the least that a generation which
prides itself on the frankness with which sexual
problems are handled, should seem almost embarrased by any reference to guilt, sin, death and judg-
ment. Yet thoughts about these concepts must play a
part in the thinking of anyone who is fully alive.

It is my belief that many turn to the study of
psychology because of the pressure of these great
problems, which seem to be part of the phenomena
with which the instruction should deal. They will feel
a sense of frustration if their teachers have nothing to
say on such matters. If they find psychology confining
itself to averages and statistics and experiments on

rats running in mazes. Then on the other side too I think it is valuable for the student of philosophy to have one of the experimental sciences as part of his curriculum; and experimental psychology is eminently suitable to play this role. Experimental psychology, besides giving good examples of the difficulty of devising crucial experiments, is replete with concepts that are in urgent need of dialectical development. All in all, then, I regret this tendency for the faculty of psychology to break away from its previous companions and become an independent study.

I am afraid I may be giving the impression that I attach very little importance to the study of experimental psychology. If so, I would now like to correct that imputation and say where I think the real importance of these experiments lies. I believe that experimental psychology has made and will continue to make very significant contributions to the study of neuro-physiology. Pavlov always described his work as 'the *physiology* of the higher nervous activity', and he eschewed the claim to be a psychologist. Yet Eysenck has called Pavlov the greatest of experimental psychologists. There is only a verbal difference here. It has interested me to see over the years how Eysenck's own books have taken on more and more a physiological terminology to replace a previous psychological one. In his first book we had the twin dimensions of extraversion–introversion, and neurotic–normal. Now these dimensions are defined in physiological terms. The extravert is one who finds difficulty in establishing positive conditioned reflexes, and can easily inhibit those already formed; whereas the introvert quickly establishes positive conditioned reflexes but finds the subsequent inhibition of those so formed harder to achieve. The neurotic-normal dimension is defined in terms of the degree of reactivity of the autonomic nervous system. Psychologists may dispute as to whether this theory is yet established, but the direction that the investigation has taken seems to me the correct one.

I mentioned earlier that Hebb's book on the 'organisation' of behaviour has had considerable influence. This I believe is due to the fact that Hebb brings out clearly how experiments in psychology have forced an elaboration of previous neurological constructs which are too simple to account for all the facts. For instance Lashley's search for the engram produced evidence that made all simple 'stimulus-response' connectionship, such as Pavlov, Thorndike, and Lashley himself believed in, impossibly simple. Similarly the perceptual phenomena that the Gestalt school drew attention to have made us revise considerably a too simple theory of sensory representation in the cerebral cortex. Lichtenberg in one of his aphorisms says that 'Materialism is the asymptote of Psychology'. I am not sure that I understand what he meant. But I would certainly say that neurophysiology is the asymptote of experimental psychology. The more rigorous experimental psychology becomes the more it will need to translate its findings into physiological terminology. Hebb seems to me to make this very point admirably in his book. But then he goes on to say:

Modern psychology takes for granted that behaviour and neural function are perfectly correlated, that one is completely caused by the other. There is no separate soul or life force to stick a finger now and then into the brain and make neural cells do what they would not otherwise.

Now while I would agree that *some* forms of behaviour are correlated with neural function and that in this field experimental psychology and neuro-physiology can with profit co-operate, I would most emphatically deny that *all* behaviour is so correlated. Nor would I conceive it a necessary alternative to believe in a 'soul or life force sticking its finger into the brain.' Why should there not be some areas of behaviour which just have no neurological counterpart? Let me put it this way. I feel hungry, and I have good experimental evidence to think that this particular sensation is correlated with a lowered blood glucose level and peristaltic contractions of the stomach. I study the menu and select certain foods; now there is some evidence from experimental psychology that animals deprived of certain necessary dietary elements will instinctively select those foods which will correct their deficiency. It may be true that human beings select their food on such a physiological basis, though this has never been proved, and the evidence of man's dietary indiscretions are all against it. After the meal I feel a desire to listen to some music; maybe with the further development of the electro-encephalogram this desire may be found to be correlated with some particular pattern of electrical wave formation. But then from my records I select, say, Bach's fourth Brandenburg Concerto. Now it seems plain nonsense to me to say that this individual selection is *physio-*

logically determined. I may or may not be able to give *reasons* for my choice, but it does not make sense to ask at the same time for the *cause* of my choice. Hebb, for example, in his book gives the evidence and the reasons which have led him to his particular theories; I imagine he would be justifiably annoyed if we then asked him to give the causes of his beliefs. For if it is not possible for us to choose between truth and error, between right and wrong, then the whole possibility of scientific discussion is reduced to an absurdity. The very possibility of speech, of intelligent discourse, of well reasoned books, depends on the certainty that a very large and important part of mental life is not determined and is not correlated with specific neural function. This certainly does not imply that a finger is thrust into the brain to compel neural cells to do what they otherwise would not. Nothing is compelled because nothing is correlated. You couldn't carry on a discussion with a tape recorder where everything is correlated and compelled; you can carry on an argument with another human being because he is able to *choose.* If I may say so, Hebb's error here is an excellent example of the point I was trying to make about the importance of a student of psychology having an acquaintance with logic. For any modern student of logic will immediately remember Wittgenstein's aphorism that 'Belief in the causal nexus is *superstition.*'

Psychology a new science with wonderful promises of future power and mental transformations: psychology determining through the study of animal behaviour the laws of learning which apply equally to 'neurotics, college students and rats'. So then I would end with this quotation written now nearly 2,500 years ago. At the end of his dialogue, the *Philebus*, Plato puts into the mouth of Socrates these words, Socrates speaks:

> Our discussion then has led to this conclusion, that the power of pleasure takes the fifth place. But certainly not the first, even though all the cattle and horses, and every other living creature seem to imply otherwise by their pursuit of enjoyment. Those who appeal to such evidence in asserting that pleasures are the greatest good in this life, are no better than augurs who put their trust in the flight of birds. They imagine that the desires we observe in animals are better evidence than the reflections inspired by a thoughtful philosophy.

A new science?

CHAPTER 3

CONCERNING BODY AND MIND

W HAT an odd situation the soul is in when it
reads an investigation about itself, when it looks
in a book to find out what itself might be. Rather like
the predicament of a dog with a bone tied to its
tail – said G.C.L., truly but a little ignobly.

LICHTENBERG

Ladies and gentlemen,

When I had completed this paper I had doubts as to
whether I should read it to you. For our Society is
properly concerned with those particular problems of
diagnosis and treatment which are daily met with in
our work. And much that I have written here will seem
at first to you as so much barren metaphysics. I don't
believe that it is barren metaphysics; indeed I hope
to show you before I conclude that the thoughts here
developed have important practical consequences, if
not for the details of our work, at least for the general
ethical background against which our work must be
carried out.

I do not see how anyone can practice the profession
of a physician, still less of a psychiatrist, without soon
coming face to face with the deepest philosophical
problems as distinct from scientific ones. Problems

which by their very nature cannot be answered by any future development of scientific discovery, but require an altogether different method of investigation. And if we do not at some time or other stop to ponder these problems, the very facts with which we come face to face will necessitate some answer in our actions. And so I venture to read this paper. But if to some of you it seems out of place, I can only assure you that I share in your disquietude.

Some months ago I was reading a translation of one of Pavlov's Wednesday morning conferences. Every Wednesday Pavlov used to meet his students and assistants, and other visiting scientists, for a general and informal discussion about any topic connected with his work in neuro-physiology. A stenographer kept a record of these conversations and they have now been translated in part. I have found some of them very interesting reading.

On Wednesday 19 September 1934, Pavlov arrived at the conference with his bushy whiskers fairly bristling with indignation. He had been reading a book by the famous English physiologist Sherrington. In this book Sherrington had used the words 'if nerve activity have relation to mind'. Pavlov was so shocked that any physiologist should doubt the absolute dependence of mind on brain, that he thought he must have read a mis-translation. He got a friend who had a better knowledge of English to check the words for him: but there they were in all their scandal – 'if nerve activity have relation to mind'.

How is it possible, said Pavlov, that in these days any scientist, let alone a distinguished neuro-physiologist, could for one moment doubt the com-

plete dependence of the mind on the healthy functioning of the organic nervous system? After some discussion he summed up his conclusion in these words:

> Gentlemen, can anyone of you who have read this
> book say anything in defence of the author? I believe
> this is not a matter of some kind of misunderstanding,
> thoughtlessness, or mis-judgment. I simply suppose
> that he is ill, although he is only seventy years of age,
> that there are distinct signs of senility.

For Pavlov, then, after thirty years of studying conditioned reflexes, the complete dependence of mind
and brain was axiomatic.

Mind dependent on brain. I suppose that we who
use daily physical methods of treatment in psychiatry,
and too often see the disastrous effects that organic
disease of the brain can produce both on intellect and
character, would feel inclined to agree with Pavlov.
To think of the mind and its activities as in some way
the product of that complex tissue we call the brain.
But I would also guess that if we were asked we might
well find ourselves at a loss to say how exactly we
conceived this precise dependence.

In the previous century that great biologist T. H.
Huxley, lecturing to an audience, told them: 'The
thoughts to which I am giving utterance, and your
thoughts regarding them, are the expression of molecular changes in that matter of life which is the source
of our other vital phenomena.' Is that clear to you?
I must say that I can attach no clear meaning to it.
Sherrington recalls that as a student in Germany the
Professor put one of the Betz cells from the cerebral
cortex under the microscope, and labelled it 'the

organ of thought'. A few days later a tumour of the brain was being demonstrated in the pathology department and one of the students asked: 'And are these cells also engaged in thinking, Herr Professor?' Now this I think was a really witty remark. For it made a piece of concealed nonsense obvious nonsense.

But to come to something written nearer our own time. Professor J. C. Eccles published in 1953 a book entitled *The Neuro-physiological Basis of Mind*. Professor Eccles is a recognised authority on neurophysiology; let us hear what he has to say.

In the Introduction to his book the Professor states his programme as follows:

> As indicated by the sub-title of this book, 'The Principles of Neuro-physiology', the scope may be described as covering the whole field of neurophysiology. The reactions of the single nerve or muscle fibre, the reactions of the single neurone, the reactions of the simpler synaptic levels of the nervous system, the plastic reactions of the nervous system and the phenomena of learning, the reactions of the cerebral cortex, and finally the relation of the brain to the mind. Broadly speaking it is an attempt to see how far scientific investigation of the nervous system has helped us to understand not only the working of our own brains, but also how liaison between brain and mind could occur. As such it tries to answer as far as is present possible some of the most fundamental questions that man can ask. What manner of being are we? Are we really composed of two substances, spirit and matter? What processes are involved in perception and voluntary action? How are conscious states related to events in the brain? How can we account for memory and the continuity of mental

experience which gives the self? How is that entity called the self interrelated to that thing called the body? Descartes failed to answer these questions because his science was too primitive, and his dualistic inter-actionist explanation has consequently been discredited. The remarkable advances that have been made possible largely by electronic techniques, now make it worth while to answer these questions in at least some of their aspects.

This is surely a most ambitious programme that Professor Eccles has set himself. And if it really is true that recent advances in neuro-physiology aided by electronics can tell us, to use his own words, 'what manner of being we are'; then surely this subject and these techniques are the most important science that anyone could choose. We would be wise to leave aside all other studies for this. But before we make such a serious decision it might be wiser first to see what conclusions Professor Eccles himself has come to on these weighty matters. To see indeed whether he has in any degree at all been able to fulfil the task he has proposed himself.

The first 260 pages of his book are taken up entirely with the early part of his programme. The structure, biochemistry and electrical phenomena of the individual neurons and synaptic junction; and then the more general anatomical organisation and histology of the cerebral cortex. Here as one would expect there is much original work of great interest and ingenuity. It is only in the last twenty-six pages of his book that he passes from positivistic natural science to more speculative matters. He starts his final chapter as follows:

We now come to the problem posed at the beginning of this book, which may be covered by the general question: 'who are we'? The answer to this question is according to Schrodinger 'not only one of the tasks of science, but the only one that really matters.'

But surely we don't need a distinguished physicist, or even a Professor of neuro-physiology, to tell us how important this question is. Centuries ago a certain unknown Greek wrote over the door of the temple of Apollo at Delphi γνῶθι σεαυτόν, 'know thyself'. This injunction 'know thyself' did not mean know your own personality and peculiar idiosyncrasies, but know what it means to be a human being, what is the nature of men as such: the very question indeed that Professor Eccles mentioned in his Introduction – 'what manner of creature are we?' Let us then look first at what he as a neuro-physiologist has to tell us. He writes:

The usual sequence of events is that some stimulus to a receptor organ causes the discharge of impulses along afferent nerve fibres, which after various synaptic relays, eventually evoke specific spatio-temporal patterns of impulses in the cerebral cortex. The transmission from receptor organ to cerebral cortex is by a coded pattern that is quite unlike the original stimulus, and the spatio-temporal pattern evoked in the cerebral cortex would again be different. Yet because of this cerebral pattern of activity we experience a sensation (more properly the complex constructs called percepts) which are projected outside the cortex, it may be to the surface of the body or even within it, or as with visual, acoustic and olfactory receptors to the outside world. However the only necessary condition for an observer to see colours, hear sounds, or experience the existence of his own body, is that appropriate patterns of neuronal activity should appear in appropriate regions of his brain, as was first clearly seen by Descartes. It is immaterial whether these events are caused by local stimulation of the cerebral cortex or some part of the afferent nervous pathway; or whether they are, as is usual, generated by afferent impulses discharged by receptor organs. In the first instance then the observer will experience a private perceptual world which is an interpretation of specific events in his brain. This interpretation occurs according to conventions acquired and inherited, that, as it were, are built into the micro-structure of the cerebral cortex, so that all kinds of sensory inputs are co-ordinated and linked together to give some coherent synthesis.

What an amazing state of confusion for an intelligent man to have arrived at! Of course something similar has been said many times before. It seems to be a fatal pitfall for anyone who is too preoccupied with the details of sensory perception. Thus Professor Eccles is able to quote such a distinguished neurologist as Sir Russell Brain in support of his conclusion; he quotes Sir Russell as saying: 'Mental experiences are the events in the universe of which we have the most direct knowledge.'

Now I went to do three things. I want first to bring out clearly the confusions and inconsistencies in such a view as Professor Eccles has here put forward. Secondly to show how easy it is for such a confusion to arise, how easy it is for anyone of us to find ourselves thinking along these lines, and thirdly and most important, how to get this sort of confusion out of our system once and for all.

I say that Eccles's theory is both inconsistent and confused. Throughout all his account he is quite certain of both the meaning and truth of certain statements he makes. His final theory is in fact a conclusion drawn from these data. He starts off by using the phrase 'the usual sequence of events'; how does he know that this is the usual sequence of events? He mentions stimuli acting on receptor organs. But if, as he states, the observer experiences 'a private perceptual world', how is it that he can even begin to talk about external stimuli and receptor organs? Eccles iscertain that the coded pattern in the afferent nerves and that evoked by them in the cerebral cortex is quite unlike the original stimulus. But then how does he know what these original stimuli were like?

To put it briefly then, if as Eccles asserts, the only necessary condition for an observer to see colours, hear sounds, etc., is that appropriate patterns of neuronal activity should occur in appropriate regions of his brain; then I do not see why or how we should ever come to believe in, or even understand the meaning of, still less logically infer, the existence of a real objective world outside. And if, furthermore, 'seeing' is taken to be the same thing as 'experiencing a private perceptual world', why should we even believe in neuronal activity in the brain itself?

Eccles is vaguely aware of this difficulty. And in fairness to him, and because it brings out the confusion even more clearly, we should consider his attempted solution. He writes:

We report our mental experiences to others and find they have like experiences to report to us. Such procedures serve to assure us that our private experiences are not hallucinations, or more strictly we may say that hallucinatory experiences are discovered by this procedure. We may conclude then that our mental experiences cannot be rejected as hallucinations, nor is solipsism a tenable explanation. Mental experiences are reported by all human beings with whom we take the trouble to communicate at the appropriate level.

But here once again Eccles is assuming the very truth he wants to regard as a justifiable inference. For if we really begin by being shut up in our own private perceptual world, how do we ever come to know that there are other observers? How could we have ever come to talk to them and to share a common language? If the only reason for regarding our sensory experiences as not hallucinatory is that we hear other voices, why should not these voices also be hallucinations (after all we know only too well that hearing voices is the most usual form of hallucination).

We have seen a very distinguished and competent experimental neuro-physiologist writing a lot of nonsense. But this particular brand of nonsense is very close to all of us. We have no cause to flatter ourselves at his expense. Let us go over the ground again and see how easy it is to get into the same sort of confusion. For only by looking at this problem from every angle will the essential and necessary clarity appear.

By accident, say, I touch the top of a hot stove and sustain a painful burn. Now we know that if, for instance, I had such a disease of the spinal cord such

FDW

as Syringomyelia; I would see both the stove and the blister on my finger but would feel neither the heat nor the pain. And so we make a distinction: the stove, my finger, the blister, these are real external things; but the feeling of heat and pain is subjective and in the mind of the percipient.

Or again I come into a room where there is a vase of roses, and I enjoy the perfume from them. But if my nose is stuffed up by a heavy cold, the smell is lost to me. So once again we say that although the bowl and the roses which are before our eyes are real enough, the smell and the pleasure I take in it are somehow in the mind of the observer. And we attribute this smell to minute particles given out by the roses which cause a chemical reaction on the nerve endings of the olfactory nerves in the nose. Here notice we have had to introduce something purely hypothetical, the minute particles.

Once more, I am listening to a concert on the radio. I have to leave the room. The radio set we are sure remains there just as it was, and also the sound waves in the air set up by the vibrations of the loud-speaker. But the music and all that it had meant to me, that surely leaves the room when I do. The symphony we would be inclined to say is the effect of the waves of air impinging on my eardrum, moving the ossicles of the middle ear, and transmitting nerve impulses to the auditory cortex via the eighth cranial nerve.

But now notice what we have been doing all along. We have been drawing a radical distinction between the sense of sight and what it reveals, and all the other sensory organs. At an unreflective and 'common sense' level it would appear as if the senses of touch, smell, hearing and taste were all dependent, as Eccles expresses it, on 'receptor organs'. But to the naïve observer the eyes are almost forgotten when in use. We are inclined to think of the eyes as in some sense a pair of windows through which we look *out* on the external world; not as organs of sensation *intervening* between us and the world of real things. But if we are to base any conclusions on physiology, the eyes are as much receptor organs as any one of the other senses. There is the transparent cornea, the lens with its possible defect of accommodation and transparency, the highly complicated nervous and photo-chemical structure of the retina, the optic tract with its decussation, the synaptic relay at the level of the geniculate bodies, and finally the radiation to the calcarine fissures of the occipital lobes. No wonder then that the physiologist finds himself in the position of saying that 'In the first place the observer will experience a private perceptual world which is an interpretation of events in his own brain.' We are back again at that complete subjectivism which we saw contained so much contradiction.

Let us go over the ground once more and see if we can track down this error to its source. We, like Professor Eccles, have been basing our conclusions on the certainty that we know a good deal about the anatomy of the sense organs and the nervous pathways to and in the brain. How did we acquire this knowledge? Well, think back for a moment to that day in the school of anatomy when you first removed the calvarium of the skull, and saw before your own eyes that marvellous structure the human brain. And then at once we had to get down to the laborious task of memorising the names of all those many, many fissures and lobes, of the areas of grey matter and white matter, and the cranial nerves which proceeded from them. But scarcely had we completed this task than the physiologist was upon us. This structure which you see with the naked eye is not, so he told us, the real nervous system; just look here beneath the microscope, see these different nerve cells, Betz cells, Purkinje cells, neuroglia, axions, dendrites, and the multitude of synaptic junctions between them. This immense neuronal network, every brain containing many more cells than there are inhabitants of this earth, this neuronal network is the real nervous system.

Not at all says the biochemist and geneticist. The dead and stained specimens on the microscope slide are largely artefacts; we know that the real nervous system is a living, growing, constantly changing thing, the seat of most complex chemical transformations and electrical phenomena which continue both by day and by night. So once again we had to get down to the task of learning the Eberden-Meyerhof process for the anaerobic utilisation of glucose, and the Krebs cycle for the oxidation of pyruvic acid. Do you remember now those benzene rings with their long side chains of carbon, hydrogen, and oxygen? And now more recently the geneticists have produced the double helix structure of the fundamental substance D.N.A. and seen in this, so they say, the key to the genetic code. Here, of course, we have passed out of the field of even microscopical vision. The various molecular structures can only be shown to us by drawings on the blackboard. And, if you were like me, I imagine that you could not help thinking that these macroscopic patterns were a reproduction of a similar one in the infra-microscopical world. I am sure the geneticist really *believes* in his double helix. And then as you placed the various atomic symbols in their correct place in the structural formula, you thought of this *C* representing a real discrete particle of carbon, and this *S* as representing a real discrete particle of sulphur, and so on. In fact you thought, to use a phrase of the great Sir Isaac Newton, of 'Little particles of matter so hard as to be indivisible.'

But now if an atomic physicist had come your way he would indeed have laughed at you. 'Little hard particles of matter? My dear fellow, don't you know that we exploded that theory long ago; one fine day over Hiroshima.' The ultimate and real constituents of matter are the fundamental particles, protons, electrons, neutrons, and now the less stable ones that keep coming on, neutrinos and anti-neutrinos, mesons, and pi-mesons, and I don't know what else.

To me it is never clear when these are spoken of as particles what they are particles *of*; and when these particles are said to pass from one orbit to another without passing through the intervening space then my mind gives up. Merciful heavens, what has happened to that nice solid brain we saw in the anatomy room? Three times now we have found ourselves ending up in a morass of confusion. There must be something radically at fault in our thinking, some original sin that has led us into repeated error. I believe this is so, and I want now to try to show this error to you. But I am in some doubt if I can do so, for the difficulty is not one of explaining something very complicated and profound, but of showing the immense importance of something so simple that it continually escapes our notice. However, let me at least try.

You remember Professor Eccles's original programme. He said he was going to investigate the whole field of the nervous system. Not only the structure and organisation of particular neurones and their synapses, but also 'the working of our brains', 'how liaison between brain and mind could occur'. He was going to investigate 'the process of perception', 'to give an account of memory and of that continuity of experience that gives the self', and finally 'decide what manner of creature we really are'.

'Investigate'. This is indeed a great word. We live in an age of investigation, when everything is investigated, both in the heavens above and the earth beneath and the waters under the earth; often with great interest and to the relief of man's estate. So what could seem more natural than to investigate perception and memory and the true nature of the self 'in the same way'. There is no more dangerous phrase in philosophy than that one 'in the same way'. Are you sure that this same way is still open? Perhaps there is a limit to what can be investigated by Science. One of the main tasks of philosophy is to show the limits of what at first sight seems limitless. So let us enquire more closely into the real nature of scientific investigation. That means taking a concrete example and seeing what we really *do* when investigating. The patient, say, has a temperature of 102°F., and I say to Sister we must investigate this. And so we go through the routine procedure of inspection, palpation, percussion, and auscultation, and then proceed to certain laboratory and X-ray examinations. But now notice what we are completely dependent on, what we assume as perfectly valid, in such investigations. We depend entirely in every one of these procedures, even the most recondite laboratory ones, on perception and memory. Sight, touch, hearing, memory, language, these are the *instruments* of scientific investigation. Therefore they themselves cannot in turn be investigated. If I may use a crude metaphor; I can look at any object on earth or in the sky through my telescope, except the telescope itself.

It therefore does not make sense, it is really a piece of concealed nonsense, when Eccles proposes to investigate perception, memory, the self, and in general the relationship between mind and body. We can indeed investigate in more and more detail the *anatomy* of the sense organs; but the 'nature of perception', 'the liaison between mind and brain', 'the transition from nerve impulse to consciousness' – investigation makes no sense here. I am not saying that these matters are so complicated that we cannot attain unto them. That would only be a challenge to try harder. Nor am I saying that these things are so commonplace that we can take them for granted. But I am saying that however much we learn concerning the physiology of the eye and optic tract this will never explain how seeing is possible. Perhaps someone would like to interrupt me here by drawing my attention to the vast literature that already is in being concerning the psychology of perception, memory, language. I think here particularly of such books as Vernon's on *Visual Perception*, Broadbent's book entitled *Perception and Communication*, and Bartlett's work on *Remembering*.

How then can I state so emphatically that perception, memory, language cannot be investigated? But now notice in these books that the psychologist is largely concerned with experiments on subjects other than himself. He has to take as given the seeing, hearing, remembering, describing, which are his own observations; these form no part of the investigation. It is possible for a psychologist sometimes to act as his own subject; one thinks at once of Ebbinghaus and his laborious work on learning and forgetting strings of nonsense syllables. But here again the same dichotomy occurs. When Ebbinghaus came to write his book, the memory of these self-experiments, the interpretation of his own notes made at the time, these were fundamental data and were not themselves in need of investigation. All I am saying is that in every investigation there will always be that which is not itself investigated; in every experiment there will be data which are not the result of experiment; in every enquiry there will always be that which is not enquired into.

This for me is such a simple yet important and far-reaching truth that I would come to the same point by another route. Suppose you showed a clock to one who had never seen such a mechanism before. You could explain in detail to him the working of the mechanism, and the use of the machine. But now imagine one born stone deaf; he could carry out a complete dissection of the outer, middle, and inner ear, and could become a master in the cytology of the auditory cortex; and nothing in all this would ever explain to him what hearing was like. Similarly one born blind could by reading Braille answer correctly all questions con-

erning the structure of the eye and the optic tract, but
would never come to an understanding of what was
meant by sight. Then again I could give an account of
how I came to learn a foreign language; but who
among us could describe how he came to speak his
native tongue?

I said that these were such simple truths that their
importance is too easily overlooked. It was forgetting
these truths that led us into all the confusions of
complete subjectivism. Simple truths, yes, but not
platitudes. If we were to lose our sight we would indeed
bemoan our fate; should we not then sometimes pause
and wonder at the miracle of sight? I want to say that
every time you open your eyes a miracle occurs. If we
should become deaf, think what we would lose in the
way of friendly communication and intelligent discussion. So should we not wonder at, and be grateful
for, the miracle of hearing? Every time you wake up
in the morning and return to consciousness a miracle
occurs.

Much speculation is going on as to the nature of the
memory trace and how it is to be explained at the
physiological level. A perpetuating cycle of activity in
a complex of neurones? A facilitation at synaptic
junctions? A molecular coding by the complex molecules of R.N.A. or D.N.A.? But whatever comes of
these speculations it will still be true that:

> When to the sessions of sweet silent thought
> I summon up remembrance of things past

a miracle occurs. It is correct to speak of progress in
science and in our scientific understanding of the
world. May that progress continue. I hope that

nothing that I say in this paper will be taken as an 'attack on science'. The greater part of my life has been taken up with an attempt to think scientifically about the problems of mental pathology, their cause and their treatment. But I am sure it is an error which is disastrous to our philosophy if we forget this great truth: that however much the realm of what is explained is extended, the realm of the inexplicable is never reduced by one iota. It would seem from much that is written nowadays that perhaps in the far distant future everything will be explained and controlled by scientific understanding. I have been trying to emphasise that this, thank God, will never be the case. Those fundamental data which we use in giving explanations: perception, memory, language, these remain for ever in the realm of the inexplicable. In an age such as this in which technological sophistication increases daily, there is a great danger that we lose the precious gifts of wonder and gratitude for the common and simpler foundations of our being.

Eccles, you will remember, spoke of the rudimentary nature of Descartes's physiology, making it impossible for him to solve the problem of the relation of mind to body. Perhaps you may have thought that in concentrating my criticism on a book published in 1956, I was already a bit out of date; after all there have been remarkable discoveries in neuro-physiology in this last decade. But my choice was deliberate. Professor Eccles was in no better position than Descartes, and we or any subsequent generation will not be in any better position than Professor Eccles, to solve a problem to which the notion of a 'solution' does not make sense. I have no need to fear that tomorrow some new discovery will invalidate everything that I have written here. 'In the idea now is always.'

At the risk of being prolix I am going to give two further examples from other writers of the type of misunderstanding I am concerned to eliminate from our thinking. (1) Suppose you take up such an excellent book as Ranson's *Anatomy of the Nervous System*. And suppose you want to learn the sensory pathway from the tips of the fingers to the cerebral cortex. You learn the details of the end organs in the fingers, the sensory nerves in the arm, their rearrangement in the brachial plexus, their separation from the motor nerves and entry into the cord through the posterior nerve roots. Then the arrangement of the sensory tracts in the spinal cord, their decussation at the level of the brain-stem, their relay to the various nuclei in the thalamus, and the connections to and from the cortex to the thalamus. All this can be described in positivistic language and we can if needs be verify each statement in the antomy room. But then you find, even in Ranson, a reference to the question at what point the nerve impulse 'enters' consciousness. Notice the complete change of language here; this is no longer descriptive and verifiable, but metaphorical and speculative. In everyday language if we use the word enter we imply a threshold both sides of which can be observed and entering means passing from one side of this threshold to the other. But in this sense, the common everyday sense, of 'entering', you cannot speak of anything entering consciousness. For consciousness has no boundary, no threshold which can be observed. If it had then there would have to be a third form of consciousness which was conscious of both what was conscious and what was not yet so. This is obvious nonsense. Consciousness is not just one of the many things we are conscious of: the mind has no particular place in nature.

(2) In a book recently published I found the following sentence:

> Some thoughts we keep to ourselves. But man being a gregarious animal seeking companionship and co-operation with his fellows, naturally wanted to pass on a great many of his thoughts. This led him through countless ages of endeavour to develop a means of communicating thought. Laboriously he built up language.

But this is surely nonsense. First thoughts and then the gradual development of words in which to express them! But can any of us think without using words already to ourselves? Thinking and language are not separable in this way. And what does 'laboriously build up' mean here? Nowhere in the world, nor in the study of extinct languages, do we find gradations of language, but only different languages. Indeed both primitive and extinct languages are often of the greatest complexity, and 'progress' is often in the nature of simplification and reduction in the vocabulary. To talk of countless ages of endeavour is to invoke a 'deus ex machina' here that just won't work. I want to say that the existence of language, and the development of the ability to speak in a child is a miracle, something that the notion of explanation as to how it came, and comes to be, does not make sense. It is something indeed for us to wonder at and be thankful for.

If Pavlov had been listening to what I have said so

far I am sure his patience would have passed all bounds, and he would have been convinced of my advanced senility. And perhaps your patience is becoming exhausted too. Surely you would say that if our sight is troubling us we go to an ophthalmologist and he by his knowledge of the anatomy and physiology of the eye and optic system may be able to correct our vision. Similarly if deafness troubles us we go to an otologist. We would not think much of such specialists if they told us that seeing and hearing were miracles. Surely we must then say that sight and hearing are dependent on the physical structure of the sensory organs and their nervous connections with the brain. Once more, in the last two decades the power of physical methods of treatment in psychiatry have been increasingly demonstrated. How then can I dare to criticise one who states that mind is dependent on brain?

Now I need hardly say that I accept as much as anyone the physical treatments of the ophthalmologist, the otologist, the psychiatrist, etc. All that I am criticising is the vagueness and the many misleading interpretations which that word 'dependent on' can give rise to. I want to fix a more precise meaning to that word, to determine its *limits*. I have tried to show how much of confusion and error comes into our thinking if we do not fix and determine these limits. But more than that only, I want to make 'wonder secure'. There is a danger, with the ever increasing development of natural science, its powerful applications, and its inevitable specialisation, that we come to forget the realm of the inexplicable. 'The mysteriousness of our present being.'

At the common-sense level we found ourselves tempted to speak of an outer world revealed by sight and an inner world of feeling, hearing, remembering, etc. I hope I have been able to make you see the misunderstandings that are contained in this unreflective use of the words 'outer' and 'inner'. The words compelled us to picture a boundary which had to be crossed and yet somehow we were to be conscious of both sides of this boundary. There is no such boundary. Experience is experienced as one continuous whole. What we see, the distant hills and their colouring, the sound of a bird calling, the smell of the pine trees, the feel of the sand beneath our feet, and the memories of previous visits to this place, and the pleasure which accompanies these things, this is all given as one and undivided. For various practical necessities we break up this undivided whole, and attend now to this aspect and then to that. If I am doing anatomy it is sight that must be my guide. But if I am listening to music it may be well to close my eyes. These are matters of expediency and depend on a deliberate shift of attention. Now the advances in natural science have been due to a wise and deliberate selection of certain aspects of the total given whole, and the ignoring of others. The division of qualities into primary and secondary was a great discovery in methodology, not a metaphysical discovery. For instance I use spectacles to overcome my astigmatism, but if I am interested in the physiology of the eye it is these very distortions that interest me. Both the corrected vision and the distorted vision are equal in their ontological status, they both belong to that which is real. Everything that comes to us by way of the senses is part of reality and worthy of attention at times, what aspect we choose to study in detail is a matter of choice.

There is a flash of lightning and a clap of thunder. We are all startled by them and make comment. Here surely you would say is an 'outer experience'. The thunder has made me feel nervous but I manage to conceal this feeling from the others, here surely you would say is an 'inner experience'. Of course I am not denying such a familiar distinction as this. I am denying nothing. I am pointing out the very real dangers and confusions that those words 'outer' and 'inner' produce in philosophy. They force on us a picture of reality, of the mind and its place in nature, which is of no use at all.

The distinction between seeing the flash of lightning and my feeling of fear is not that the vision lies on one side of a barrier and my feeling on the other. For me there is no barrier between them, they are together. We have learnt by experience that if there is lightning others see it too (but remember not always); we have also learnt by a long process of training to conceal our emotions. A small child cannot conceal its terror, such an emotion is as much 'outer' as anything seen; it is *seen*. I sometimes have a high pitched ringing noise in my ears, this I constantly mistake for the telephone ringing; only experience has taught me that I really have '*Tinnitus aurium*'. I know now that the sound is 'inner', but at one time it was 'outer', and it has not changed its quality.

Once we have grasped the necessary limitations that must be imposed on the words 'inner' and 'outer' when used in epistemology, then the confusion we got into when describing the different conceptions of the brain can be disentangled. The anatomist describes the brain which he sees with his naked eyes. The physiologist describes the stained specimens he sees under the microscope. The biochemist describes those experiments which have led him to postulate such and such a molecular structure. The pure physicist has his own complicated apparatus for investigating the structure and constituents of the atom. But once again I must insist every one of these investigators depends in the last resort on sensory perception, memory, language; these are the tools with which he investigates and whose validity he has to assume. He cannot in turn investigate these.

No one of the pictures that these various investigators build up to direct them in their work has any claim to priority over the other. All are necessary for a full knowledge of the subject. A radiologist trying to locate a brain tumour from the appearance of his X-ray will necessarily use the gross terms of the anatomist. The neurologist trying to account for an area of anaesthesia or paresis, will be guided by the knowledge he has of neuronal structure, and will speak in terms of nerve centres and nerve tracts. The expert in mental deficiency is being increasingly helped by the development of the biochemistry and genetics of the brain. And finally it is the pure scientist who has over the past centuries provided us with the microscope, the chemical stains, the X-ray apparatus on which these other investigators depend. At no level of investigation can we say, 'Ah! now we have reached the real thing in itself; before, all that we were concerned with was mere appearance.'

Part Two

And yet, and yet; when Professor Eccles promised to answer that question 'what manner of being are we?', did not this arouse our interest in a deep and serious sense? We have seen, I hope, in the previous section, that this is a problem that no empirical investigation can ever answer. Schrödinger was right in describing this as the most important of questions, but then he went all astray when he added 'the most important question that *science* can ask.' It is not a problem in natural science; neither neuro-physiology, psychology, or any other empirical investigation can help us here. And yet we must both ask and give an answer at once. The fact that we have to live and make decisions demands an answer.

It was a Greek who first posed this question in words. Suppose then that for a moment we forget about our present scientific achievements and go back in history to the fifth century B.C., to Athens: one of the greatest centuries in the history of human thought. But first we must set the scene aright. The scene is set in prison. Socrates has been condemned by his fellow citizens on a charge of atheism, impiety, and corrupting the young by his sophistry. In a few hours he is to be given poison to drink. He spends these last hours in discussion with his friends over this very problem of the relation of the mind to the body. He tells them a little of the development of his own thoughts on this subject. Let us listen for a moment to him. Socrates speaks:

GDW

When I was young I had a great desire to know that department of philosophy which is called 'natural science'. To understand the causes of things. To understand why a thing is, how it is created and how destroyed, this appeared to me a worthy investigation. I was always preoccupied with such questions as these: Is it some form of fermentation which causes heat and cold to bring forth living creatures? Is the blood the essential element without which thinking could not occur, or is it respiration, or the natural heat of the body? Or perhaps none of these but the brain may be the natural seat of our senses of hearing and sight and smell; and from these sensations memory and opinion arise, and then when memory and opinion are firmly established natural science may be built up. Then I went on to consider how these powers are lost, and this led me to consider all phenomena in heaven or on earth. Finally I came to the conclusion that I had no aptitude for these studies, and I will tell you what led me to this conclusion. For I found that my preoccupation with these investigations had so blinded my eyes to things which before had seemed to me and others self-evident.

Doesn't this sound very familiar to you? Pavlov, Eccles, you and I, starting off with the enthusiastic conviction that the investigations of natural science will provide us with answers to the deepest questions. And then as our investigation proceeded we found ourselves bewildered and in doubt over what at first had seemed so certain and well established. This bewilderment and confusion we found at last arose because we were trying to solve a philosophical puzzlement by an irrelevant empirical investigation. Socrates too discovered in good time that these sort of investigations could never answer for him the most important question as to the nature of man and his destiny. I will not here discuss the method of philosophical enquiry that he then developed, but I will proceed to tell you of the conviction he finally came to, and with which he went willingly to his death. Socrates speaks again:

So long as we keep to the body and our soul is contaminated with this imperfection, there is no hope of our attaining our object, which we assert to be absolute truth. For the body is a source of endless trouble to us by reason of the mere requirement of food; and is liable also to diseases which overtake us and impede us in the search after true being: it fills us full of loves and lusts and fears and fancies of all kinds, and endless foolery, and in fact, as men say, takes away from us the power of thinking at all. Whence come wars and factions and fighting? Whence but from the body and the lusts of the body? Wars are occasioned by the love of money, and money has to be acquired for the sake and in the service of the body; and by reason of these impediments we have no time to give to philosophy; and last and worst of all, even if we are at leisure and betake ourselves to some speculation, the body is always breaking in on us causing turmoil and confusion in our enquiries, and so amazing us that we are prevented from seeing the truth. It has been proved to us by experience that if we would have pure knowledge of anything we must be quit of the body, the soul in herself must behold things in themselves; and then we shall attain the wisdom which we desire and of which we say we are lovers. Not while we live but after death. For if while in the body, the soul cannot have pure knowledge, one of two things follows, either knowledge is not to be attained at all, or, if at all, only after death. For then and not till then, the soul will be parted from the body and exist in herself alone. In this present life I reckon that we make the nearest approach to knowledge when we have the least possible intercourse with the body and are not surfeited with the bodily nature, but keep ourselves pure until the hour when God himself is pleased to release us. And thus having got rid of the foolishness of the body we shall be pure and hold converse with the pure, and know of ourselves the clear light everywhere, which is no other than the light of truth.

But o, my friend if this be true there is great reason to hope that, going where I go, when I have come to the end of my journey, I shall attain that which has been the pursuit of my life.

For Pavlov 'mind dependent on body': for Socrates the body a hindrance, a source of distraction and deceit, an imprisonment for the mind. Socrates of course, or maybe Plato speaking in the name of Socrates, is ennunciating a conception which already had had a long history in Greek thought. There was indeed a familiar Greek proverb σῶμα σῆμα, 'the body a tomb'. And it would have been no paradox to his audience when Euripides put into the mouth of his chorus these lines:

Who knows if life is not death
and death is considered life in the other world.

What has interested me though, and what I now want to draw your attention to, is the way this Pythagorean-Socratic-Platonic conception of the relationship of the soul to the body finds perfect expression in the most unexpected places. An Elizabethan actor-dramatist, a man described as knowing little Latin and less Greek; a man living in an age of intense religious controversy who yet nowhere in his many writings gives us so much as a hint as to where his own allegiance lay. And then suddenly this: *The Merchant of Venice*, Act V, Scene 1. Lorenzo and Jessica have come out into the garden, it is a bright starlit Italian night. Lorenzo speaks:

> Sit, Jessica; look how the floor of heaven
> Is thick inlaid with patines of bright gold:
> There's not the smallest orb which thou behold'st
> But in his motion like an angel sings:
> Still quiring to the young-eyed cherubims;
> Such harmony is in immortal souls;
> But while this muddy vesture of decay
> Doth grossly close in, we cannot hear it.

Ah! there you see it comes again, 'This muddy vesture of decay doth grossly close us in. The mind prevented by the body from perceiving the truly real in all its wonder and beauty.

And if anyone should reply that Shakespeare is only putting words into the mouth of one of his many characters, listen to this sonnet of his where he is surely speaking for himself.

> Poor soul, the centre of my sinful earth,
> Fool'd by these rebel powers that thee array,
> Why dost thou pine within and suffer dearth,
> Painting thy outward walls so costly gay?
> Why so large cost, having so short a lease,
> Dost thou upon thy fading mansion spend?
> Shall worms, inheritors of this excess,
> Eat up thy charge? Is this thy body's end?
> Then, soul, live thou upon thy servant's loss,

And let that pine to aggravate thy store;
Buy terms divine in selling hours of dross;
Within be fed, without be rich no more:
So shall thou feed on Death, that feeds on men,
And Death once dead there's no more dying then.

For me though the most impressive and deepest
expression of this Socratic-Platonic conception in all
literature is found in the most unlikely of places.
Victorian England; a dreary Parsonage high up on
the Yorkshire moors; the mother long since dead; the
father a man of no great ability; the brother already
a victim of alcohol; and then three sisters of superlative
imagination. Of Emily Brontë her sister said: 'Stronger
than a man, simpler than a child, her nature stood
alone.' So then hear this, which must surely reflect a
personal experience:

But first a hush of peace, a soundless calm descends;
The struggle of distress and fierce impatience ends;
Mute music soothes my breast, unuttered harmony
That I could never dream till earth was lost to me.

Then dawns the invisible, the unseen its truth reveals;
My outward sense is gone, my inward essence feels:
Its wings are almost free, its home its harbour found,
Measuring the gulf it stoops and dares the final bound.

O dreadful is the check, intense the agony,
When the ear begins to hear and the eye begins to see;
When the pulse begins to throb, the brain to think again;
The soul to feel the flesh, and the flesh to feel the chain!

Yet I would lose no sting, would wish no torture less;
The more that anguish racks, the earlier it will bless;
And robed in fires of hell, or bright with heavenly shine
If it but herald death, the vision is divine.

Poetry! Poetry! What am I doing quoting it here? Am
I not speaking to a society dedicated to scientific
investigation and the sober weighing of experimental
evidence? I tried to demonstrate to you in the first
part of my paper that the methods of scientific investigation were not and never could be applicable to this
great question, the relation between mind and body.
And that which seemed so obvious to Pavlov was far
from being self-evident, that indeed when rigorously
pursued it led us into obvious nonsense. I am certainly
not claiming that the conception which Socrates discussed at his death, and which these poets so un-
expectedly echoed, is one that can be proved or verified. The very notion of proof or verification is misunderstanding and superficiality here. I can only say
that this 'idea is like an arrow in the mind. Once it has
lodged there it cannot be extracted. That is the reason
why poetry is its true formulation. Perhaps this is
what Goethe meant when he said that he who does not
believe in the world to come is already dead in this
one.

But concerning that which can be neither proved
nor verified is not a healthy agnosticism the proper
attitude in a scientific age? Yes certainly, a healthy
agnosticism concerning that which has not yet been
ascertained but may perhaps in the future be known,
for instance the possibility of life on other planets. But
agnosticism has no meaning when applied to those
questions which by their very nature will never be a
matter of scientific investigation. These are questions,
I say, that the conduct of life demands an answer from
us now, at once. To suppose that conduct can be
divorced from speculation or that we may do good

without caring about truth, is a danger that is always tempting.

So now let me draw your attention to certain broad principles in our own field of psychiatry where a decision on this ethical question is urgent and imperative. And yet where neither common sense, nor further information, nor any scientific discovery, can ever come to our aid. Where the will alone must decide the truth it will believe.

Some of us have to take care of and do as much as lies in our power for those who either by genetic defect or birth trauma will never develop into maturity. Some indeed who will never learn to speak or even be able to carry out the simplest acts of self-preservation. Now if Pavlov was correct and mind was dependent on brain, we must assume that where there is such gross brain damage, mind is almost non-existent too. I have lived through an age in which a great and cultured nation deliberately acted as if this were so; and counted it wise and praiseworthy to destroy such apparent monstrosities. Knowing the history of man I see no reason to be optimistic that our children, or our children s children, may not have to fight this same battle over again. But suppose that what Socrates contended for was indeed the truth. That the soul is *imprisoned* within the body. Then we can say nothing concerning the hidden life of these sufferers; they are shut off from us by barriers that neither we nor they can break; but we do not know yet what they shall be. I state this not as an hypothesis that one day might be proved, nor as anything that some special insight could reveal, but as a decision of the will, a decision of ethics where neither physiology nor any other science can come to our aid. In the practice of psychiatry we are dealing every day with those whose personality has undergone a change. People who have become morose and depressed; people who have become wildly excited and overactive; people who have become withdrawn and suspicious; people who have become deluded and even dangerous; and so on through all the range of mental illnesses. We have been discovering these last thirty years to what extent these disorders can be cured by purely physical methods of treatment (methods which require, however, patience and explanation in their application). But I think the very success of these methods are to some degree a danger to those who employ them. Whatever advances are made in the future regarding the treatment of mental illness, however close the work of a psychiatrist becomes to that of a general physician, we should never forget that there is, and always will be, a mystery about mental ill-health which makes it different from any disease of the body. Every mentally ill patient is an individual enigma, and we should always think of him as such. There is something more disturbing and puzzling in a dissolution of the personality than in any bodily disease. I think that great and good man Dr Samuel Johnson spoke for all mankind when he described his own experience: 3 a.m. on the morning of 16 June 1783.

> I felt a confusion and indistinctness in my head which lasted I suppose about half a minute. I was alarmed and prayed God that however He would afflict my body He would spare my understanding. This prayer that I might try the integrity of my faculties, I made

in Latin verse. The lines were not very good, but I knew them not very good: I made them easily and concluded myself to be unimpaired in my faculties. Soon after I perceived that I had suffered a paralytic stroke, and that my speech was taken from me. I had no pain and so little dejection in this dreadful state that I wondered at my own apathy, and considered that death itself when it should come would excite less horror than now seems to attend it.

I think Dr Johnson's relief that only his body was affected and not his reason is something that we who have to treat those who mind *is* affected should constantly remember. For the patient a mental disease is and always will be, whatever advances in treatment are made, a more terrifying and humiliating experience. I think we should make it clear that although we do not share their pessimism about the outcome, we do appreciate their natural alarm.

It was once said to me, 'What I should fear if I became mad would be your common-sense attitude, that you would seem to take it as a matter of course that I was suffering from delusions.' I think I understand what he meant, and I think he was referring to an attitude that it is only too easy for those dealing daily with mental illness to fall into. I believe that we must let our psychiatric patients see that we understand that they are in a state of affliction which is not comparable to any bodily pain however severe. To communicate such an understanding is not easy.

When I was a medical student, the treatment of mental illness was largely a matter of protective custody, attention to physical health, and a patient hopefulness. You younger psychiatrists of today can hardly imagine the mental hospitals of those days. Now on all sides there are treatments to be got on with and you can feel a genuine optimism concerning the ultimate recovery of most of your patients. There is perhaps a danger that we should take all this too much for granted. Many generations of physicians have desired to see the things that you see and have not seen them. I know that with any scientific discovery in time it must lose its wonder; but if what I have been saying concerning the relation of mind and body has carried any conviction to you, then I think these methods of treatment should always be a source of wonder. There is something to wonder at here in the return of sanity; these treatments are on a different plane than any other medical procedure. As time goes on it is probable that we will come to know, and make use of, considerably more about the biochemistry of the central nervous system. The information that the electro-encephalogram can give us is still perhaps only in its infancy. Yet assuming that the steady therapeutic progress of the last thirty years will continue (and remember this is an assumption), there will always be in psychiatry the realm of the inexplicable. An inexplicable which does not exist in any other branch of medicine. There is still, for instance, a great deal to learn about, say, the action of the tri-cyclic drugs on the biochemistry of the brain. But no discovery can ever be made as to how these drugs can relieve melancholia and change nihilistic delusions. This leap from the physical to the mental will remain always in the realm of the inexplicable. Concerning this may I not once again use the word 'the miracle'? I might mention at this point a matter of less importance,

yet which is relevant to what I have been con-
tending for. I am sorry that the word 'psychiatrist' has
come into general use to denote those physicians who
are concerned in the treatment of mental illness. It
suggests I think to the general public, and we may
even deceive ourselves by it, that we have both more
power and understanding than we really possess. None
of us are able to 'heal the soul' as the word psychiatrist implies. I prefer that old-fashioned word 'alienist'.
We are concerned with those who in some way are
alienated from their real selves. We have found in
recent years certain ways of treating the body that
hastens in many cases the return from alienation, but
why this should be so is a matter that will always
defy explanation, just because consciousness and
personality are matters which the notion of 'explanation' is not applicable to.

We have been talking about drugs, their known
action on the human nervous system, and their inexplicable action on the mind and on personality.
There has been talk in recent years of drugs that
might provide new and deeper 'insight' into the real
nature of the world; opening as it were 'the doors of
perception'. There have been those who have advised
and attempted to use such drugs as mescaline and
lysergic acid to obtain a vision of the world freed
from the everyday categories through which we
normally perceive it. In so far as I may have seemed
to speak of and quote those who longed for some such
release –

Its wings are almost free, its home its harbour found,
Measuring the gulf it stoops, and dares the final bound.

– it might seem, I say, as if I would be in favour of such experimentation. I must explain the terrible errors that are present in this way of thinking, which is perhaps also becoming a way of acting. I will leave aside the purely pharmacological aspects of this use of drugs, merely mentioning that at present we have no such drugs whose influence is always beneficial and which carry no risk of addiction. For myself I doubt whether any substance that consistently produced euphoria could be free from the risk of addiction. But suppose in the future a chemical substance was discovered that had all the advantages which Aldous Huxley wrongly claimed for mescaline. I will just remind you of these claims by quoting Huxley's own words:

> These better things may be experienced (as I experienced them) outside or 'in here', or in both worlds, the inner and the outer simultaneously or successively. That they are better seems to be self-evident to all mescalin takers who come to the drug with a sound liver and an untroubled mind.

The fact that Huxley's claim for mescaline is inaccucurate is not the most important point here; it is the enormous ethical error that is most in need of exposition. The escape from the body and its limitations that Socrates spoke to his friends about, that Shakespeare and Emily Brontë so impressively expressed in poetry this in its very essence was something that was given, unearned and unexpected. If it was something that we human beings could manipulate, that was ours to achieve as and when we wanted, then it is not that of which these wrote and of which I was speaking. This

is that which must be longed for in expectation and
patience. All pleasure-seeking is the search for an
artificial paradise, an intoxication, but of this freedom
it was truly said 'The wind bloweth where it listeth,
and thou canst not tell whence it cometh or whither
it goeth.'

You remember the quotation from Socrates' speech
finished: 'If no pure knowledge is possible in the
company of the body, then it is either totally impossible to acquire knowledge, or it is only possible after
death.' The sonnet of Shakespeare and the poem of
Emily Brontë both spoke of death with a certain
longing and sense of expectation. An entrance into
that state for which they longed.

As practitioners of medicine we have to be
acquainted with death. It is our duty to fight to the
last for the lives of our patients. But we have another
duty too, one that is hard to combine with the previous
one. And that is to recognise the signature of death
when it is inevitable. Did you ever read Macaulay's
account of the death of Charles the second? It is a
horrid picture. How the Royal physicians clustered
round him like flies; they bled him, they repeatedly
purged him, and gave him disgusting emetics, until
at last the poor king said wanly, 'You must pardon
me gentlemen, I seem to be an unconscionable time in
dying.' How one would have liked to drive those
leeches out of the sick-room and let the poor soul
depart in peace.

If what I have said concerning the relation of mind
and body is the truth (and remember I have made it
my principal endeavour to show that nothing in the
nature of proof or reasonableness or evidence has any

place here. The will must decide). But if this is your decision, then the moment of death is the supreme moment of life. The moment when the prisoner escapes out of the prison house, as it were a bird out of the snare of the fowler. Then I say we, as physicians, must have insight to know when our work is done to the uttermost. When it is our duty to stand aside and interfere no more.

I would end this paper with one more quotation from Plato; from the dialogue *Phaedrus*. I choose this quotation because it expresses for me so profoundly the mystery of mind and body; the mysteriousness of our present being.[1]

Thus far I have been speaking of the fourth and last kind of madness, which is imputed to him who, when he sees the beauty of earth, is transported with the recollection of true beauty; he would like to fly away, but he cannot; he is like a bird fluttering and looking upward and careless of the world below; and he is therefore thought to be mad. And I have shewn this of all inspirations to be the noblest and highest and the offspring of the highest to him who has or shares in it, and that he who loves the beautiful is called a lover because he partakes of it. For, as has been already said, every soul of man has in the way of nature beheld true being; this was the condition of her passing into the form of man. But all souls do not easily recall the things of the other world; they may have seen them for a short time only, or they may have been unfortunate in their earthly lot, and, having had their hearts turned to unrighteousness through some corrupting influence, they may have lost the memory of the holy things which once they saw. Few

[1] Jowett's translation.

only retain an adequate remembrance of them; and they, when they behold here any image of that other world, are rapt in amazement; but they are irnorant of what this rapture means, because they do not clearly perceive.

CHAPTER 4

HYPOTHESES AND PHILOSOPHY

> DO not call it hypothesis, even less theory, but the manner of presenting it to the mind.
>
> LICHTENBERG

Ladies and gentlemen,

I am going to begin with a quotation from Macaulay's essay on Francis Bacon. It is as follows:

Suppose that Justinian when he closed the schools of Athens, had asked the last few sages who haunted the Portico, and lingered round the ancient plane trees, to show their title to veneration: suppose that he had said: a thousand years have elapsed since in this famous city Socrates posed Protagoras and Hippias; during those thousand years a large proportion of the ablest men of every generation has been employed in constant efforts to bring to perfection the philosophy which you teach; that philosophy has been munificently patronised by the powerful; its professors have been held in the highest esteem by the public; it has drawn to itself all the sap and vigour of the human intellect; and what has it effected? What profitable truth has it taught us that we should not equally have known without it? What has it enabled us to do which we should not have been

HDW

equally able to without it? Such questions we suspect would have puzzled Simplicius and Isidore.

Ask a follower of Bacon what the new philosophy, as it was called in the time of Charles the second, has effected and his answer is ready. It has lengthened life, it has mitigated pain; it has extinguished diseases; it has increased the fertility of the soil; it has given new security to the mariner; it has furnished new arms to the warrior; it has spanned great rivers and estuaries with bridges of form unknown to our fathers; it has guided the thunderbolt innocuously from heaven to earth; it has lighted up the night with the splendour of the day; it has extended the range of human vision; it has multiplied the power of the human muscles; it has annihilated distance; it has facilitated intercourse, correspondence, all friendly offices, all dispatch of business; it has enabled men to descend to the depths of the sea, to soar into the air, to penetrate securely into the noxious recesses of the earth; to traverse the land in cars which whirl along without horses, and the ocean in ships which run against the wind.

You may well be wondering what this long bit of Victorian rhetoric has to do with the title of my paper, Hypotheses and Philosophy. I have chosen it because it illustrates so superbly the central error I want to discuss with you. The confusion as to what the proper function of philosophy is. Why we human beings need it so much, and perhaps particularly in this present age. And why it never hands over a finished result to be transmitted from one generation to another.

My main thesis is this. That a philosophy which takes no cognizance of science becomes empty; and a natural science which is not subjected to philosophical criticism becomes blind. I have chosen the modern mutation-selection theory of evolution to illustrate this thesis. Not that the theory of evolution has any special status in this respect. Modern astronomy when it talks about the ultimate nature of the universe, modern physics when it talks about the fundamental constituents of matter, modern psychology when it talks about the scientific study of persoanlity – any one of these would have served my purpose as well.

But at the present moment the theory of evolution is particularly in need of a little dose of philosophic doubt. It is one of those recent advances in knowledge which appear to be so much more important than they really are. It is a subject in which it is so difficult to say only just as much as we really know.

Perhaps I can make clearer what I want to say if I begin by stating the main line of my argument in rather general terms, and only later fill in the concrete details: as it were formulate the charge against the prisoner at the bar and then proceed to examine the witnesses.

The great philosophical danger in every natural science is to confuse an hypothesis with a fact. A new branch of natural science begins because of new observations, new phenomena not noticed before. Often this is due to the discovery of a new instrument, a telescope, a microscope, an electric cell, a Wilson cloud chamber. But always the new data are perceptions. There is nothing in science which was not first in the senses. Now to communicate these new discoveries and to pass them on to the next generation, a new language is required, new words, new concepts, but most important of all new schemata: models, pictures, maps. These new models, pictures, maps are scientific hypotheses. They are not given to us as necessities, never dictated by the facts, never forced upon us, but invented by us as ingenious abbreviations to summarise the complexities of the mass of a new factual data. Which of a large number of possible hypotheses we accept is at first a matter of choice. It is determined to a great extent by the spirit of the age in which the new discoveries are made.

But then when an hypothesis has become generally accepted and shown its usefulness, it forgets its humble origin. It begins to masquerade in the logical status of a fact. Something we can't query. Something which is the reality behind phenomena. Something which has enabled us to see behind the curtain of sensation. And so the hypothesis which is our own useful creation, dazzles our view of things. We fail to see much that the hypothesis doesn't include; we extend the limits of our hypothesis into regions of phantasy. Reality which lies before us at every moment is replaced by the abstract picture we have ourselves created. Reality we are told is nothing but a fortuitous concatenation of atomic particles. Reality we are told is the immense system of extra-galactic nebulae. Reality we are told is that long process of evolution from amoeba to consciousness. In speaking like this we have become dazzled by our picture making.

Now to make this specific charge more precise by considering in detail the modern mutation-selection theory of evolution.

I bow to no one in my admiration for Charles Darwin. Where else will you find such close and accurate observation of plants and insects, of birds and mammals, and the constant interrelation in the lives and deaths of all these creatures? What powers of observation he had!

I bow to no one in my admiration for Gregor Mendel.

Those simple but painstaking experiments with his dwarfed, wrinkled, yellow, tall and short peas. Mendel's demonstration of how already existing characteristics emerged or failed to emerge in the offspring of a particular union; this was indeed a new field of observation. It shows what a real talent for research can do with the simplest of material, and with no financial endowment.

But now on the basis of Darwin's and Mendel's work has grown up what is known as the mutation selection theory of evolution. The theory that the development of all the multitude of living forms both in the vegetable and animals world can be explained in terms of genetic mutation and the survival of the fittest. New forms arise by mutation and survive by natural selection.

For instance in a recent popular book on the evolution of man, I find it stated that 'biologists are no longer interested in finding a proof of this theory, it is now only a matter of filling in the details.'

In more scientific language Professor Medawar states,

It is the great strength of the Darwinian selection theory that it appeals to the working of no mechanisms which are not severally well understood and demonstrable. Selection does occur, that is the members of a population do make unequal contributions to the ancestry of future generations; new variants do arise by the process of mutation.

But Julian Huxley is even more bold; he writes:

> One of the major achievements of modern biology has
> been to show that purpose is apparent only, and that
> adaptation can be accounted for on a scientific basis
> as the automatic result of mutation and selection
> operating over many generations. In Darwin's time
> natural selection was only a theory, now it is a fact.

Thank you, Mr Huxley, for putting so concisely the
logico-philosophical error I wish to refute. A theory
can never become a fact. An hypothesis remains an
hypothesis to all eternity. It always contains an
element of choice, one way of looking at things; one
way of arranging an arbitrary selection of material
into a coherent picture.

The danger of forgetting this is that we proceed to
overlook the facts that *won't* fit into the picture; and
we extend the picture to cover aspects of experience
to which it has *no* relevance. Let me illustrate these
dangers in the case of the mutation-selection theory
of evolution.

First the facts which won't fit into the picture. In
this part of my paper I am largely borrowing from an
important book by Professor C. P. Martin of McGill
University. Time will only allow reference to some of
the salient points in his work.

The two most effective ways of producing mutations
experimentally are the use of X-rays and of nitrogen-
mustard. These are at the same time two of the most
powerful protoplasmic poisons known. All mutations
produced by these agents, that is all experimentally
produced mutations, lower the fertility and viability
of the species so changed. I can find no reference to a

mutation produced by human interference that is not either lethal or sublethal. For instance it is possible to produce by experimental mutation a tailless variety of mouse. But such a breed cannot be continued for more than one or two generations; not that the loss of a tail is so serious a disability, but because the process of mutation has so undermined the viability of the species.

Yet geneticists continue to assert that the millions of variations found in nature arose by mutation; and that these mutations had in certain circumstances increased viability and adaptive value. This is pure guess-work. Fisher, a leading exponent of the mutation-selection theory, really admits as much when he has to write as follows:

> We may reasonably suppose that other less obvious mutations are occurring which at least in certain surroundings or in certain genetic combinations might prove themselves to be beneficial.

Notice those words, 'suppose', 'might', 'at least'. How can Huxley claim that the hypothesis has now become a fact?

Dobzhansky, another protagonist for the theory I am criticising, goes so far as to say:

> The genetic theory of evolution would be embarrassed if anyone were to observe the origin of a mutant superior to the ancestral type in the environment in which the latter normally live.

I therefore assert that what we really know is that mutation is a pathological process, and we are only guessing when we say that it has ever been otherwise.

Now consider the process of natural selection. The

survival of the fittest. Undoubtedly at certain times and under certain circumstances such selection has occurred. And the study of the way in which form and function, structure and coloration, adapt an organism to the complexities of its environment is a fascinating study. But that all the immense variety spread out over the whole face of nature; that all this multiformity of shape and pattern and habit; that all this is due entirely to a process of natural selection – this seems to me to be the most far-fetched assumption.

Indeed there are many cases where we can see patently that this could not be true. Once again I am borrowing largely from Professor Martin. He devotes a whole chapter to the universal phenomenon of the atrophy of disused organs. Such atrophy proceeds by steps too small for any of them to count as an advantage, and proceeds far beyond the point at which any process of selection could apply.

Herbert Spencer was much intrigued by the size of a whale's femur. Buried deep in the huge carcase of the whale is a tiny bone weighing about two ounces. It is the exact homologue of the femur, the largest bone in the mammalian skeleton. We know nothing about the process by which certain mammals reverted to a purely marine existence. The earliest skeletons of whales are found in the Oligocene formations, and differ little from our present species. Before this period the geological record is completely silent. But suppose they are descended from animals that at one time had legs, and that as the legs became an encumbrance in their new aquatic environment, they gradually atrophied. It could surely make no difference to the survival of the whale if its femur weighed twenty ounces instead of two. The atrophy has proceeded far beyond the point where natural selection could apply. Exactly the same line of argument applies to the atrophy of the wings of flightless birds. On isolated oceanic islands flightless birds are found which belong unmistakably to species which elsewhere have the power to fly. If a bare incapacity to fly was what natural selection favoured (and it is difficult to see how such an incapacity could be an advantage) natural selection cannot explain an atrophy which has proceeded far *beyond* the capability to fly.

Such considerations lead one on to consider the vexed question of the inheritance of acquired characteristics. The mutation-selection theory seems to consider any such supposition as utterly unscientific. Since the time of Weissman it has been a scientific dogma that all inheritance must be transmitted through the germ cells; and as these are uninfluenced by any experience in the life history of an organism, no acquired characteristic can be inherited. But I can see no reason to believe that all inheritance must be via the germ cells. I see no reason why there should not be psychological factors in inheritance as well as physical. Why certain tendencies, habits, likes and dislikes, should not be directly inherited without being dependent on any material structure for that inheritance. Professor Martin has put this point so well that I would like to quote him. He writes:

All living creatures form habits. They develop preferences in all their activities and these preferences are transmitted in a measure from generation to generation to generation. In this way biological races are formed. The distinguishing characteristics of these biological races are not simple modifications, that is individual characteristics, for they do not appear fully in the first generation placed in the environment concerned. They develop progressively in the course of several generations if the race continues to reside in the appropriate environment, and fade out in a similar way if a biological race is transferred to a different environment.

What Professor Martin is here saying seems to me to be of the greatest importance. There is much factual evidence that all living creatures can inherit a psychological aptitude to develop with increasing ease a new habit. What is inherited is the ease in acquiring an acquired characteristic.

Let me give you an example. For about one hundred years the wild Norway rat has been used in laboratory experiments. It has gradually become easier and easier to tame each new born generation. Richter describes the difference between the wild and laboratory rat in these words:

> The wild rat is fierce and aggressive, attacks at the least provocation, and is highly suspicious of everything in its environment. The domesticated rat is tame and gentle and will not bite unless actually injured.

Tameness is an acquired characteristic. But tameability is inherited. A rigid dichotomy of characteristics into those that are either genetically inherited or acquired during the life-time of the individual is inadequate to describe the facts. It is sheer dogmatism to assert that all inheritance must be transmitted through the genes of the germ cells: that psychological traits must be dependent on anatomical structure. Weissman's theory is nothing but the old fallacy of epiphenomenalism dressed up as a piece of biological science. I would like to say, that the mind has genes of its own that the germ cells know nothing about.

I have been illustrating the danger that arises when a scientific hypothesis takes to itself the airs and graces of a fact. It blinds us from seeing much that won't fit into the hypothesis. But the second danger is more serious.

An hypothesis which is taken for a fact easily assumes an ontological status apart from the data which gave it birth. It becomes a hidden reality behind phenomena. And so we get, in the case of our chosen example, Evolution spelt with a capital E. A recent book by a famous palaeontologist illustrates this confusion very well. I refer to De Chardin's *Phenomenon of man.* In his Introduction to this book Julian Huxley tells us that De Chardin was delighted with the phrase 'In modern scientific man evolution is at last becoming conscious of itself.' The fundamental idea in the book, if I understand it rightly, is that the long centuries of evolution have at last produced a phenomenon 'consciousness' which is able to understand the process from which it has arisen. Julian Huxley regards this as such a profound conception that he sees in it the foundation of a new humanistic religion. Evolution having become conscious of itself can now plan its own future.

But what a mix up of categories is here. Animal, vegetable, mineral, and – consciousness. Don't you feel there is something wrong about a classification like this? Go back to first principles. Every scientific hypothesis depends on data. And, whatever instruments we use to obtain these data, they are in the end dependent on the use of our senses. There is nothing in science which was not first in the senses. The data of every natural science are data for consciousness. You cannot then bring consciousness in as one of the items of the hypothesis. The material used in the foundation cannot at the same time form the coping stone of the roof. Consciousness is not just one of the things we are conscious of.

Look at it this way. I suppose we have all some time or other been fascinated by looking at one of those pictures of the world as it was, say, in the Carboniferous age, when the coal measures were laid down. Those strange tree-like ferns growing in the swampy deltas of the carboniferous rivers. And as we look at these pictures we almost seem to feel the warmth of those sub-tropical times, and hear the wind rustling that strange foliage, and smell the putrefaction of that marshy land, and to see the play of colours as the sunlight comes streaming down through the matted vegetation. But then at once those old familiar questions come crowding in. Were there any smells there when there was no nose to smell them? And were there any sounds there when there was no ear to hear them? And were there any colours there when there was no eye to see them? And if I now try to take refuge in a theory of primary and secondary qualities, then I am reminded of what I once read in the first chapter of Bradley's *Appearance and Reality*. For this chapter showed me conclusively that such a theory cannot be taken as more than a working hypothesis.

It is doubtless scientific to disregard certain aspects when we work; but to urge that such aspects are not fact, and that what we use without regard to them is an independent real thing – this is barbarous metaphysics.

A pre-historic world which was only a re-arrangement of electrons and protons would be one that we could scarcely attach much meaning to, and it would have certainly lost all its imaginative compulsiveness. You see, what we picture when we construct in imagination the theory of geological evolution, is how the world would have looked to a *mind* capable of being a spectator of all time and all existence. So once again you can't bring consciousness in right at the end and say that it itself is the product of evolution.

We have in immediate experience our one sole contact with reality, and everywhere this immediate experience cries aloud that it is incomplete and fragmentary. Then we go on to construct in imagination the conception of an experience which would be more adequate, more satisfying. That is what every scientific hypothesis, apart from its practical usefulness, attempts to be. And in so far as such a process of inference does bring a greater sense of unity into our experience, it is so far legitimate. What is not legitimate is to think that the process of inference is at an end and the ideal is now reached. In the long run I would say that no purely spatial or temporal picture, no picture of the world consisting of a lot of things scattered about in space and time, can satisfy our demand for a final resting place. For every spatial and temporal picture goes to pieces completely at its edges.

I keep coming back to the fundamental thought of

this paper, the logical status of a scientific hypothesis. That it is always a transitory, incomplete affair. Never finished, final, factual. Every scientific hypothesis is always at the mercy of new evidence and may require indefinite modification in the light of this evidence.

Somewhere between Athens and Marathon there is a great outcrop of Jurassic limestone. The surface of these rocks, so I am told, is studded with fossil shells and bones of the mesozoic period: the age of the great reptiles. Aristotle must have passed this place many times. Yet I believe I am correct in saying that nowhere in the biological writing of Aristotle is the existence of this place even mentioned. So much the worse for Aristotle you say. All right, so much the worse for Aristotle. But what is sauce for the goose is sauce for the gander. Considering the vast complexity of the matrix of nature, isn't it certain that there is still much evidence, lying before our eyes and beneath our hands, which we have failed to notice as yet? And may not such evidence in the future transform our idea of nature as much as the new biology has transformed the Aristotelian concepts? The great thinkers of the Middle Ages are often criticised in popular works for their subservience to Aristotle. This of course is a gross historical over-simplification. But in so far as it is true, it represents a universal human tendency to take transitory concepts as final and absolute. Huxley and De Chardin, when they make the idea of evolution the basis of their philosophy, even of their religion, are making just the same error. Hypotheses, as Kant said, are contraband in philosophy.

I began this paper with Macaulay's eulogy of natural science. Now at almost the same date that Macaulay was writing this essay a much greater European thinker, Kierkegaard, was writing in his journal this passage:

> There is no use in going in for natural science. There is no more terrible torture for a thinker than to have to live under the strain of having details constantly uncovered, so that it always looks as though the thought is about to appear, the conclusion. If the natural scientist does not feel that torture, he cannot be a thinker, a thinker is as it were in hell until he has found spiritual certainty.

But not only is every scientific hypothesis at the mercy of new data. They all also contain an element of choice. The data we do have can always be interpreted in a number of ways. Consider again the evidence on which the mutation-selection theory of evolution is based: the geological formations and the fossil record. Hegel in his philosophy of nature puts forward the suggestion that the organic forms found in early geological strata never really lived. They are merely anticipations in stone of what was later to be clothed in living flesh and blood. Why do we reject such an hypothesis as foolish and jejune? It is not that we can produce some concrete piece of evidence that refutes it. We do not *know* that a Brontosaurus ever breathed or a pterodactyl ever flew. Hegel's hypothesis accounts for all the data. We reject it for two reasons. First because of the way we have been educated. We have been brought up in the Darwinian tradition. Our popular books, our encyclopaedias, our natural history museums, have presented this one hypothesis as a *fait accompli*. It is an hypothesis that is now so familiar that it is mistaken for a fact. But secondly and more important, there is no doubt that the theory of evolution has an immense appeal to our imagination. This appeal is vividly shown by the fact that Tennyson was able to translate these ideas into poetry.

> There rolls the deep where grew the tree.
> Oh earth, what changes has thou seen!
> There where the long street roars, has been
> The stillness of the central sea.
>
> The hills are shadows, and they flow
> From form to form, and nothing stands;
> They melt like mist, the solid lands,
> Like clouds they shape themselves and go.
>
> .   .   .
> 'So careful of the type?' but no.
> From scarped cliff and quarried stone
> She cries, 'A thousand types are gone:
> I care for nothing, all shall go.'
>
> .   .   .
>   And he, shall he
> Who loved, who suffered countless ills,
> Who battled for the True, the Just,
> Be blown about the desert dust,
> Or sealed within the iron hills?

Spengler claimed that the scientific world view which appeals to the late stages of a culture is closely connected with the architectural forms which inspired the spring time of that culture. The compact, symmetrical, perfectly proportioned Greek temple. And then an historian like Thucydides on the first page of his history saying: 'Before our time nothing much of

importance had happened in the world.' So I find
myself wondering whether the imaginative appeal, the
sense of awe, with which some modern scientific
hypotheses fascinate us, those infinite astronomical
distances, those long corridors of time peopled with
strange monsters, whether this fascination may not be
related to the fact that not many generations ago our
ancestors found their inspiration in Gothic architecture. Those tall spires reaching into the sky. Those
long dark interior perspectives fading into obscurity,
where the gargoyles peered out from the stones.

Be that as it may. What I am in earnest about is
this. Every scientific hypothesis is a transitory and
to some extent arbitrary affair. It must never be
allowed to solidify into a pseudo-fact. But why not?
What harm is done?

So it is time we got back to Justinian and the
question Macaulay puts into his mouth.

'What profitable truth has philosophy taught us
that we should not equally have known without it?
What has it taught us to do which we could not have
equally done without it?'

I would like to think that Isidore replied in the true
spirit of Socrates. Good sir, you mistake our purpose.
We add nothing to the sum total of human cleverness
and skill. Our function is otherwise. When the Delphic
oracle told our father founder that he was the wisest
man in Athens, he understood this to mean that he
alone knew how little he understood. That still remains
our function in society. To insist that people say
only just as much as they really know; that when,
as happens in every generation, new advances in
knowledge are made, they are not taken to be more

IDW

important than they really are. You ask what is the value of such scepticism, such agnosticism, such carping criticism? One value only. It keeps wonder secure. That sense of wonder that Samuel Johnson wrote of in these words:

> We all remember a time when nature gave delight which can now be found no longer, when the noise of a torrent, the rustle of a wood, had power to fill the attention and suspend all perception of the course of time.

That sense of wonder that Wordsworth wrote of:

> There was a time when meadow, grove, and stream,
> The earth and every common sight,
> To me did seem
> Apparelled in celestial light,
> The glory and the freshness of a dream.

But remember how Wordsworth ends:

> Turn where so ere I may,
> By night or day,
> The things which I have seen I now can see no more.

May I end then with a little parable? It is not really mine; it is taken from one of the novels of Charles Morgan.

You are sitting in a room and it is dusk. Candles have been brought in that you may see to get on with the work in hand. Then you try to look up and out to the garden which lies beyond; and all you can see is the reflection of the candles in the window. To see the garden the candles must be shaded.

Now that is what philosophy does. It prevents us from being dazzled by what we know. It is a form of thinking which ends by saying, don't think – look.

CHAPTER 5

MADNESS AND RELIGION

S O what can a man do where he sees so clearly that
what lies before him is not the whole plan?
Answer: No more than work faithfully and actively
on that part of the plan which lies before him.

LICHTENBERG

During the last thirty years a remarkable change has
taken place in the practice of psychiatry. When I was
a medical student there was no known form of treatment for what are called the major psychoses, melancholia, mania, schizophrenia, paranoia. Patients
suffering from these diseases were admitted to hospital
and their physical well-being looked after, but their
recovery from the disease itself was a matter that had
to be left to time and chance. Even in the more fortu-
nate cases this was usually a matter of months or
years. Now for each one of these diseases we have a
specific form of therapy: restraint and seclusion are
things of the past, and duration of stay in hospital is
measured in weeks rather than in months and years.

To most people's surprise these treatments have
turned out to be physical and chemical in nature, and
have not arisen from any deeper understanding of the

psychological processes causing the symptoms manifested. The fact that a person's mood and content of
thought can be so profoundly and rapidly altered by
the administration of a few pills or injections, or by an
artificially induced convulsion, seems to me to raise
important questions both in philosophy and ethics.
These questions I do not find anywhere adequately
discussed. For two reasons I think. Those who are
using these treatments are so delighted to be able at
last to do something positive and effective for their
patients, that they have neither the time nor the
training nor the inclination to raise questions about
first principles and ultimate objectives. Whereas those
who are trained to think dialectically have little opportunity to see the dramatic way these treatments work.

I am therefore very grateful to you for giving me
the chance to discuss my problems with you. I think
the best way to begin would be to tell you in some
detail about four case histories which I have taken
from the records of the hospital where I work. I would
emphasise that there is nothing very unusual about
the first three cases. I am sure any busy mental
hospital could produce similar ones. The fourth case
is unusual but I have included it as it brings out one
aspect of my problem very clearly.

The first case I want to describe to you is that of a
man aged fifty-four, a priest. We will call him Father
A. This priest had for some years been directed by his
Superior to conduct retreats, a type of work for which
he was considered to have great gifts. A few months
prior to my seeing him he had begun to feel very
depressed about his work, that he could not longer
put any feeling into what he was preaching; that he

was asking people to believe and do things which he himself had lost faith in. It was a great burden for him to say Mass or read his daily office. He felt that he ought never to have been ordained, that he had no vocation. When he visited his brother, a happily married man surrounded by his family, he felt *that* was the sort of life he was meant for. In addition he began to lose weight and to have very disturbed sleep, he would wake about three in the morning and lie awake till dawn worrying about his spiritual state. He developed a feeling of great tension and discomfort in the pit of his stomach. He could not eat. These symptoms led him to believe that he had cancer, to hope indeed that he had cancer and that he would soon be dead. He consulted a physician who advised admission to a general hospital for investigation. After the usual X-rays and biochemical tests had been done he was told that there was no evidence of any organic disease. But he felt no better for this information. It was at this stage a psychiatrist was called in, who diagnosed an involutional depression, and recommended admission to a mental hospital for treatment. So it was he came under my care. When I first saw him he was resentful and suspicious. His condition was a spiritual one, he stated, and no doctor could aid him. He had brought it on himself and must bear the blame for it. I concentrated on his insomnia and his abdominal pain and asked him to let me treat these symptoms, leaving the whole question of his spiritual state in abeyance for the time being.

I gave him a course of what is known as electric convulsive therapy. It consists in giving the patient an anaesthetic and then passing a current of 150 volts for

about one second through the frontal lobes of the
brain. This causes a generalised epileptic-like convulsion which lasts about two minutes. Within fifteen
minutes the patient is awake and fully conscious
again.

After the first treatment the pain in the abdomen
had gone. He began to eat better, he needed less drugs
to obtain a full night's sleep. Within a week he came
spontaneously to ask if he could say Mass again. By
the time he had seven such treatments he stated he
was feeling very well. He was sleeping soundly without
any drugs and had gained ten pounds in weight. But
this is what is significant: his spiritual problem had
disappeared too. He was saying Mass every morning,
and could read his daily office again with devotion.
He felt ready to return to his work and to conduct
retreats as before. This is what he is now doing, though
his Superior has been advised to see that he has
proper intervals of rest.

A straightforward case of involutional melancholia
properly treated, most of my colleagues would say.
Why do I say that it raises important philosophical
and ethical questions? Well, now listen to this piece
of autobiography, written nearly a hundred years
ago, by a man about the same age as Father A:

I felt that something had broken within me on which
my life had always rested, that I had nothing left to
hold on to, that morally my life had stopped. An
invincible force impelled me to get rid of my existence,
in one way or another. It cannot be said that I wished
to kill myself, for the force which drew me away from
life was fuller, more powerful, more general than any
mere desire. It was a force like my old aspiration to

live, only it impelled me in the opposite direction. It was an aspiration of my whole being to get out of life.

Behold me then a happy man in good health, hiding the rope in order not to hang myself to the rafters of the room where every night I went to sleep alone; behold me no longer going shooting, lest I yield to the too easy temptation of putting an end to myself with my gun.

I did not know what I wanted. I was afraid of life; I was driven to leave it; and in spite of that I still hoped for something from it.

All this took place at a time when so far as all my outward circumstances went I ought to have been completely happy. I had a good wife who loved me and whom I loved, good children and a large property which was increasing with no pains taken on my part.

I am sure that you feel with me the similarity between this man's state of mind and that of Father A. And having seen several hundred such cases recover with the same treatment that I gave Father A, I cannot help concluding that had such treatment been available in those days this man's two years of suffering could have been terminated in as many weeks.

But would it have been right to do so?

For the writer of that piece of autobiography was Count Leo Tolstoy. It occurs in a book which he calls *My Conversion*. The thoughts and convictions which eventually delivered him from this misery were to determine his whole future manner of life and writing. He says expressly that he was in good health, and I am sure that like Father A he would have resented any interference by a doctor.

Again going back a little further in history; when I

read some of the great spiritual directors of the seventeenth and eighteenth centuries, such writers as Fenelon and De Caussade, they seem to me to be writing sometimes to people in just such a state of mind as Father A or Tolstoy. They speak about states of aridity and dryness, of loss of the faith. Here for instance is Father Gratry describing his own experience of such a state:

> But what was perhaps more dreadful was that every idea of heaven was taken away from me. I could no longer conceive of anything of that sort. Heaven did not seem to me to be worth going to. It was like a vacuum, a mythological elysium, an abode of shadows less real than the earth. I could conceive no joy or pleasure in inhabiting it. Happiness, joy, love, light, affection, all these words were now devoid of sense.

Yet these spiritual directors universally teach that such states, these dark nights of the soul, are necessary stages in the growth of spiritual maturity. They are sent by God, and are to be accepted willingly and patiently; they are a proof that the soul has now passed the beginner's stage of sensible consolation, and is being educated by suffering.

But today it would seem a psychiatrist can treat such states of mind not out of the abundance of his spiritual wisdom and experience, but by mechanical and materialistic means: electrical stimuli to the brain, drugs which alter the biochemistry of the nervous system. Such treatments can be given by some recently qualified young man to whom the spiritual agony of the patient is something quite outside his comprehension.

That is why I say such a case as that of Father A raises for me philosophical and ethical problems. Can we differentiate between madness and religion? Can we say of one such state: 'This is a mental illness and is the province of the psychiatrist? And of another: 'This is a spiritual experience sent by God for the advancement of the soul and is the province of a wise director?

My second case is that of Miss B, forty-three years of age, living in the west of Ireland and employed as the housekeeper by the parish priest. She was admitted to hospital in a state of elation and excitement. She had had a personal revelation from 'the little flower', St Therésè of Lisieux. This had occurred when she was visiting a holy well near her home. She had seen lights in the sky which conveyed a special message to her. She had been ordered to convert all the protestants in Ireland. In the ward she rushed across to preach to two non-catholic patients who are there. Some of the junior nurses wore a pink uniform. This was a sure proof that they were half-communists, and she would receive neither food nor medicine from their hands. She denied emphatically that her experiences were in any way due to an illness and resents being in a mental hospital.

Her treatment consisted in a short course of electric convulsive therapy followed by the administration of large doses of a comparatively new chemical substance which has been found to control rapidly such states of exaltation. In three weeks' time her behaviour and conversation were completely normal. She never referred spontaneously to her experiences and only seemed embarrassed when they were mentioned. But she was never willing to admit that it had all been a matter of illness. She was able to go into the city alone and always returned to hospital as requested. And now at the present moment I hope she is cooking Father Murphy's supper among the quiet hills of County Mayo.

Nowadays, seeing this patient's state of mind, few people would hesitate to describe her as mentally ill. Certainly her parish priest who brought her to hospital had no doubts on the matter. But in previous ages and among simpler folk might she not have been regarded as indeed the recipient of a divine revelation? We were inclined to smile at her delusion about the nurses' pink uniforms, but now listen to this:

> It was commanded by the Lord of a sudden to untie my shoes and put them off. I stood still for it was winter, but the word of the Lord was like a fire in me so I put off my shoes, and was commanded to give them to some shepherds who were nearby. The poor shepherds trembled and were astonished. Then I walked about a mile till I came into the town, and as soon as I was got within in the town, the word of the Lord came to me again to cry 'Woe to the bloody city of Lichfield'. So I went up and down the streets crying with a loud voice, 'Woe to the bloody city of Lichfield.' And no man laid hands on me; but as I was thus crying through the streets there seemed to me a channel of blood flowing down the streets and the market place appeared to me like a pool of blood.
>
> And so at last some friends and friendly people came to me and said, 'Alack, George, where are thy shoes?' I told them it was no matter.

That was George Fox, the founder of the Society of Friends. Madness or religion?

My third case is this. Guard C was twenty-seven years of age, a policeman on motor-cycle patrol in the city of Dublin. One day his sergeant was horrified to see Guard C's motor cycle propped up against some railings and the guard himself kneeling in prayer on the pavement. He was taken to hospital in a car and on arrival there was at first quite mute. He appeared to be listening intently to something coming from one corner of the ceiling. His lips moved silently as if in prayer. Later in the ward he stated that a voice from heaven had told him that he had been chosen by God to drive the English soldiers out of the Province of Ulster. He was to be made a commissioner in the Guards and after his death he would be canonised as a saint.

Once again the treatment of this patient consisted in the administration of a powerful chemical substance both by mouth and by injection. Within six weeks he was able to admit that his ideas had been delusions due to illness, and after a proper period of convalescence he was able to return to duty.

But in 1429 when Joan of Arc came to Vancouleurs she stated that the voices of St Michael and St Catherine had ordered her to drive the English soldiery from the fair Kingdom of France. Robert de Baudricourt gave her a horse and a suit of armour; and then – but we all know what happened then. My question is this. Supposing Robert de Baudricourt had been able to give Joan a stiff dose of phenothiazine instead of the panoply of a knight at arms, would she have returned in peace to the sheep herding at Domremy?

The fourth and final case history is this. It came to

my notice over fifteen years ago, when many of the methods of treatment we now have were not known. Mr D was sixty-seven years of age, a retired civil servant, a man of great piety who devoted his retirement to prayer and works of charity. His wife had no sympathy for what she regarded as a morbid religiousness. One morning at Mass he heard read the words of the Gospel: 'Go and sell all that thou hast and give to the poor and thou shalt have treasure in heaven, and come and follow me.' These words spoke to him like a command. And straightaway he left the church, putting all the money that was on him into the poorbox at the door. He set off to walk the 135 miles to Lough Derg, a famous place of pilgrimage in Ireland since earliest times.

When he did not return for his breakfast and the morning passed without news of him, his wife became alarmed and notified the guards. Eventually that evening he was stopped by a policeman in a small village about thirty miles from Dublin. He was seen by a doctor and put on a Temporary Certificate for admission to a mental hospital. He made no protest at entering hospital, told his story clearly, and accepted what had happened as God's will. I gave this man no treatment other than insisting that he had his breakfast in bed and allowed us to restore a rather emaciated frame. I learnt more from talking to him than he did listening to me. There was at first some difficulty in getting his wife to take him home. She was convinced that he suffered from a condition she called religious mania, but eventually after some weeks she agreed to his discharge.

But now go back a little over sixteen hundred years

and to a church in Alexandria. Another man hears these same words read from the altar. And straightaway he goes out into the desert around Thebes and lives there until his death a life of heroic austerity. Soon thousands are to follow him; to form themselves into communities, to draw up a rule of life. It is the beginning of Christian Monasticism with all that it was to mean for European religion and culture. And so Anthony was canonised and Mr D was certified.

Madness or Religion?

But why should I be quoting from Fenelon and George Fox, from St Joan and St Anthony? I suppose no psychiatrist can read the Bible without sometimes hearing a disturbing echo of what he has just heard said to him on his ward round.

> Behold I was shapen in wickedness and in sin did my mother conceive me.

Was this written by someone in a state of melancholia, and would a course of electroplexy have given him a more sanguine estimate of man's estate?

> Thou makest my feet like hart's feet and setteth me up on high. He teacheth my hands to fight and mine arms shall break even a bow of steel. I will follow upon mine enemies and overtake them, neither will I turn again until I have destroyed them.

Was this written in a state of manic elation and was a sedative called for here?

> Thou art about my path and about my bed and spiest out all my ways. For lo there is not a word in my mouth but Thou knowest it altogether.

Schizophrenics often complain that all their inmost

thoughts are being read and controlled by some power outside themselves.

The prophet Ezekiel, the most ecstatic and visionary of the prophetic writers, gives an account of a catatonic state with functional aphonia such as could be duplicated by reference to any standard textbook of psychiatry:

> But thou, son of man, lay thyself on thy left side and I shall lay the guilt of the house of Israel upon thee; the number of days that thou shalt lay upon it shalt thou bear their guilt. And behold I shall lay cords upon thee that thou shalt be unable to turn from one side to the other, till thou hast ended the days of thy boundness.

And in three other passages occur the words:

> In that day shall thy mouth be opened and thou shalt speak and be no more dumb.

In the New Testament too the same problem is thrust upon us:

> And I heard behind me a great voice as of a trumpet speaking, saying: what thou hearest write in a book.

Was the author of Revelations hallucinated? 'Paul, thou art mad,' said Festus, 'thy great learning hast made thee mad.' And did not the Pharisees, those religious experts, say of our Lord, 'Say we not well that thou art a Samaritan and hast a devil?'

Then there is that strange account in St Mark's Gospel, which the other Evangelists omit:

> And when his friends heard of it they sought to lay hands on him, for they said he is beside himself.

Most commentators agree that the friends mentioned here refer to his mother and his brethren who had been mentioned in the previous verse. So you see this problem of ours is one that can deceive even the very elect.

I am sure that by now all sorts of possible answers to the problem have been coursing through your minds. Let us look at some of these answers and see will they do.

One answer cuts the knot straightaway. For Freud there is no problem here. The distinction between the pathological and religious state of mind cannot be made because it does not exist. In his books *Totem and Taboo, The Future of an Illusion,* and *Moses and Monotheism,* Freud argues that it is obvious to anyone trained in psycho-analysis, that religious beliefs and practices are a racial neurosis. The conviction with which such beliefs are held without scientific evidence for them, is the same conviction with which a paranoic clings to his systematised delusion in spite of any proof. The strictness with which religious ceremonies are observed, is the same as that with which an obsessional carries out his profitless repetitions.

I find this simple solution of Freud's entirely unacceptable. Freud never comes to grips with the central problem of ethics. It is clear from reading his biography and personal letters that the man himself was more than his theory. He had a strong sense of duty, and a system of absolute values about which he was not prepared to compromise. A passion to find out the truth, a courage to stand against unpopularity and hostility, a love of nature and art, a lifelong devotion to his wife and children. There is an amusing but I think significant story which Ernest Jones records about Freud.

At the time when the relations between Freud and Jung were almost at breaking point, Jung was still secretary of the psycho-analytical association. He sent Jones an announcement of the next meeting but made an error in the date, so that if Jones had not had other information he would have missed the meeting entirely. Jones knowing Freud's interest in these slips of the pen and tongue showed the letter to him. But Frued was neither interested or amused. No gentleman, he said, *ought* to have an unconscious like that.

Ought? Ought? Ought? What is that ought doing there on the lips of a psycho-analyst? Of course, we like Freud all the better for this human touch. You see, however much we may exclude oughtness from our theories, we cannot get it out of our lives. Oughtness is as much an original datum of consciousness as the starry vault above. Both should continue to fill us with constant amazement.

Freud's solution of our central problem is, for me, altogether too one-sided to satisfy. It omits entirely to take into account an essential aspect of life – our sense of duty – an aspect which is the very source of the problem itself. When is it *right* to treat this man as mad and when to say let be, let his spiritual growth proceed without meddlesome interference?

I mentioned the Swiss psychiatrist, Carl Gustav Jung, a moment ago. After his break with Freud, Jung developed a doctrine almost diametrically opposed to that of his former teacher. This is what he says in one of his later books: 'Among my patients in the second half of life there has not been one whose problem in the last resort was not that of finding a religious outlook.'

So once again the problem which I raised as to the criterion between madness and religion does not arise for Jung. Madness is religion which has not yet come to an understanding of itself. Madness is the protest of those unconscious needs and forces which the patient has not allowed to find any expression in his life. These unconscious needs are not sexual as Freud taught but religious: all that side of human nature which in the past has found expression in myths and cults and symbols.

I must say that as a theoretical solution this appeals to me. My difficulty arises when I try to make use of it in practice. I would like to be able to cure my patients by discussion, advice, wise counsel, and from an understanding of their spiritual needs. But my experience has been that in all the serious disturbances of the mind such as find their way into a mental hospital, the word has lost its power. Take those first three cases I described to you. I do not know how anyone could talk Father A out of his depression; could convince Miss B that her vision was an hallucination; demonstrate to Guard C that his sense of mission was a delusion. Whereas I do know that by means of these physical methods of treatment I can at least restore them to their former equanimity and return them to their gainful occupations. It is precisely the limitations of these methods that I am debating with you. When to say, 'This man is mad and we must put a stop to his raving,' and when to say, 'Touch not mine annointed and do my prophet no harm.'

One solution which for some time seemed to me to

KDW

offer at least a practical solution of our problem was this. You remember that in the case of Father A there was a disturbance of his physical health. Pain, loss of appetite, loss of weight and insomnia. It was these symptoms that enabled me to get his consent to treatment. May we not say then that where there is an obvious failure of physical well-being then we may diagnose morbidity and not spirituality?

But I now find that I must reject this source of distinction. For these bodily disturbances, though common, are not a constant feature in all mental illness. Besides, every psychiatrist knows that these are secondary phenomena. The crux of the matter is the emotional disturbance which has caused them. It is to this that the treatment is directed. Remove the depression, subdue the excitement, get rid of the hallucinations, and sleep and appetite and physical health are restored too.

And then looking at this matter from the other side; the lives of the saints are not free from just these same disturbances of physical health. Von Hügel in his great two-volume study of St Catherine of Genoa has to devote a whole chapter to what he calls her psycho-physical peculiarities. This is what he has to say:

Now as to those temperamental and neural matters to which this chapter shall be devoted, the reader will no doubt have discovered long ago that it is precisely here that not a little of the 'Life and Teaching' is faded and withered beyond recall, or has even become positively repulsive to us. The constant assumption and frequent explicit assertion on the part of nearly all the contributors, upon the immediate and separate significance, indeed the directly miraculous character of certain psycho-physical states; states which taken thus separately would now be inevitably classed as most explicable neural abnormalities. Thus when we read the views of nearly all her educated attendants that 'her state was clearly understood to be supernatural when in so short a time a great change was seen and she became yellow all over, a manifest proof that her humanity was being entirely consumed in the fire of divine love', we are necessarily disgusted.

I have quoted Von Hügel at some length to emphasise that someone writing not from a medical but from a theological standpoint, finds this same problem requiring attention.

The reason why we, looking back on history, are able to make the distinctions we do is because of what was achieved. After his conversion Tolstoy, both by his manner of life and his writings, exercised a profound influence on all Europe. George Fox was the founder of the Society of Friends and his influence is with us to this day. And Joan of Arc went forward with the royal banners to the crowning of her king at Rheims. So is it not true that by their fruits ye shall know them, and that it is in this that the distinction we have been looking for will be found?

But we are surely treading on dangerous ground if we introduce results and success into the religious category, and make this our absolute criterion. What sort of results? What sort of success? Is failure and defeat always to be a condemnation? Let me put this matter quite concretely with a particular example.

That great mathematical genius, Blaise Pascal, would almost certainly have preceded Newton and

Leibniz in the discovery of the infinitesimal calculus, if it had not been for what happened on the night of Monday 23 November 1654. You remember his own description:

> From about half past ten to half after midnight,
>
> FIRE
>
> God of Abraham, God of Isaac, God of Jacob, not of the philosophers and wise. Security, Security. Feeling, Joy, Peace. Forgetfulness of the world and of all save God. O righteous Father, the world has not known Thee, but I have known Thee.

And so Pascal turned from his mathematical studies to write his defence of the Gospel. These fragments we now have in his *Pensées*. Those to whom the *Pensées* are a source of depth and wonder will see in them a proof of the authenticity of that night of pentecostal fire.

But then I take up a recent history of mathematics in which the author bewails what he calls Pascal's nervous breakdown on that fatal night – leading him to forsake his true genius for what this writer calls meaningless mysticism and platudinous observations. So an attempt to find the distinction we have been looking for in the results achieved, once again fails us. For who is to be the judge of the results?

When in philosophy you keep coming up against a dead end, such as we have so far, in our search for a principle of differentiation between madness and religion, it is often because we are looking for the wrong type of answer. And this indeed is what I believe we have been doing in our search. For we were sitting back in a cool hour and attempting to solve this problem as a pure piece of theory. To be the

detached, wise, external critic. We did not see ourselves and our own manner of life as intimately
involved in the settlement of this question. Now there
can indeed be experts and critics in all the arts and
sciences, but their writ does not run in the realm of the
religious. It is not possible to adopt a detached and
purely theoretical attitude in these matters. It is not
given to any man to be an honorary member of all
religions.

I suppose most thoughtful people have realised that
sooner or later they may be afflicted with some painful, perhaps mortal, disease, and have considered how
they hope to comport themselves under this trial.
But to face clearly the possibility of a mental illness –
that is both too terrible and too much an unknown to
accept. That we, you and I, might one day have to be
admitted to a mental hospital in a state of despairing
melancholia, or foolish mania, might become deluded
or hallucinated – that is a thought not easily to be
entertained. We like to think that either our intelligence, or our will-power, or our piety, would save us
from such a fate. I heard a sermon some time ago in
which the preacher stated that the great increase in
mental illness at the present time was due to the
decay of faith. Anyone, he said, who had a firm belief
in God would never suffer from nerves or a mental
breakdown. Alas his premises were false and his conclusion erroneous. For just those qualities of personality in which we trust, which we regard as peculiarly
our own for keeps, our intelligence, our will-power,
our piety, these are all dependent on the proper
functioning of a very complicated and delicate neuro-
humoral mechanism over which we have no control.

Some slight disturbance of an endocrine secretion, a hardening of some arterial wall, a failure of an enzyme to catalyse an essential chemical reaction, and all in which we have put our trust is gone. Our sanity is at the mercy of a molecule.

So now if we really face these facts squarely the whole problem we have been debating changes, we find *ourselves* closely involved. The problem now is not how as external observers we are to distinguish between madness and religion, but how are we to reconcile the existence of madness, and the ever present threat of madness, with our religious convictions and beliefs.

And then the answer is not far to seek. For it has always been a central doctrine in Christian ethics that the greatest danger to man as a spiritual being does not come from the animal side of his nature, his lusts and passions or even their perversion, but comes precisely from those qualities which distinguish him from the brute creation, his intelligence and efficiency. Pride, self-sufficiency, smugness, 'Lord I thank Thee that I am not as other men are', it is these sins that are utterly stultifying and soul destroying.

Towards the end of his life Kierkegaard wrote in his Journal these words:

> Sometimes in moments of despondency it strikes me that Christ was not tried in the suffering of illness, at least not in the most painful of all where the psychological and the physical touch each other dialectically, and consequently as though his life was easier in that respect. But then I say to myself: Do you think if you were perfectly healthy, you would

easily or more easily become perfect? On the contrary you would give in all the more easily to your passions, to pride if no other, to an enormously heightened self sufficiency.

To lead a really spiritual life while physically and psychologically healthy is altogether impossible. One's sense of well being runs away with one. If one suffers every day, if one is so frail that the thought of death is quite naturally and immediately to hand, then it is just possible to succeed a little; to be conscious that one needs God. Good health, an immediate sense of well being, is a far greater danger than riches, power, and position.

Simone Weil had the same thought too. She writes:

To acknowledge the reality of affliction means saying to oneself: I may lose at any moment through the play of circumstance over which I have no control anything whatsoever I possess, including those things which are so intimately mine that I consider them as being myself. There is nothing that I might not lose. It could happen at any moment that what I am might be abolished and be replaced by anything whatsoever of the filthiest and most contemptible sort. To be aware of this in the depths of one's soul is to experience non-being. It is the state of extreme and total humiliation which is also the condition for passing over into truth.

It is a common prejudice, and one hard to get free from, that a mental illness in a degradation of the total personality; that it renders the sufferer to some degree subhuman. Thus many people would feel that if Tolstoy really suffered from melancholia his challenge to our whole western way of life would be largely blunted and nullified. And if Joan of Arc was a schizophrenic she could not at the same time be a saint. But these are prejudices. A mental illness may indeed utterly disable the patient for the daily commerce of social life, but the terrifying loneliness of such an experience may make him more aware of the mysteriousness of our present being.

A short time ago I was called to see a patient who had just been admitted to hospital for the fifth time. When I came to her she was sitting up in bed reading her Bible with the tears streaming down her face. I thought to myself, this woman understands that book better than I do, or indeed many a learned theologian. 'They that are whole need not a physician but they that are sick.'

Many years ago Ludwig Wittgenstein asked me if I could arrange for him to have conversations with some mental patients. Of one of them, a certified and chronic inmate of the institution, he observed, 'I find this man much more intelligent than any of his doctors.'

There was an old pagan saying, 'Quem deus vult perdere prius dementat.' Perhaps we should baptise that saying. 'Sometimes those whom God intends to save he first has to make mad.'

Every death-bed can be a religious experience both for him who is dying and for those who had loved him and watch beside him. Every mental illness can be a religious experience both for him who is afflicted and for those that loved him. Conversely every religious belief and practice where it is deep and sincere is madness to those who trust in themselves and despise others. That distinction we spent so much time looking for was nothing but a will-o'-the-wisp.

But then what about those mechanical methods of treatment I mentioned at the commencement? Are they not sometimes at least a gross interference with what should be left to the wisdom of God? Are we always right to use them?

Of course we are. A doctor who tries to prolong life and ease the pains of the dying in no way detracts from the majesty and significance of death. A doctor who attempts to shorten and relieve the suffering of the mentally ill in no way diminishes the lesson of madness. If we are to take the doctrine of the creed seriously, 'by whom all things were made', then we must accept that madness in all its horror is as much part of God's creation as the tubercle *bacillus* and the cancer cell. We do not know why these things should be, and if we did they would not be what they are. We are right to fight against them with all the energy and all the weapons that we have. For this energy and these weapons are also part of His creation. But this we must never forget, good physical health, good mental health are not the absolute good for man. These can be lost and yet nothing be lost. The absolute good, the goal and final end of our being is in heaven and not here; and all earthly things as though they get us but thither.

And so to all of us, in sickness or in health, in sanity or in madness, in the vigour of youth or in the decrepitude of senility, God speaks these words which He spoke once to St Augustine.

Currite, ego feram, et ego perducam, et ibi ego feram.

Run on, I will carry you, I will bring you to the end of your journey and there also will I carry you.

INDEX

FACT AND HYPOTHESIS
from *The Human World*, vol. 15–16 (1974)
by M. O'C. Drury

Correspondence & Comment

Fact and Hypothesis

Mr Dilman's thoughtful review of my book *The Danger of Words* (*Human World* 14) has shewn me that the epistemology I there hinted at was too briefly expressed and lacked adequate examples to avoid misinterpretation. I am therefore grateful to him for giving me an opportunity to expound in greater detail the theory I now hold. "In a few places I find a tension between a kind of empiricism which is reminiscent of Hume and Mach and a more profound strand that owes much to Wittgenstein." (Dilman)

I regret now that I used the expression: "There is nothing in science that was not first in the senses." This was slovenly and vague. I would now say this. Every scientific hypothesis, if it is to be meaningful, must be begotten of observation and give birth to verifiable predictions. And these initial observations and subsequent verifications must be capable of being described in terms of immediate sensory perception. If this is not done the hypothesis is liable to float freely and to give rise to all manner of confusions.

Two books: One Wittgenstein often praised to me the other he ridiculed. The first was Faraday's *Natural History of a Candle*. The second Jeans's *The Mysterious Universe*. What is the striking difference between these two books? Whenever Faraday uses hypothetical language he immediately goes on to describe in minute detail the actual experiments on which the hypothesis is based (and in the original lectures demonstrated the experiments before the eyes of his audience). But Jeans on the other hand makes startling assertions about the nature of the Universe (The Universe is like a rapidly expanding soap bubble) but never tells us what the Astronomer actually *does* and *observes*. It is the skills and techniques which scientists make use of that constitute the very soul of each particular science. Let me exemplify.

1. Chemists tell us that a molecule of Water consists of two atoms of hydrogen and one of oxygen. This means that we can perform the familiar experiment of decomposing a given volume of water, by means of electrolysis, into two parts of hydrogen and one of oxygen. And in a further experiment recombine these gases in suitable proportions to form once again water. But now if we don't mention these experiments the statement about a molecule of water is liable to make us feel that science has discovered new *entities*, molecules and atoms, and that our senses are too crude, and somehow deceive us, so that we do not see the real nature of things. But everything is what it is and not another thing. Water is water, neither

molecule or atom. It is that wonderful substance that quenches our thirst and delights our eyes in rivers and lakes.

The atomic theory consists of two things. First the discovery of some remarkable experiments, something we can now *do*. Then secondly an ingenious notation by means of which these experiments can be concisely recorded and further experiments suggested. It did not conduct us behind the curtain of sensation.

2. Physicists tell us that light has a velocity of 187,000 miles per second. This was first begotten by Romer's observation that there was a delay between the expected time of an eclipse of Jupiter's moon and the actual observed time. This delay being a function of the distance at the time between the earth and Jupiter. Here it must be said that a very high degree of skill and instrumentation had first to be developed before such an observation could be made. Then much later Fizeau devised an ingenious terrestial experiment in which the light returning from a distant mirror was occluded by a rapidly rotating spoked wheel. To construct such an apparatus and to use it was no amateur matter.

But now again if these highly skilled and technical matters are not mentioned and the phrase "the velocity of light" is left bare, imagination comes into play. Velocity! surely then there must be *something* that moves. A stream of photons? A wave motion in an unknown medium? Yet the experiments reveal no such entities. Everything is what it is and not another thing. Light is light, neither particle nor wave. It is the glory of a sunrise, the serenity of a full moon, and the amazement of the stars.

3. Popular books on astronomy tell me that when I look at the great nebula in Andromeda I am really seeing something that was contemporary with a period millions of years ago, before man had yet appeared on the earth. This I take to be nonsense. What I see is always simultaneous with my seeing it. And if you deny that, what criterion of simultaneity do you use? Here again the word velocity has led us astray. We imagine some *thing* that leaving the nebula travels through the immensity of space to impinge on my retina and be conveyed via the optic tract to my visual cortex. But this as I tried to shew in my book makes nonsense of all perception. Here I imagine an indignant astronomer would intervene—"my dear fellow, we can now measure the distance between us and the nebula in Andromeda, what more can you want?" I would reply that if you talk of measurement you must tell me the *method* of measurement used. In this particular case it all depends on an ingenious speculation (Leavitt, 1912) that always and everywhere throughout the universe the absolute luminosity of a Cepheid Variable can be deduced from observing its periodicity. Now photographs taken with the largest telescopes reveal that there are Cepheid Variables in the Andromeda nebula. The discrepancy between the apparent luminosity and the calculated absolute luminosity enables us to estimate the immense distance involved. This is speculation; only a very clever mind and a

highly trained observer would have thought of it. But speculation remains speculation and should be labelled as such. It should not be put before a gullible public as the very latest discovery of scientific certainty.

4. When at the end of the last century such distinguished physicians as Charcot and Janet, Bernheim and Liebault thought that the phenomena of hypnosis were worthy of scientific study they soon discovered that under hypnosis patients could recover memories that were not available in the waking state. Also that commands given to a hypnotised patient would be carried out meticulously although the subject was not aware that they were so being obedient, and would invent a fictitious motive for their behaviour. Now having used hypnosis in suitable cases for the last twenty years I know that these are indeed facts. They are facts which the language of every day life is not equipped to describe except in terms of a long circumlocution. So it became convenient to introduce a special terminology and to speak of "unconscious" memories and "unconscious" motives. But every adjective is in deadly danger of being transformed into a substantive. So it came about that psychologists began to speak of "the unconscious mind", as if some new *entity* had been discovered. A mysterious second self that accompanied us all at all times and was the "real" source not only of dreams and neuroses, but of art and mythology, history and religion. This is superstition and has done infinite harm.

Wittgenstein once made the remark that "physics is what physicists do." And one could go on to say that chemistry is what chemists do, astronomy is what astronomers do, psychology is what psychologists do. These various "doings" are highly skilled procedures requiring years of apprenticeship. To communicate these skills from one generation to another each science develops its own technical language. To join in the activities one must learn the appropriate language. The danger arises when one learns the language without mastering the skills it is meant to mediate. It is as if a man should memorise a musical score without understanding that it was meant to be performed! In my book I quoted a long passage from Macaulay's Essay on Bacon in which he extolled all the harvest of useful inventions which were the fruit of the Baconian philosophy. But Macaulay overlooked something Bacon once wrote: "Without doubt the contemplation of things as they are without superstition or imposture, without error or confusion, is in itself a nobler thing than the whole harvest of inventions." (*Novum Organum*, Book I, Aphorism 129)

The attainment of this contemplative ideal is the true goal of philosophy. This is no aberration of certain minds but a passion without which a man is not fully awake. The danger is that in our haste to reach this goal we tend to take the discoveries of natural science as an answer. Or if we cannot accept this to think there is yet another science, metaphysics, which will bring us satisfaction. But philosophy is an ascetic discipline, a via negativa; by insisting that everywhere and always we say only so much as we really know, it potentiates the "inquietum cor nostrum".

"There is a reality outside the world, that is to say outside space and time, outside man's mental universe, outside any sphere whatsoever that is accessible to human faculties. Corresponding to this reality, at the centre of the human heart, is the longing for an absolute good, a longing which is always there and is never appeased by any object in this world."

—Simone Weil, *Draft for a Statement of Human Obligations*, 1943

M. O'C. Drury

SOME NOTES ON
CONVERSATIONS WITH
WITTGENSTEIN

SOME NOTES ON CONVERSATIONS WITH WITTGENSTEIN

M. O'C. Drury

In his Biographical Sketch of Ludwig Wittgenstein Professor G. H. von Wright speaks of the multiplicity of the interpretations that have been put on Wittgenstein's writings, and that such interpretations have little significance. He ends his Sketch with the thought-provoking sentence: 'I have sometimes thought that what makes a man's work classic is often just this multiplicity, which invites and at the same time resists our craving for a clear understanding.' Now in what I have to say here I will be concerned with this multiplicity, with this resistance to a clear understanding. I am going to suggest that there are dimensions in Wittgenstein's teaching that are still ignored or 'watered down' (to use his own expression).

I will begin by drawing attention to two aspects of Wittgenstein's personality which all who knew him will at once recognize.

First then this. Wittgenstein knew that he had an exceptional talent for philosophical discussion. He once said to me: 'It made an enormous difference to my life when I discovered that there really was a subject for which I had a special ability.' Yet whilst knowing this, for the greater part of his life he was making plans to forsake this work and to live an entirely different mode of existence to that of an academic philosopher.

After the First World War he worked for a time as a village schoolmaster in a remote part of Austria. He worked as an architect building a house for his sister. (On one occasion he said to me: 'You think philosophy is hard enough, but I can tell

you it is nothing to the difficulties involved in architecture.')
Later he thought seriously of going to live in Russia, but not to
teach philosophy there, and he took the trouble of becoming
competent in speaking Russian. Later he considered studying
medicine and asked me to make enquiries about the possibility
of his entering the medical school here in Dublin. During the
Second World War he worked first as a hospital porter in London and then later, when requested to do so, did some independent work in the physiology of shock. Dr Grant, the chief of the
team who had requested Wittgenstein to do this research, said
to him: 'What a pity you are a philosopher and not a physiologist.'

Now we may indeed be glad that nothing final came of these
various plans, and that he continued to work at his philosophical writings up to a few days before his death. But I am certain
that we will not understand Wittgenstein unless we feel some
sympathy and comprehension for this persistent intention to
change his whole manner of life. These plans of his were not
just a transitory impatience but a conviction that persisted for
years until the time came when he realized that such a change
was no longer a possibility. I once got an inkling as to what was
behind this intense desire to change his manner of life when he
said to me: 'I thought when I gave up my professorship that I
had at last got rid of my vanity. Now I find I am vain about the
style in which I am able to write my present book.' (This
remark referred to the style of Part II of the *Philosophical Investigations*, which Professor von Wright thinks will one day rank
among the classic examples of German prose.)

Intellectual vanity, whether in himself or in others, was
something that Wittgenstein detested. I believe he considered
it more important to be free from all trace of vanity than to
achieve a great reputation in philosophy. He once said to me:
'Wounded vanity is the most terrible force in the world. The
source of the greatest evil.' And again on another occasion: 'A
philosopher should enjoy no more prestige than a plumber!' But
then as against this I must record him saying: 'Don't think I
despise metaphysics. I regard some of the great philosophical
systems of the past as among the noblest productions of the
human mind.'

At one time when we were out walking together he discussed with me what title he should give to the book he was then writing (the work that was later called *Philosophical Investigations*). I foolishly suggested that he should call it 'Philosophy'.

WITTGENSTEIN: [angrily] Don't be such an ass – how could I use a word like that which has meant so much in the history of human thought? As if my work was anything more than just a small fragment of philosophy.

*

Then secondly this, though closely connected with what I have just said. Throughout his life Wittgenstein was convinced that he could not make himself understood. Thus in a letter to Russell about the manuscript of the *Tractatus* he wrote: 'In fact you would not understand it without a previous explanation as it's written in quite short remarks. (This of course means that *nobody* will understand it; although I believe, it's all as clear as crystal . . .)' (L 68). In the introduction to the *Philosophical Remarks* he wrote:

I would like to say, 'This book is written to the glory of God', but nowadays this would be the trick of a cheat, i.e. it would not be correctly understood. It means the book was written in good will, and so far as it was not but was written from vanity etc., the author would wish to see it condemned. He cannot make it more free of these impurities than he is himself. [R 7, translated by Rush Rhees]

I would dwell on this quotation for a moment. It implies that words which in one age could be correctly used can at a later date be 'the words of a cheat'; because if these words are constantly used in a superficial way they become so muddied that the road can no longer be trodden. (This metaphor of a road that has become so muddied that it can no longer be trodden was one of Wittgenstein's own expressions.)

When Wittgenstein sent a copy of the typescript of the 'Blue Book' to Russell he said in the covering letter: 'two years ago I held some lectures in Cambridge and dictated some notes to my pupils so that they might have something to carry home with them, in their hands if not in their brains . . . (I think it's very difficult to understand them, as so many points are just hinted at . . .)' (B v). Again the emphasis on the difficulty of making himself understood. Then in the Preface to the *Philosophical Investigations* comes the sentence: 'It is not impossible that it should fall to the lot of this work, in its poverty and in the darkness of this time, to bring light into one brain or another – but of course it is not likely' [P p. x]. These words, 'of course it is not likely', must not be taken as the expression of a temporary petulant pessimism. They are the expression of a lifelong conviction concerning all his writing. When he was working on the latter part of the *Philosophical Investigations* he told me: 'It is impossible for me to say in my book one word about all that music has meant in my life. How then can I hope to be understood?' And about the same date:[1] 'My type of thinking is not wanted in this present age, I have to swim so strongly against the tide. Perhaps in a hundred years people will really want what I am writing.' Again in the same conversation: 'I am not a religious man but I cannot help seeing every problem from a religious point of view.'

Now these remarks at once raise for me the question as to whether there are not dimensions in Wittgenstein's thought that are still largely being ignored. Have I seen that the *Philosophical Remarks* could have been inscribed 'to the glory of God'? Or that the problems discussed in the *Philosophical Investigations* are being seen from a religious point of view?

In the prolegomena to his 'Lecture on Ethics' Wittgenstein says something that enables me to understand why I get lost in the difficulty of his writings. He says:

My third and last difficulty is one which, in fact, adheres to most lengthy philosophical lectures and it is this, that the hearer is incapable of seeing both the road he is led and the goal which it leads to. That is to say: he either thinks: 'I understand all he says, but what on earth is he driving at?, or else he thinks 'I see what he's driving at, but how on earth is he going to get there?' All I can do is again to ask you to be patient and to hope that in the end you may see both the way and where it leads to. (LE 4)

Here I think we have a clear pointer to the reason why there have been such a multiplicity of interpretations of Wittgenstein's thought, and why, as Professor von Wright says, they have been largely without significance. Some interpreters get lost on the road and do not make us see the goal. Others avoid the labour of the road and try to jump ahead to a summary conclusion.

There are two words which were frequently used by Wittgenstein, 'deep' and 'shallow'. I remember him saying: 'Kant and Berkeley seem to me to be very deep thinkers'; and of Schopenhauer: 'I seem to see to the bottom very quickly.' On another occasion when we had been listening to a discussion on the Third Programme between Professor Ayer and Fr Copleston he remarked when it was over: 'Ayer has something to say, but he is incredibly shallow. Fr Copleston contributed nothing at all to the discussion.'

I told Wittgenstein that I had been to a lecture by Professor A. E. Taylor, the subject being 'Hume's Essay on Miracles'. Taylor had ended his lecture with the remark: 'I have never been able to make up my mind as to whether Hume was a great philosopher or only a very clever man.'

WITTGENSTEIN: As to Hume I can't say, never having read him. But the distinction between a philosopher and a very clever man is a real one and of great importance.

Here again I would say the categories of 'deep' and 'shallow' are implied. A very clever man can be shallow, but a true philosopher must be a deep thinker. So that if we are to understand the goal of Wittgenstein's road and not merely a few steps on the way we must be clear as to the meaning of these two categories. For myself if I had to give a brief definition of this distinction I would say that a shallow thinker may be able to say something clearly but that a deep thinker makes us see that there is something that cannot be said ('all that music has meant in my life').

In one of the earliest conversations I had with Wittgenstein

he told me: 'Philosophy is like trying to open a safe with a combination lock: each little adjustment of the dials seems to
achieve nothing; only when everything is in place does the door
open.' In the 'Blue Book' he compares philosophy to having to
arrange a confusion of books in a library (B 44–5); there are
numerous little changes to be made before the final arrangement is arrived at. In the *Philosophical Investigations* he compares his method to that of teaching someone his way about a
strange city; numerous journeys have to be made in which the
same place is constantly approached by different routes. Only
when many journeys have been made can the learner say 'now
I can find my way about' (P 18, 123, 203; cf. p. vii). Now in all
these comparisons there is the constant idea of a long and even
tedious process, which at times must seem trivial, in which the
final objective is out of sight, but there is a real goal. A goal,
however, which cannnot be gained without the labour of the
route. It is therefore hazardous, ultimately wrong, to even try to
point to the goal without the detail of the method. Yet I am
going to try to give some indication as to what I have understood for myself as to the ultimate objective.

We are now all familiar with the fact that in writing to Ficker
Wittgenstein said of the *Tractatus*:

> My book draws limits to the sphere of the ethical from the
> inside as it were, and I am convinced that this is the ONLY
> *rigorous* way of drawing those limits. In short, I believe that
> where *many* others today are just *gassing*, I have managed in
> my book to put everything firmly into place by being silent
> about it. [LF 94–5, translated by B. F. McGuinness][2]

Now I am going to venture to state that all the subsequent
writings continue this fundamental idea. They all point to an
ethical dimension. And they do this by a rigorous drawing of
the limits of language so that the ethical is put firmly into
place. This limitation has to be done from the inside so that
whereas nothing is *said* about the ethical it is shown by the
rigour of the thinking. All the sciences, and what is known as
common sense, attempt to say more than we really know. (In
the 'Blue Book' occurs the key sentence, 'The difficulty in
philosophy is to say no more than we know' (B 45).) This rigor-

ous drawing of the limits of language demands a form of self-denial, an ethical demand, a renunciation of a very strong tendency in our nature. Once when I was talking to Wittgenstein about McTaggart's book *The Nature of Existence* he said to me: 'I realize that for some people to have to forsake this kind of thinking demands of them an heroic courage.' I believe that the difficulty that should be found in understanding Wittgenstein's writing is not merely an intellectual difficulty but an ethical demand. The simple demand that we should at all times and in all places say no more than we really know.

What I have just been saying is made clearer for me when I read again the 'Lecture on Ethics'. This is the only piece of writing we have where Wittgenstein is speaking to a general audience who had no particular interest or training in philosophy. I will quote some of the passages which are particularly relevant to the point I am trying to make.

> probably many of you come to this lecture with slightly wrong expectations. And to set you right in this point I will say a few words about the reason for choosing the subject I have chosen: When your former secretary honoured me by asking me to read a paper to your society, my first thought was that I would certainly do it, and my second thought was that if I was to have the opportunity to speak to you I should speak about something which I am keen on communicating to you and that I should not misuse this opportunity [by giving] you a lecture about, say, logic. (LE 3–4)

Here we have the definite assertion that he is going to say something that he thinks should be understood by all. Now consider what is the central thought and final conclusion of this lecture. Again I quote:

> we cannot write a scientific book, the subject matter of which could be intrinsically sublime and above all other subject matters. I can only describe my feeling by the metaphor, that, if a man could write a book on Ethics which really was a book on Ethics, this book would, with an explosion, destroy all the other books in the world. Our words used as we use them in science, are vessels capable only of containing

and conveying meaning and sense, *natural* meaning and sense. Ethics, if it is anything, is supernatural and our words will only express facts; as a teacup will only hold a teacup full of water [even] if I were to pour out a gallon over it. (LE 7)

Then later on near the end of the lecture he says:

I at once see clearly, as it were a flash of light, not only that no description that I can think of would do to describe what I mean by absolute value, but that I would reject every significant description that anybody could possibly suggest, *ab initio*, on the ground of its significance . . . My whole tendency and I believe the tendency of all men who ever tried to write or talk Ethics or Religion was to run against the boundaries of language. This running against the walls of our cage is perfectly, absolutely hopeless. (LE 11–12)

I would draw attention to the fact that he speaks of 'my tendency', that is of something in himself which he feels deeply but has to curb and discipline. This drawing of a firm and unbreakable boundary around the sphere of what can be said significantly is not done to condemn or ridicule those who have tried to overleap this boundary; on the contrary, it is done to intensify the very impetus and desire to break out of our cage.

To give an example of this. That deeply religious and truly wonderful personality, Simone Weil, starts her essay entitled 'Draft for a Statement of Human Obligations' with the sentences:

There is a reality outside the world, that is to say outside space and time, outside man's mental universe, outside any sphere whatsoever that is accessible to human faculties. Corresponding to this reality, at the centre of the human heart is the longing for an absolute good, a longing which is always there and is never appeased by any object in this world.[3]

When I first read this it was indeed the case that 'Os meum aperui, et attraxi spiritum',[4] but suppose someone was to say to me, 'What in the world do you mean, outside space and time?' The word "outside" only has a meaning *within* the categories of space and time.' This is a perfectly logical objection: the words 'outside space and time' have no more meaning than Plato's beautiful expression 'the other side of the sky'. Again if someone was to object, 'I don't feel any longing for an absolute good which is never appeased by any object in this world', how could you arouse such a desire? What right have you to make the psychological assertion that such a desire lies at the centre of every human heart? Yet I believe that Simone Weil is right when she goes on to say that we must never *assume* that any man, whosoever he may be, has been deprived of the power of having this longing come to birth. But how then can this desire for the absolute good be aroused? Only, I believe, by means of an indirect communication. By so limiting the sphere of 'what can be said' that we create a feeling of spiritual claustrophobia.* The dialectic must work from the inside, as it were. There is a latent metaphysics underlying all the natural sciences and even the expressions of everyday speech: this must be exposed and done away with. Then, 'commonplace materialism and commonplace theology vanish like ghosts'. But this vanishing is painful and makes an ethical demand.

I suspect many will feel that I am reading an interpretation into Wittgenstein's writing that is not really to be found there. And in view of my own disagreement with much that has been written about him, perhaps I am. I come back again to what Professor von Wright describes as the 'multiplicity' of interpretations. Of course it is obvious that Wittgenstein was interested in many aspects of philosophy: the foundations of mathematics, symbolic logic, the language of psychology, etc. I am only wishing to maintain that alongside of these specific interests there is to be found an ethical demand, if we are to understand the implications of his work to their full extent. It is this watching brief in the interests of the absolute that gives a depth to his work that I do not find in those who have followed after him or tried to simplify the complexity of his thought.

* 'Diese Angst in der Welt ist aber der einzige Beweis unserer Heterogenität' ['But this anxiety in the world is the only proof of our being different from it'] (J. G. Hamann).

My conviction that this is so is reinforced for me by the vivid recollections of some of the conversations I once had with him. I emphasize the word 'recollection'. I do not believe that my memory deceives me in quoting these remarks and I quote them in direct speech to avoid the constant repetition of 'he said' etc. But every time I do so quote him the reader should add the rubric 'if I remember rightly he said something to this effect'. (When I gave Wittgenstein a copy of Boswell's *Life of Johnson* he particularly commended the way Boswell was careful to guard his quotations with a similar precaution.)

To prevent these memories being too much a record of scattered occasions I will try and bring some order into them by making use of a quotation from Professor von Wright's Biographical Sketch. He writes:

> Wittgenstein received deeper impressions from some writers in the borderland between philosophy, religion, and poetry, than from the philosophers, in the restricted sense of the word. Among the former are St Augustine, Kierkegaard, Dostoevsky and Tolstoy. The philosophical sections of St Augustine's Confessions show a striking resemblance to Wittgenstein's own way of doing philosophy. Between Wittgenstein and Pascal there is a trenchant parallelism which deserves closer study. It should also be mentioned that Wittgenstein held the writings of Otto Weininger in high regard.

I will, then, take the above-mentioned names as so many pegs to bring together my recollections of conversations which reinforce my belief that the interpretation I have already tried to indicate is not too far from the mark. I will arrange the names in the chronological order that I remember him first mentioning them to me and not in the order given above.

Dostoevsky and Tolstoy

In the first serious conversation I ever had with Wittgenstein I told him I had come up to Cambridge with the intention of being ordained as a priest in the Anglican Church.

WITTGENSTEIN: I don't ridicule this. Anyone who ridicules these matters is a charlatan and worse. But I can't approve, no I can't approve. You have intelligence; it is not the most important thing, but you can't neglect it. Just imagine trying to preach a sermon every Sunday: you couldn't do it, you couldn't possibly do it. I would be afraid that you would try and elaborate a philosophical interpretation or defence of the Christian religion. The symbolism of Christianity is wonderful beyond words, but when people try to make a philosophical system out of it I find it disgusting. At first sight it would seem an excellent idea that in every village there should be one person who stood for these things, but it hasn't worked out like that. Russell and the parsons between them have done infinite harm, infinite harm.

He then went on to say that there had been only two European writers in recent times who really had something important to say about religion, Tolstoy and Dostoevsky. (It is of interest that on this occasion he did not mention Kierkegaard.) He advised me in the coming vacation to read *The Brothers Karamazov*, *Crime and Punishment*, and the short stories of Tolstoy collected under the title *Twenty-three Tales*.

We met again after the vacation and he asked me what impression I had got from this reading.

WITTGENSTEIN: When I was a village schoolmaster in Austria after the war I read *The Brothers Karamazov* over and over again. I read it out loud to the village priest. You know there really have been people like the Elder Zosima who could see into people's hearts and direct them.

DRURY: I found Dostoevsky more to my liking than Tolstoy.

WITTGENSTEIN: I don't agree with you. Those short stories of Tolstoy's will live for ever. They were written for all peoples. Which one of them was your favourite?

DRURY: The one entitled 'What Men Live By'.

WITTGENSTEIN: My favourite is the story of the three hermits who could only pray, 'You are three we are three have mercy upon us.'

It soon was after this conversation that he mentioned to me that when Tolstoy's brother died, Tolstoy, who by then was very far from being an Orthodox believer, sent for the parish priest and had his brother buried according to the full Orthodox rite. 'Now', said Wittgenstein, 'that is exactly what I should have done in a similar case.' (Years later, on the evening on which Wittgenstein died, his friends whom he had sent for, Miss Anscombe, Mr Smythies, Dr Richards and myself, had to decide what should be done about Wittgenstein's burial. No one would speak up. I then mentioned the above conversation and it was unanimously agreed that a Roman Catholic priest should say the usual committal prayers at the grave-side. This later gave rise to false rumours and I have been troubled ever since as to whether what we then did was right.)

Kierkegaard

During a discussion after a meeting of the Moral Science Club at Cambridge Wittgenstein mentioned the name of Søren Kierkegaard. I had already come across some quotations from this author in the writings of Baron von Hügel. These quotations had so impressed me that I had anxiously searched the catalogues of the University Library to see if anything by Kierkegaard had been translated into English. My search had been fruitless. So the next day when we were alone I asked Wittgenstein to tell me more about Kierkegaard.

WITTGENSTEIN: Kierkegaard was by far the most profound thinker of the last century. Kierkegaard was a saint.

He then went on to speak of the three categories of life-style that play such a large part in Kierkegaard's writing: the aesthetic, where the objective is to get the maximum enjoyment out of this life; the ethical, where the concept of duty demands renunciation; and the religious, where this very renunciation itself becomes a source of joy.

WITTGENSTEIN: Concerning this last category I don't pretend to understand how it is possible. I have never been able to deny myself anything, not even a cup of coffee if I wanted it.

Mind you I don't believe what Kierkegaard believed, but of this I am certain, that we are not here in order to have a good time.

When some years later Kierkegaard was translated into English, largely by Walter Lowrie, Wittgenstein was displeased with the poor style of this translator. He completely failed to reproduce the elegance of the original Danish.

Again at a later date Wittgenstein told me that one of his pupils had written to him to say that he had become a Roman Catholic, and that he, Wittgenstein, was partly responsible for this conversion because it was he that had advised the reading of Kierkegaard. Wittgenstein told me he had written back to say: 'If someone tells me he has bought the outfit of a tight-rope-walker I am not impressed until I see what is done with it.'

Nearer the end of his life, during his last stay here in Dublin, I remember that during a walk the subject of Kierkegaard's writing came up again.

DRURY: Kierkegaard seems to me to be always making one aware of new categories.

WITTGENSTEIN: You are quite right, that is exactly what Kierkegaard does, he introduces new categories. I couldn't read him again now. He is too long-winded; he keeps on saying the same thing over and over again. When I read him I always wanted to say, 'Oh all right, I agree, I agree, but please get on with it.[5]

I have recently been reading again Kierkegaard's *Concluding Unscientific Postscript*, and certain sentences in this book seem to me to be illustrative of that ethical dimension which I have been trying to draw attention to in Wittgenstein's writings. And so to try to clarify my point I will quote these sentences here, using David Swenson's translation.

The very maximum of what one human being can do for another in relation to that which each man has to do solely for himself, is to inspire him with concern and unrest.

To be outstanding in the religious sphere constitutes a step backward, by virtue of the qualitative dialectic which separates the different spheres from one another.

Ethically it would be perhaps the highest pathos to renounce the glittering artistic career without saying a single word.

It is rather remarkable that one may precisely by talking about something, prove that one does not talk about that thing; for it would seem that this could only be proved by not talking about it.

Dialectics itself does not see the absolute, but it leads, as it were, the individual up to it.

I feel inclined to add that, although I never discussed this point with him, I do not think that Wittgenstein would have agreed with Kierkegaard's frequent use of the words 'the paradox' and 'the absurd'. Here surely is an attempt to get beyond the barrier of language.

St Augustine

I had begun to attend Professor Moore's lectures. At that time I was unable to appreciate what could be learnt from Moore. At the commencement of his first lecture Moore had read out from the University Calendar the subjects that his professorship required him to lecture on; the last of these was 'the philosophy of religion'. Moore went on to say that he would be talking about all the previous subjects except this last, concerning which he had nothing to say. I told Wittgenstein that I thought a professor of philosophy had no right to keep silent concerning such an important subject. Wittgenstein immediately asked me if I had available a copy of St Augustine's *Confessions*. I handed him my Loeb edition. He must have known his way about the book thoroughly for he found the passage he wanted in a few seconds.

WITTGENSTEIN: You are saying something like St Augustine says here. 'Et vae tacentibus de te quoniam loquaces muti sunt.' But this translation in your edition misses the point entirely. It reads, 'And woe to those who say nothing concerning thee seeing that those who say most are dumb.' It should be translated. 'And woe to those who say nothing concerning thee just because the chatterboxes talk a lot of nonsense.' 'Loquaces' is a term of contempt. I won't refuse to talk to you about God or about religion.

He went on to say that he considered St Augustine's *Confessions* possibly 'the most serious book ever written'. He had tried to read *The City of God* but had been unable to get on with it.

A short time after this I mentioned to Wittgenstein that I was reading Dr Tennant's book entitled *Philosophical Theology*, which had just been published.

WITTGENSTEIN: A title like that sounds to me as if it would be something indecent.

DRURY: Tennant tries to revive in a complicated way the 'argument from design'.

WITTGENSTEIN: You know I am not one to praise this present age, but that does sound to me as being 'old-fashioned' in a bad sense.

DRURY: Tennant is fond of repeating Butler's aphorism, 'Probability is the guide of life.'

WITTGENSTEIN: Can you imagine St Augustine saying that the existence of God was 'highly probable'!

Soon after this conversation he sent me a copy of the Vulgate New Testament, advising me to read the Latin text. He said that in reading the Latin he thought I would get an entirely new impression. He also told me that at one time he and Moore had planned to read St Paul's Epistle to the Romans. But after a very short time they had had to give it up. (Many years later when he was living in Dublin he told me that at one time he thought the religion of the Gospels was entirely different from that found in St Paul's Epistles, but that now he saw that he had been wrong, it was the same religion in each.)

Before I leave these few remarks about St Augustine I would quote the last few sentences of the *Confessions*, for here it seems to me is a text on which the 'Lecture on Ethics' might be regarded as a commentary.

Tu autem bonum nullo indigens bono semper quietus es . . . Et hoc intellegere quis hominum dabit homini? Quis angelus angelo? Quis angelus homini? A te petatur, in te quaeratur, ad te pulsetur: sic, sic accipietur, sic invenietur, sic aperietur.[6]

Otto Weininger

Professor von Wright mentions the high regard that Wittgenstein had for the writings of Otto Weininger. I think a certain qualification is called for here. He did advise me to read Weininger's *Sex and Character*,[7] saying it was the work of a remarkable genius. He pointed out that Weininger at the age of twenty-one had recognized, before any one else had taken much notice, the future importance of the ideas which Freud was putting forward in his first book, the one in which he had collaborated with Breuer, *Studies on Hysteria*. When I had read *Sex and Character* I spoke to Wittgenstein.

DRURY: Weininger seems to me to be full of prejudices, for instance his extreme adulation of Wagner.

WITTGENSTEIN: Yes, he is full of prejudices, only a young man would be so prejudiced.

And then with regard to Weininger's theme that women and the female element in men was the source of all evil he exclaimed: 'How wrong he was, my God he was wrong.' On another occasion he asked me to read out loud to him a passage in Weininger's book where he quotes from the Renaissance scholar Pico della Mirandola. As it may be that this fine piece of Latin prose is not as well known as it deserves, and as it delineates a view of man's nature that Wittgenstein found admirable, I will quote it in full.

'Nec certam sedem, nec propriam faciem, nec munus ullum peculiare tibi dedimus, o Adam, ut quam sedem, quam faciem, quae munera tute optaveris, ea, pro voto, pro tua sententia, habeas et possideas. Definita ceteris natura intra praescriptas a nobis leges coercetur. Tu, nullis angustiis coer-

citus, pro tuo arbitrio, in cuius manu te posui, tibi illam prae-
finies. Medium te mundi posui, ut circumspiceres inde com-
modius quicquid est in mundo. Nec te caelestem neque
terrenum, neque mortalem neque immortalem fecimus, ut
tui ipsius quasi arbitrarius honorariusque plastes et fictor, in
quam malueris tute formam effingas. Poteris in inferiora
quae sunt bruta degenerare; poteris in superiora quae sunt
divina ex tui animi sententia regenerari.'
O summam Dei patris liberalitatem, summam et admiran-
dam hominis felicitatem! cui datum id habere quod optat, id
esse quod velit. Bruta simul atque nascuntur id secum affer-
unt . . . e bulga matris quod possessura sunt. Supremi spiritus aut ab initio aut paulo mox id fuerunt, quod sunt futuri
in perpetuas aeternitates. Nascenti homini omnifaria semina
et omnigenae vitae germina indidit Pater; quae quisque exco-
luerit illa adolescent, et fructus suos ferent in illo. Si vegeta-
lia, planta fiet. Si sensualia, obrutescet. Si rationalia, caeleste
evadet animal. Si intellectualia, angelus erit et Dei filius, et
si nulla creaturarum sorte contentus in unitatis centrum
suae se receperit, unus cum Deo spiritus factus, in solitaria
Patris caligine qui est super omnia constitutus omnibus
antestabit.[8]

When I had finished reading this to him Wittgenstein
exclaimed, 'That is so fine that I would wish to read more of
Pico.'

Pascal

Professor von Wright speaks of a 'trenchant parallelism'
between the writings of Pascal and those of Wittgenstein. I do
not have any recollection of a discussion about Pascal with
Wittgenstein. But I think there is something of importance that
I can add here. Certainly Pascal's intensity, his seriousness, his
rigorism, these find a parallel in Wittgenstein. It has been well
said that Pascal has had 'the rare privilege never to meet with
indifference' (Laberthionère). The same encomium could be
given to Wittgenstein. Pascal is a writer who arouses concern
and unrest. Conversations with Wittgenstein were equally dis-

turbing, and if his writings do not produce the same unrest they have been misunderstood.

I feel, though, more inclined to point out where I consider there are important differences between Pascal and Wittgenstein. The *Philosophical Investigations* appear to be a haphazard arrangement of remarks and aphorisms such as Pascal's *Pensées* undoubtedly are. It is generally believed that if Pascal had written the book he intended the *Pensées* would have been arranged in an entirely different order from that in which we now have them. But we know that Wittgenstein was constantly rearranging the material found in his book, that he spent a lot of time and thought in obtaining the precise order we now have. To grasp the significance of the *Investigations* it is essential to see the order of development of the thoughts.

Secondly this. For Pascal there was only one true religion, Christianity; only one true form of Christianity, Catholicism; only one true expression of Catholicism, Port-Royal. Now although Wittgenstein would have respected this narrowness for its very intensity, such exclusiveness was foreign to his way of thinking. He was early influenced by William James's *Varieties of Religious Experience*. This book he told me had helped him greatly. And if I am not mistaken the category of *Varieties* continued to play an important part in his thinking.

WITTGENSTEIN: The ways in which people have had to express their religious beliefs differ enormously. All genuine expressions of religion are wonderful, even those of the most savage peoples.

In the *Remarks on Frazer's Golden Bough* he writes:

Was St Augustine mistaken then, when he called on God on every page of the *Confessions*? Well – one might say – if he was not mistaken, then the Buddhist holy-man, or some other, whose religion expresses quite different notions, surely was. But *none* of them was making a mistake except where he was putting forward a theory. [F 1]

Thirdly and most important this. Pascal has been accused by some of 'fideism'. And there are places in the *Pensées* where this accusation might seem justified: 'Il faut s'abêtir'; 'Le pyrrhonisme est le vrai.' Wittgenstein could never have written that.

WITTGENSTEIN: Drury, never allow yourself to become too familiar with holy things.

Now the essential fault of what has been called 'fideism' is that it dodges all difficulties by adopting a too familiar acquaintance with holy things.

Kierkegaard spoke of faith as 'immediacy *after* reflection' and I do not think Wittgenstein would have found fault with this expession.

Dr Samuel Johnson

I will add one more name to the list I quoted from Professor von Wright's Biographical Sketch: that of Dr Samuel Johnson.

We were talking one day about prayer and I mentioned to Wittgenstein how very impressive I found the ancient liturgical prayers of the Latin rite and their translation in the Anglican Prayer Book.

WITTGENSTEIN: Yes, those prayers read as if they had been soaked in centuries of worship. When I was a prisoner of war in Italy we were compelled to attend mass on Sundays. I was very glad of that compulsion.

He went on to say that he had at one time begun each day by repeating the Lord's Prayer, but that he had not done so now for some time. He did not say why he had discontinued this practice.

WITTGENSTEIN: It is the most extraordinary prayer ever written. No one ever composed a prayer like it. But remember the Christian religion does not consist in saying a lot of prayers, in fact we are commanded just the opposite. If you and I are to live religious lives it must not just be that we talk a lot about religion, but that in some way our lives are different.

A short time later he sent me a copy of Dr Johnson's little book entitled *Prayers and Meditations*. I have it before me now. On the flyleaf Wittgenstein has written: 'Dear Drury, this is not a

nice edition at all but it is the only one I could get. I hope you
will like it all the same.'

Professor Malcolm in his Memoir mentions that Wittgenstein also gave him a copy of this book. I have an idea that it
was a present that he gave others too. I believe the reason why
this book appealed to him so strongly was because of the short-
ness of the prayers, their deep seriousness, and Johnson's
repeated appeal that he might have grace to amend his life.

*

I have been trying to give some indication of the conversations
I had with Wittgenstein concerning ethics and religion. I do not
think I could end this attempt in a better way than by quoting
a letter he once wrote me. It was at a time when I was doing my
first period of residence in hospital and was distressed at my
own ignorance and clumsiness. When I mentioned this to him
he at first dismissed it with the remark that all I lacked was
experience, but the next day I received the following letter from
him.

Dear Drury,

I have thought a fair amount about our conversation on
Sunday and I would like to say, or rather not to say but write,
a few things about these conversations. Mainly I think this:
Don't think about yourself, but think about others, e.g. your
patients. You said in the Park yesterday that possibly you had
made a mistake in having taken up medicine: you immediately added that probably it was wrong to think such a thing
at all. I am sure it is. But not because being a doctor you may
not go the wrong way, or go to the dogs, but because if you do,
this has nothing to do with your choice of a profession being
a mistake. For what human being can say what would have
been the right thing if this is the wrong one? You didn't make
a mistake because there was nothing at the time you knew or
ought to have known that you overlooked. Only this one
could have called making a mistake; and even if you had
made a mistake in this sense, this would now have to be
regarded as a datum as all the other circumstances inside and
outside which you can't alter (control). The thing now is to

live in the world in which you are, not to think or dream about the world you would like to be in. Look at people's sufferings, physical and mental, you have them close at hand, and this ought to be a good remedy for your troubles. Another way is to take a rest whenever you ought to take one and collect yourself. (Not with me because I wouldn't rest you). As to religious thoughts I do not think the craving for placidity is religious; I think a religious person regards placidity or peace as a gift from heaven, not as something one ought to hunt after. Look at your patients more closely as human beings in trouble and enjoy more the opportunity you have to say 'good night' to so many people. This alone is a gift from heaven which many people would envy you. And this sort of thing ought to heal your frayed soul, I believe. It won't rest it; but when you are healthily tired you can just take a rest. I think in some sense you don't look at people's faces closely enough.

In conversations with me don't so much try to have the conversations which you think would taste well (though you will never get that anyway) but try to have the conversations which will have the pleasantest after-taste. It is most important that we should not one day have to tell ourselves that we had wasted the time we were allowed to spend together.

I wish you good thoughts but chiefly good feelings.

CONVERSATIONS WITH WITTGENSTEIN

M. O'C. Drury

During the years I knew Wittgenstein and was having discussions with him, I made entries in my day-book, from time to time, of remarks which I wished to remember – for my own use only. Hence the abrupt nature of these conversations, the lack of any connecting narrative and the absence of precise dates. But I can state that the chronological order of these entries is correct.

Would the right thing have been to let these memories die with me? I don't know. I am certainly not of the opinion that everything Wittgenstein said ought to be recorded. Some of these incidents will seem trivial and of personal interest rather than general. But the fact that, at the time, they impressed me and remained stamped in my memory, has led me to include them. For it seemed to me that it was important that a future generation should see Wittgenstein, not merely as an important name in the history of philosophy, but as a personality – kind, generous, quick-tempered, and with his own eccentricities.

The reader will be disapppointed that there are no long discussions of specific philosophical problems. The truth is that these did not occur. He allowed me to attend his lectures and to join in discussions with him at the Moral Science Club, but when we were alone he did not want to discuss philosophy with me. Indeed when I became a medical student he expressly told me he would not do so. I think he felt that his own thinking was so much more developed than mine that there was a danger of swamping me and of my becoming nothing but a pale echo of himself. He did constantly exhort me to think for myself.

Many of these conversations are concerned with religion. So

here it must be said that he frequently warned me that he could only speak from his own level, and that was a low one.[1] He sometimes used in this connection a vulgar French proverb which is perhaps too coarse to print here. It will be seen that as the years developed his views on some religious matters changed and deepened, so that some remarks in the earlier part of this essay he would later have repudiated. Once, near the end of his life, I reminded him that in one of our first conversations he had said that there was no such subject as 'theology'; and he replied, 'That is just the sort of stupid remark I would have made in those days.'

The reader will be annoyed, as I am disgusted, by my frequent dumbness and stupidity in these discussions. If only I had been able to stand up to him and insist on further elucidation, how much more interesting these conversations might have been! But to argue with Wittgenstein required an alacrity of mind and speech, and a certain obstinate courage, and these were virtues I did not possess. After Wittgenstein's death I became acquainted with the writings of Simone Weil. These have had as profound an influence on my subsequent thought as Wittgenstein had had on my earlier life. So I hope he who now puts together these memoirs is not quite the superficial person who is heard speaking in them.

I regret the constant repetition of the word 'I' in these conversations. But if I did not give the context of Wittgenstein's remarks they would lose their significance. In nearly every case his words are associated in my mind with particular places, times, moods. I have included these. Johnson exhorted Boswell not to leave out the details. I have followed his advice. But the memory, even the most recent, is deceitful. We only record what we are able to receive. So that it may well be that I have distorted or misinterpreted what he actually said. The reader must have this rubric in mind throughout the essay.

To sum up: This essay is an album of snapshots taken by an amateur photographer with a mediocre camera. If to those who knew Wittgenstein some of these pictures seem out of focus, I should not wish to argue the point with them. It is not a portrait of Wittgenstein – I had not the ability for that.

1929

A meeting of the Moral Science Club in Dr Broad's rooms. Prichard from Oxford read a paper on 'Ethics'. The discussion had only just got under way when someone whom I couldn't see began making very pertinent criticism of the paper. The discussion became much more animated than was usual at these meetings. I asked my neighbour who it was that was raising these objections. He replied that it was Wittgenstein, the author of the *Tractatus Logico-Philosophicus*. So far as I could follow it, Wittgenstein's point was that although two people could always discuss the best means to an agreed end, there could be no argument about what were absolute ends in themselves. Hence there could be no science of ethics.

*

Invited Wittgenstein to have lunch with me and asked Donaldson to come and meet him. We waited half an hour and when Wittgenstein hadn't arrived we decided to start. We had nearly finished lunch when he arrived. He said he didn't want anything to eat. Conversation very difficult, Wittgenstein saying little and obviously ill at ease. Realized that he disliked being 'lionized' and that I had made a mistake in thinking that he was the sort of person who could join in the ordinary chit-chat of a Cambridge luncheon.

Donaldson had to leave early and after he had gone Wittgenstein and I went and sat down by the fire. He asked me why I was studying philosophy.

DRURY: When I was still at school I saw in the public library at Exeter the two volumes of Alexander's book entitled *Space, Time, and Deity*. This title so aroused my interest that I could hardly wait until I had purchased the books for myself. When I came to read them I couldn't understand a word. I thought that if I studied philosophy I might be able to understand this sort of writing.

WITTGENSTEIN: Oh, I can understand that. If it is right to speak about the 'great problems' of philosophy, that is where they lie: space, time, and deity. When I was a student in

Manchester I thought at one time of going to see Alexander, but decided no good would come of it.

DRURY: Then I went on to read Mill's *Logic*, starting it with great excitement, but being bitterly disappointed, when I finished it, at how little I had learnt.

WITTGENSTEIN: Of course, if you thought there was a book that would teach you how to think, it would seem the most important book in the world; but that is not how things are.

We went on to discuss the recent meeting of the Moral Science Club. He said he thought Prichard's paper was very poor. He had stayed behind afterwards to talk to Broad and had expressed the same opinion to him. Broad had received him very coldly and had merely replied that he had a very high opinion of Professor Prichard.

*

Wittgenstein asked me this afternoon to come out for a walk with him.We walked to Madingley and back. He asked me about my childhood. I found we had both had the same game of inventing an imaginary country and writing its history in a private code we had invented. He said he thought that this was very common among children.He then went on to tell me that as a child he had suffered greatly from morbid fears. In the lavatory of his home some plaster had fallen from the wall and he always saw this pattern as a duck, but it terrified him: it had the appearance for him of those monsters that Bosch painted in his *Temptations of St Anthony*. Even when he was a student at Manchester he suffered at times from morbid fears. To get from his bedroom to his sitting-room he had to cross over a landing, and sometimes he found himself dreading making this crossing. We were at that time walking quite briskly, but he suddenly stopped still and looked at me very seriously.

WITTGENSTEIN: You will think I am crazy, you will think I have gone mad, when I tell you that only religious feelings are a cure for such fears.

I replied that I didn't think that was crazy at all; that comming from Ireland I knew something of the power of religion. He seemed displeased with this answer as if I hadn't understood him.

WITTGENSTEIN: I am not talking about superstition but about real religious feeling.

After this we walked on in silence for some time.

*

In view of our conversation on the way back home from Madingley I thought it necessary to tell Wittgenstein that, after leaving Cambridge, I intended to be ordained as an Anglican priest.

WITTGENSTEIN: Don't think I ridicule this for one minute, but I can't approve; no, I can't approve. I would be afraid that one day that collar would choke you.

We went on to talk about the Bible. I said that for me the Old Testament was no more than a collection of Hebrew folklore and that whether it was true history didn't matter at all. But I felt quite differently about the New Testament: that lost its significance if it wasn't an account of what really happened.

WITTGENSTEIN: For me too the Old Testament is a collection of Hebrew folklore – yes, I would use that expression. But the New Testament doesn't have to be proved to be true by historians either. It would make no difference if there had never been a historical person as Jesus is portrayed in the Gospels; though I don't think any competent authority doubts that there really was such a person.

*

Today a further discussion with Wittgenstein about my intention to be ordained.

WITTGENSTEIN: Just think, Drury, what it would mean to have to preach a sermon every week; you couldn't do it. I don't mean that there haven't been people in the past who were great preachers, but there are no such people today.

I told him that as a boy I had been greatly influenced by the seriousness and deep piety of an Anglo-Catholic priest in Exeter (Fr E. C. Long, rector of St Olave's Church).

WITTGENSTEIN: I know how impressive such a person can be. I have only one objection: that there is a certain narrowness about them. There are some subjects you feel you can't discuss with them. In one point I do agree with Russell: I like to feel free to discuss anything with anyone I am with. [Then, after a pause, he sighed and said:] Russell and the parsons between them have done infinite harm, infinite harm.

I was puzzled by his coupling Russell and the parsons in the one condemnation.

WITTGENSTEIN: I would be afraid that you would try and give some sort of philosophical justification for Christian beliefs, as if some sort of proof was needed. You have intelligence; it is not the best thing about you, but it is something you mustn't ignore.

The symbolisms of Catholicism are wonderful beyond words. But any attempt to make it into a philosophical system is offensive.

All religions are wonderful, even those of the most primitive tribes. The ways in which people express their religious feelings differ enormously.

DRURY: I think I could be happy working as a priest among people whom I felt shared the same beliefs as I have.

WITTGENSTEIN: Oh, don't depend on circumstances. Make sure that your religion is a matter between you and God only.

After we had talked a little longer he went on to say that there had been only two great religious writers in Europe of recent times, Tolstoy and Dostoevsky. We in the West were inclined to forget the existence of the Eastern Orthodox Church with its millions of members. He advised me to read *The Brothers Karamazov*. When he was a schoolmaster in Austria he read this book constantly, and at one time read it aloud to the village priest.

*

I stayed behind after Johnson's lecture on logic today to talk to Johnson about my work. I told him I was having discussions with Wittgenstein.

JOHNSON: I consider it is a disaster for Cambridge that Wittgenstein has returned. A man who is quite incapable of carrying on a discussion. If I say that a sentence has meaning for me no one has a right to say it is senseless.

Later talked to Wittgenstein about Johnson.

WITTGENSTEIN: I admire Johnson as a man, he is a man of real culture. His life's work has been his three volumes on logic. You can't expect him now to see that there is something fundamentally wrong with what he has written. I wouldn't try and discuss with Johnson now.

The next Sunday Wittgenstein and I went to one of Johnson's Sunday afternoon tea-parties. I noticed the very cordial relations between Johnson and Wittgenstein.

After tea Johnson played some of Bach's Forty-eight Preludes and Fugues. Wittgenstein told me he admired Johnson's playing. On the way back to Trinity he told me that at one of these afternoons Johnson had played badly, and he knew it himself, but the audience had applauded loudly. This annoyed Johnson, so by way of revenge he gave as an encore the accompaniment only of a Beethoven violin sonata, which of course was meaningless without the violin part. This gesture seemed to please and amuse Wittgenstein.

*

Wittgenstein told me that I should try to get to know Lee of Corpus Christi College, who he said was by far the ablest of our present discussion group.

DRURY: I find it very hard to start a real philosophical discussion with a stranger.

WITTGENSTEIN: Of course you find it hard. You will have to spend a long time before you can begin to understand each other. You will be lucky if during your life you find even one person with whom you can have really valuable discussions. You are not an easy person to get to know.

*

Invited Lee and Wittgenstein to come with me on a visit to Ely Cathedral, a building I had come to love. Wittgenstein seemed pleased that we should do this together. Arriving at Ely we sat for some time in the Romanesque chapel on the southern side of the west front. Silence. After a time Wittgenstein leaned over and whispered to me, 'This is real architecture; this is very impressive.'

Later we went further up the nave to the great lantern over the transepts, and to the Lady Chapel with its elaborate tracery in the Decorated style.

WITTGENSTEIN: Once the arch becomes pointed, I don't understand it any more.

Outside we looked at a carving over a Norman door, depicting the serpent tempting Eve.

WITTGENSTEIN: I can hear Adam saying, 'The woman whom Thou gavest to be with me, she gave me of the tree.'

Another carving was described in the guidebook as being a humorous scene of two peasants.

WITTGENSTEIN: That must be wrong. They would never have meant this to be funny. It is the case that we forget the meaning of certain facial expressions and misinterpret their reproduction. What does it mean to us if a Chinaman smiles?

In the train on the way back to Cambridge we talked about Dickens. Wittgenstein said how much he admired *A Christmas Carol*. Another book of Dickens that was a favourite of his was *The Uncommercial Traveller*.

WITTGENSTEIN: This is a very rare thing – good journalism. The chapter 'Bound for the Great Salt Lake' was particularly interesting. Dickens had gone on board the emigrant ship prepared to condemn, but the happiness and good order he found on board made him change his mind. This showed what a real common religious movement could achieve. It was striking that when Dickens tried to draw them out as to what exactly it was they held in common, they became embarrased and tried to avoid answering.

1930

Wittgenstein came and had tea with me in my rooms today. I noticed that though he enjoyed a normal cup of coffee he would only drink the very weakest tea, so pale as to be little more than milk and hot water. He said that strong tea disagreed with him.

He went over to look at my books, and picked up a volume of Spinoza's letters.

WITTGENSTEIN: These letters are most interesting, particularly when he is writing about the beginnings of natural science. Spinoza ground lenses. I think this must have been an enormous help to him when he needed a rest from thinking. I wish I had a similar occupation when I can't get on with my work.

DRURY: I have just been reading a chapter in Schopenhauer entitled 'Man's Need for Metaphysics'. I think Schopenhauer is saying something very important in that chapter.

WITTGENSTEIN: 'Man's Need for Metaphysics.' I think I can see very well what Schopenhauer got out of his philosophy. Don't think I despise metaphysics. I regard some of the great philosophical systems of the past as among the noblest productions of the human mind. For some people it would require a heroic effort to give up this sort of writing.

DRURY: I have to read as my special authors for the second part of my Tripos, Leibniz and Lotze.

WITTGENSTEIN: Count yourself lucky to have so much time to study such a great man as Leibniz. Make sure you use this time when you still have leisure *well*. The mind gets stiff long before the body does.

DRURY: I find Lotze very heavy going, very dull.

WITTGENSTEIN: Probably a man who shouldn't have been

allowed to write philosophy. A book you should read is William James's *Varieties of Religious Experience;* that was a book that helped me a lot at one time.[2]

DRURY: Oh yes, I have read that. I always enjoy reading anything of William James. He is such a human person.

WITTGENSTEIN: That is what makes him a good philosopher; he was a real human being.

DRURY: I was recently at a lecture by A. E. Taylor in which he said that he could never make up his mind whether Hume was a great philosopher or only a very clever man. Alexander said later that he didn't know which to admire most: the wrongness of Taylor's statement or the audacity to say it.

WITTGENSTEIN: As to Hume I can't say, never having read him. But the distinction between a philosopher and a very clever man is a real one and of great importance.

Another book he noticed on my shelves was Schweitzer's *The Quest of the Historical Jesus.*

WITTGENSTEIN: The only value of that book is that it shows how many, many different ways people can interpret the Gospel story.

*

Called at Wittgenstein's rooms in Whewell's Court and asked him to come for a walk with me. He had chosen rooms at the top of the staircase so as to have no one overhead. I noticed that he had altered the proportions of the windows by using strips of black paper.

WITTGENSTEIN: See what a difference it makes to the appearance of the room when the windows have the right proportion.

You think philosophy is difficult enough but I can tell you it is nothing to the difficulty of being a good architect. When I was building the house for my sister in Vienna I was so completely exhausted at the end of the day that all I could do was go to a 'flick' every night.

Before going out we sat for a time talking. He had evidently been looking at something of von Hügel's since our conversation of a few days previously.

WITTGENSTEIN: Von Hügel seems to have been a very pure character, almost a Roman Catholic.

DRURY: But von Hügel was a Roman Catholic. He was closely connected with what was called the modernist movement at the beginning of this century.

WITTGENSTEIN: People who call themselves modernists are the most deceived of all. I will tell you what modernism is like: in *The Brothers Karamazov* the old father says that the monks in the nearby monastery believe that the devils have hooks to pull people down into Hell; 'Now,' says the old father, 'I can't believe in those hooks.' That is the same sort of mistake that modernists make when they misunderstand the nature of symbolism.

We then set off for our walk.

WITTGENSTEIN: I have been reading in a German author, a contemporary of Kant's, Hamann, where he says, commenting on the story of the Fall in Genesis: 'How like God to wait until the cool of the evening before confronting Adam with his transgression.' Now I wouldn't for the life of me dare to say, 'how like God'. I wouldn't claim to know how God should act. Do you understand Hamann's remark? Tell me what you think – I would really like to know.

DRURY: Perhaps if something terrible had happened to one at a time when one felt strong enough to bear it, then one might say:'Thank God this didn't happen before, when I could not have stood up to it.'

Wittgenstein didn't seem pleased with this answer.

WITTGENSTEIN: For a truly religious man nothing is tragic.[3]

We walked on in silence for a time. Then:

WITTGENSTEIN: It is a dogma of the Roman Church that the existence of God can be proved by natural reason. Now this dogma would make it impossible for me to be a Roman Catholic. If I thought of God as another being like myself, outside myself, only infinitely more powerful, then I would regard it as my duty to defy him.

*

Wittgenstein advised me in the coming vacation to read some of the writings both of Tolstoy and of Dostoevsky. When we met again at the beginning of term we had lunch together at the Cambridge Union. Wittgenstein was fond of this ugly old Gothic Revival building and referred to it as 'a friendly old aunt'. (Years later when the building was completely modernized he wrote to me that 'the friendly old aunt is no more'.) After lunch I told him the works of Dostoevsky and of Tolstoy I had read, and he asked me what impression I had.[4]

DRURY: I found the character of the Elder Zosima in *The Brothers Karamazov* very impressive.

WITTGENSTEIN: Yes, there really have been people like that, who could see directly into the souls of other people and advise them. Now what would really have interested me would be to have seen how a character like Smerdyakov could have been saved rather than Alesha.

DRURY: I thought the incident where a man murders a woman because she has chosen another man for her lover rather far-fetched.

WITTGENSTEIN: You don't understand anything at all. You know nothing about these matters.

DRURY: I suppose that is just my narrowness.

WITTGENSTEIN: [now much more sympathetically] Narrowness won't matter as long as you know that you are narrow.

*

Dawes Hicks read a paper to the Moral Science Club.[5] After he had talked for an hour he said, 'I haven't finished what I have written yet; do you want me to go on?' I was in the chair and I did not know how to reply to this. But I thought it only polite to tell him to finish his paper. Wittgenstein then got up and left the room.

The next day I discussed this dilemma with Wittgenstein. He said that he realized that any discussion after the paper was going to be impossible and so he left, but he didn't see what else I could have said. There should be a rule, he said, that no paper to the Club should last longer than twenty minutes.

DRURY: I mentioned my difficulty to Johnson this morning. He replied that I should have said: 'I think some of us would now like to ask a few questions.'

WITTGENSTEIN: Good old Johnson, of course that would have been the right thing to say.

*

I told Wittgenstein that my friend James, who had been working on his Ph.D. thesis for a year, had decided in the end that he had nothing original to say and would therefore not submit his thesis or obtain his degree.

WITTGENSTEIN: For that action alone they should give him his Ph.D. degree.

DRURY: Dawes Hicks was very displeased with James about this decision. He told James that when he started to write his book on Kant he had no clear idea what he was going to say. This seems to me an extraordinary, queer attitude.

WITTGENSTEIN: No, Dawes Hicks was quite right in one way. It is only the attempt to write down your ideas that enables them to develop.

*

Wittgenstein is now attending Moore's Saturday morning discussion class. This leads to a very lively exchange between Moore and Wittgenstein. Today a visiting student from Oxford started quoting from Kant in German. The irrelevance of this so annoyed Wittgenstein that he shouted at him to shut up.

Walking back to Trinity after this incident, Wittgenstein regretted what had happened.

WITTGENSTEIN: I am no saint and don't pretend to be, but I shouldn't lose my temper like that.[6]

Entering the Great Gate of Trinity we passed Dr Simpson the historian walking along in his usual abstracted manner.

DRURY: The first day I came to Trinity and saw Dr Simpson I said to myself, that must be Dr Broad whom I am to see tomorrow. I got such a shock when I called on Dr Broad, to find a chubby little man with no air of profundity.

WITTGENSTEIN: I remember that when I first went to visit Frege I had a very clear idea in my mind as to what he would look like. I rang the bell and a man opened the door; I told him I had come to see Professor Frege. 'I am Professor Frege,' the man said. To which I could only reply, 'impossible!' At this first meeting with Frege my own ideas were so unclear that he was able to wipe the floor with me.

*

Walking today across Parker's Piece I told Wittgenstein that I was not getting much help from Moore's lectures.

DRURY: It never seems to me that Moore worries if he doesn't come to any conclusion. He goes on working away at the same problem until I lose sight of what he is trying to do. Whereas you, Wittgenstein, do seem to me to have reached a real resting-place. *

This was one of those occasions where Wittgenstein suddenly stood still and looked at me intently.

WITTGENSTEIN: Yes, I have reached a real resting-place.[7] I know that my method is right. My father was a business man, and I am a business man: I want my philosophy to be businesslike, to get something done, to get something settled.

DRURY: Moore seems to think that if certain problems in epistemology were solved, everything else would fall into place. As if there was one central problem in philosophy.

WITTGENSTEIN: There is no one central problem in philo-

---

* The reader will have perceived already that I was quite incapable at this time of understanding Moore's true greatness.

sophy, but countless different problems. Each has to be dealt with on its own. Philosophy is like trying to open a safe with a combination lock: each little adjustment of the dials seems to achieve nothing; only when everything is in place does the door open.

On the way back from the walk we passed a street preacher who was proclaiming in a loud, raucous voice all that Jesus Christ had done for him. Wittgenstein shook his head sadly.

WITTGENSTEIN: If he really meant what he was shouting, he wouldn't be speaking in that tone of voice. This is a kind of vulgarity in which at least you can be sure that the Roman Catholic Church will never indulge. On the other hand, during the war the Germans got Krupps to make a steel, bomb-proof container to convey the consecrated host to the troops in the front line. This was disgusting. It should have had no protection from human hands at all.

*

We listened this evening in Lee's rooms to a performance on gramophone records of Brahms's Third Symphony. Wittgenstein's complete absorption in the music was most impressive. When it was finished he asked that we might hear it all over again – this, he said, was his favourite of the four symphonies of Brahms. We continued to talk about composers.

WITTGENSTEIN: I once wrote that Mozart believed in both heaven and hell, whereas Beethoven only believed in heaven and nothingness.

DRURY: I have never cared for any of Wagner's music.

WITTGENSTEIN: Wagner was the first of the great composers who had an unpleasant character.

DRURY: I love Mendelssohn's music. I feel at ease listening to Mendelssohn, whereas I find Beethoven and Schubert at times really frightening.

WITTGENSTEIN: Mendelssohn's Violin Concerto is remarkable in being the last great concerto for the violin written. There is a passage in the second movement which is one of the great moments in music. Music came to a full stop with Brahms; and even in Brahms I can begin to hear the sound of machinery.

DRURY: The Lener String Quartet is coming to Cambridge soon, and I intend to go and hear them.

WITTGENSTEIN: [making a face] They play like pigs.

A few days later he came to my rooms looking very distressed. So much so that I asked him what was the matter.

WITTGENSTEIN: I was walking about in Cambridge and passed a bookshop, and in the window were portraits of Russell, Freud and Einstein. A little further on, in a music shop, I saw portraits of Beethoven, Schubert and Chopin. Comparing these portraits I felt intensely the terrible degeneration that had come over the human spirit in the course of only a hundred years.

1930(?) [8]

At our discussion group today someone was inclined to defend Russell's writings on marriage, sex and 'free love'. Wittgenstein interposed with: 'If a person tells me he has been to the worst places I have no right to judge him; but if he tells me it was his superior wisdom that enabled him to go there, then I know he is a fraud.'

He went on to say how absurd it was to debar Russell from the professorship in New York on 'moral grounds'. If ever there was anything which could be called an an-aphrodisiac, it was Russell writing about sex.

'Russell's books should be bound in two colours: those dealing with mathematical logic in red – and all students of philosophy should read them; those dealing with ethics and politics in blue – and no one should be allowed to read them.'

*

I had a conversation with Wittgenstein this afternoon, when we were strolling through the Fellows' Garden of Trinity College. I told him I was reading a book about the 'Desert Fathers', the early Christian ascetics of the Egyptian Thebaid. I said something to the effect that they might have made better use of their lives – rather than, for example, the extreme asceticism of St Simeon Stylites.

WITTGENSTEIN: That's just the sort of stupid remark an English parson would make; how can you know what their problems were in those days and what they had to do about them?

I know there have been times in history when monks were nothing but a nuisance, but monasticism does correspond to a real need of some human beings . . . But you, Drury, couldn't be a monk. It would be all wrong for you to wear a monastic habit.

*

Wittgenstein advised me to read Spengler's *The Decline of the West*. It was a book, he said, that might teach me something about the age we were now living in. It might be an antidote for my 'incurable romanticism'. After I had read the book I said to him, 'Spengler wants to put history into moulds , and that you can't do.'

WITTGENSTEIN: Yes, you are right; you can't put history into moulds. But Spengler does point out certain very interesting comparisons. I don't trust Spengler about details. He is too often inaccurate. I once wrote that if Spengler had had the courage to write a very short book, it could have been a great one.

DRURY: I conceived the idea that I might write a book to try and bring out just what was important in Spengler.

WITTGENSTEIN: Well, perhaps some day you might do just that.

193?

Wittgenstein presented me with a copy of Dr Johnson's *Prayers*.[9]

We talked about the ancient liturgies, particularly the collects in the Latin mass.

DRURY: Isn't it important that there should be ordained priests to carry on this tradition? That was my idea in wanting to be ordained.

WITTGENSTEIN: At first sight it would seem a wonderful idea that there should be in every village someone who stood for these things. But it hasn't worked out that way at all. For all you and I can tell, the religion of the future will be without any priests or ministers. I think one of the things you and I have to learn is that we have to live without the consolation of belonging to a Church. If you feel you must belong to some organization, why don't you join the Quakers?

The very next morning he came to see me, to say that he had been quite wrong to suggest my becoming a Quaker. I was to forget that he ever mentioned it. 'As if nowadays any one organization was better than another.'

WITTGENSTEIN: Of one thing I am certain. The religion of the future will have to be extremely ascetic; and by that I don't mean just going without food and drink.

I seemed to sense for the first time in my life the idea of an asceticism of the intellect; that this life of reading and discussing in the comfort of Cambridge society, which I so enjoyed, was something I would have to renounce. Wittgenstein saw that I was troubled.

WITTGENSTEIN: But remember that Christianity is not a matter of saying a lot of prayers; in fact we are told not to do that. If you and I are to live religious lives, it mustn't be that we talk a lot about religion, but that our manner of life is different. It is my belief that only if you try to be helpful to other people will you in the end find your way to God.

Just as I was leaving he suddenly said, 'There is a sense in which you and I are both Christians.'

1930(?)

Last night a meeting of the Moral Science Club in Broad's

rooms. Before the meeting began, Wittgenstein and I stood talking, looking out of the window; it was a dull grey evening just getting dark. I told Wittgenstein that I had been listening to Beethoven's Seventh Symphony, and how impressed I had been by the second movement.

WITTGENSTEIN: The chord with which that slow movement opens is the colour of that sky [pointing out of the window]. At the end of the war, when we were retreating before the Italians, I was riding on a gun-carriage and I was whistling to myself that movement. Just at the very end of the movement Beethoven does something which makes one see the theme in an entirely different light.

DRURY: The slow movement of the Fourth Piano Concerto is one of the greatest things in music.

WITTGENSTEIN: There Beethoven is writing not just for his own time or culture but for the whole human race.

*

I read a paper to the Moral Science Club entitled 'Are there degrees of clarity?' My thesis was that a proposition either had meaning or it hadn't. There was not a gradual approximation from nonsense through partial confusion to perfect clarity. Moore was present at the meeting and attacked what I had written vigorously. I put up a very poor defence. The next day I told Wittgenstein that Moore had 'wiped the floor with me'.

WITTGENSTEIN: Surely you were able to stand up to Moore?[10]

Then he asked me to read the paper to him. He listened attentively without interruption; and when I had finished:

WITTGENSTEIN: You know, I rather like it. You are doing the sort of thing I am working at, trying to see how in actual life we use words. It has puzzled me why Socrates is regarded as a great philosopher. Because when Socrates asks for the meaning of a word and people give him examples of how that word is used, he isn't satisfied but wants a unique definition. Now if someone shows me how a word is used and its different meanings, that is just the sort of answer I want.

DRURY: I suppose the fact that Socrates was put to death has something to do with the fact that his memory is held in reverence.

WITTGENSTEIN: Yes, I would think that had a lot to do with it.

DRURY: It may be significant that those dialogues in which Socrates is looking for precise definitions end, all of them, without any conclusion. The definition he is looking for isn't reached, but only suggested definitions refuted. This might have been Socrates's ironical way of showing that there was something wrong in looking for one exact meaning of such general terms.

I told Wittgenstein that one of my acquaintances was working on a thesis as to why the League of Nations had failed.

WITTGENSTEIN: Tell him to find out first why wolves eat lambs!

*

Professor Schlick from Vienna was due to read a paper to the Moral Science Club entitled 'Phenomenology'.

WITTGENSTEIN: You ought to make a point of going to hear this paper, but I shan't be there. You could say of my work that it is 'phenomenology'.[11]

*

He showed me a question set in the History Tripos examinations. It read: ' "The Pope showed as little wisdom in his dealings with the Emperor as he had previously done in his dealings with Luther." Discuss.'

WITTGENSTEIN: Now that is the sort of question that teaches people to be stupid. How could a Cambridge undergraduate in this century possibly know what the Pope could have done about Luther or the Emperor – for instance, whom the Pope had to advise him?

*

A student who had come from Edinburgh with a reputation of

considerable ability never came to Wittgenstein's discussions and very rarely to the Moral Science Club.

WITTGENSTEIN: A philosopher who is not taking part in discussions is like a boxer who never goes into the ring.

*

Walked with Wittgenstein to Madingley and back. I mentioned Jeans's book, *The Mysterious Universe*.[12]

WITTGENSTEIN: These books which attempt to popularize science are an abomination. They pander to people's curiosity to be titillated by the wonders of science without having to do any of the really hard work involved in understanding what science is about. Now a good book is one like Faraday's *The Chemical History of a Candle*.[13] Faraday takes a simple phenomenon like a candle burning, and shows how complicated a process it really is. All the time, he demonstrates what he is saying with detailed experiments. There is a tendency nowadays for scientists when they reach middle age to become bored with their real work, and launch out into absurd popular semi-philosophical speculations. Eddington is an example of this. So also is Broad's interest in psychical research. Broad pretends that his interest is purely scientific, but it is obvious that he is thrilled to death by speculating and experimenting on these things in this way.

*

After a particularly foolish paper by a visiting professor of philosophy:

WITTGENSTEIN: A bad philosopher is like a slum landlord. It is my job to put him out of business.

DRURY: Joad for example?

WITTGENSTEIN: Everyone picks on Joad, nowadays; but I don't see that he is any worse than many others.

1930(?)

At lunch in the Union today:

DRURY: I think in your recent lectures you have been directly concerned with Kant's problem: How are synthetic a priori propositions possible?

WITTGENSTEIN: Yes, you could say that. I am concerned with the synthetic a priori.[14] When you have thought for some time about a problem of your own, you may come to see that it is closely related to what has been discussed before, only you will want to present the problem in a different way. These thoughts which seem so important to you now, will one day seem like a bag of old, rusty nails, no use for anything at all.

*

There was a performance of *King Lear* by a Cambridge University amateur dramatic society.

WITTGENSTEIN: You should not have missed seeing this; it was a most moving experience. You need young players to perform this play: they can put the necessary passion into it. Coming away from the theatre I was so absorbed by what I had heard that in crossing over the street I was nearly run over by a taxi.

DRURY: I am sorry I missed that play. What I do intend to do is to go with a friend to see the exhibition of Italian art now on in London.

WITTGENSTEIN: [making a face] If you must go to such an exhibition, there is only one way to do it. Walk into a room, select one picture that attracts you, look at it for as long as you want to, then come away and don't look at anything else. If you try to see everything you will see nothing.

*

We were walking in Cambridge and passed a bookshop. In the window there was a book entitled *The Bible Designed to be Read as Literature.*

WITTGENSTEIN: Now I wouldn't want to look at that. I don't

want some literary gent to make selections from the Bible for me.

DRURY: I am at present reading a Commentary on the Epistle to the Romans by a Swiss theologian, Karl Barth. It seems to me a remarkable book.

WITTGENSTEIN: Moore and I once tried to read the Epistle to the Romans together; but we didn't get very far with it and gave it up.[15]

The next day I asked him if I might read out to him something of Karl Barth's. I had with me the volume called *The Word of God and the Word of Man*. I had only been reading for a short time when Wittgenstein told me to stop.

WITTGENSTEIN: I don't want to hear any more. The only impression I get is one of great arrogance.

1931

Wittgenstein told me he had long wanted to read Frazer's *The Golden Bough* and asked to get hold of a copy out of the Union library and read it out loud to him. I got the first volume of the full edition and we continued to read from it for some weeks.[16]

He would stop me from time to time and make comments on Frazer's remarks. He was particularly emphatic that it was wrong to think, as Frazer seemed to do, that the primitive rituals were in the nature of scientific errors. He pointed out that beside these (ritual) customs primitive peoples had quite advanced techniques: agriculture, metal working, pottery etc. The ceremonies that Frazer described were expressions of deeply felt emotions, of religious awe. Frazer himself showed that he partly understood this, for on the very first page he refers to Turner's picture of the Wood of Nemi and the feeling of dread that this picture arouses in us when we remember the ritual murder performed there. In reading of these practices we are not amused by a scientific mistake but ourselves feel some trace of the dread which lay behind them.

After the reading we often went to a cinema together, a 'flick' as he always called it. He insisted on sitting in the very front row and would appear to be completely absorbed in the picture. He would go only to American films, and he expressed a dislike for all English and Continental ones: in these, the cameraman was always intruding himself as if to say, 'Look how clever I am.' I remember him expressing a special delight on the dancing of Ginger Rogers and Fred Astaire.

1931(?)

Wittgenstein staying in Norway in his hut. I had a postcard from him saying, 'Nature is wonderful in all her moods.'

When he returned from Norway he told me that he had done no writing there but had spent his time in prayer. He had felt it necessary to write out a confession of those things in his past life of which he was most ashamed. He insisted on my reading this. He had already shown it to Moore, and he said that Moore had seemed very distressed that he had had to read this. I will of course say nothing about the contents of this confession, except to state – if this is necessary – that it contained nothing about the sexual behaviour ascribed to him in a recent writing.

He told me that he had got to know some wonderful characters in Norway. A woman who had said to him how fond she was of rats! 'They had such wonderful eyes.' This same woman once sat up every night for a month waiting for a sow to farrow, so as to be on hand to help if necessary. This attention to animals seemed to have pleased Wittgenstein especially.

On his journey back from Norway, the boat bringing him down the fiord stopped at a jetty. There was a woman standing on the jetty dressed in a trouser suit.

WITTGENSTEIN: Usually I dislike seeing women wearing trousers, but this woman looked magnificent.

1931

I had now moved from my rooms in Trinity to the theological college, Westcott House. Wittgenstein came to see me there. Noticing a crucifix over my bed, he looked at me very sternly.

WITTGENSTEIN: Drury, never allow yourself to become too familiar with holy things.

We then went and sat for a while in the college chapel. There was no organ in the chapel but instead a piano in the loft. While we were sitting in silence, someone else came in and started to play the piano. Wittgenstein jumped up at once and hurried out; I followed.

WITTGENSTEIN: Blasphemy! A piano and the cross. Only an organ should be allowed in a church.

He was obviously very disturbed. I felt that my life hitherto had been superficial and aesthetic. That something much more costly was required of me. I began for the first time to have serious doubts about continuing my plan to be ordained in the Anglican Church.

*

I went to see Wittgenstein and told him I had decided to leave the theological college. He said, 'A separation has occurred in your life.' We discussed what I should do next.

WITTGENSTEIN: It is essential that you get away from Cambridge at once. There is no oxygen in Cambridge for you. It doesn't matter for me, as I manufacture my own oxygen. You need to get among ordinary people of a type that you at present know nothing about. One of my pupils, on my advice, has gone to work in Woolworth's; now that is the sort of thing you should do. Try and get a job in some large store or firm, where you will meet ordinary people. It is some such experience as this that you need.

DRURY: There is so much unemployment at present that I would feel guilty in taking a post that perhaps someone else needed more than me. Wouldn't it be best to use the education I have been given and take a teaching post in a school?

WITTGENSTEIN: That isn't the experience you need. You would still be in the same environment that you are now.

DRURY: The Archdeacon of Newcastle was recently visiting

the College, and said he wanted someone to come as a voluntary worker to help run a club for the numerous unemployed on Tyneside. Accommodation would be provided, but there would be no salary. From my scholarship I have enough in hand to keep myself for a time.

WITTGENSTEIN: If you feel you can do that, go there. But it sounds to me like trying to climb Mount Everest.

1932

I spent some months at Newcastle, and together with a group of unemployed shipyard workers we had repaired a derelict building and turned it into a social club for the neighbourhood. We had also started a boot-repairing workshop, a carpenter's shop and a canteen where cheap meals could be had at cost price. When this was under way, Wittgenstein came up to Newcastle to visit me. I took him down to Jarrow, where there was almost complete unemployment. The shipyard there had been closed for several years. The shops were mostly boarded up, and the whole area had a terrible air of dereliction.

WITTGENSTEIN: Sraffa[17] is right: the only thing possible in a situation like this is to get all these people running in one direction.

I told him that if I was to continue the work I was doing I would soon have to find some way of earning my living. For it had been made clear to me that, now that the club was well under way, I could not have free board and lodging much longer. Also, my own funds were nearly exhausted. I had seen a notice that a lecturer in philosophy was required at Armstrong College,[18] and I thought it might be the right thing to apply for it. Wittgenstein said he supposed that under the circumstances it was the only thing to do. I needed three testimonials and so I wrote to Broad, and Moore, and asked Wittgenstein for the third; which he gave me.

Later I told him that Moore, at the end of his testimonial, had said, 'He has a sense of humour.'

WITTGENSTEIN: Moore is unique: only Moore would have

thought of writing that a sense of humour is important in a philosopher.

Later I had to write to Wittgenstein and tell him that I had not obtained the post. It was given instead to Miss Dorothy Emmett. On several occasions in later years he used to say to me that I owed a great debt to Miss Emmett, in that she had saved me from becoming a professional philosopher.

1933

I was invited by a friend to come for a year to live in the settlement at Merthyr Tydfil in South Wales, where he was acting as warden. The plan was that we should use the large garden there for running a communal market garden for the many unemployed miners in the town. Wittgenstein came down for a night to visit me, and I took him round the garden, which was now producing a good crop of vegetables. He then told me that for short time he had worked as a gardener in a Benedictine monastery near Vienna.[19] One day the Abbot had passed him when he was at work and had said, 'So I see that intelligence counts for something in gardening too.'

We were sitting and talking in my bedroom when he noticed a copy of Thomas à Kempis by my bedside.

WITTGENSTEIN: Are you reading this book?

DRURY: I find it a help when I feel in a despondent mood.

WITTGENSTEIN: It wasn't written for that purpose. It was written to be remembered in all moods.

*

A close friend of mine had become seriously ill and had had to be admitted to a mental hospital. I was very distressed at this, and decided I would apply to be trained as a male nurse in a mental hospital. I arranged an interview with the medical superintendent of the hospital. He tried to dissuade me from my plan, saying that I could do much more useful work with my education if I would train as a doctor. I wrote a letter to

Wittgenstein telling him the result of this interview. Immediately I got a telegram in reply: 'Come to Cambridge at once.' Wittgenstein and Francis Skinner met me at the station at Cambridge, and I was hardly out of the train –

WITTGENSTEIN: Now there is to be no more argument about this: it has all been settled already, you are to start work as a medical student at once. I have arranged with two wealthy friends of mine to help you financially, and I shall be able to help you myself.

I was so taken aback by this announcement that I could say nothing until we arrived at Skinner's rooms in East Road.

DRURY: I think at my age I ought to stand on my own feet and not be sponging on others.

WITTGENSTEIN: You are not sponging on others. There is nothing I dislike so much as a sponger. But you never asked for this. It has been given you as a willing gift. To refuse it now would be nothing but an obstinate pride.

We then went to the Union to look at various University Calendars, to see which medical school I should try for. After some further discussion, and correspondence, it was decided that I should go to Trinity College, Dublin.

1934

After my first year in the school of anatomy, I spent the summer in my brother's cottage in Connemara, at the mouth of the Killary harbour, nine miles from a shop and twenty miles from the nearest railway station. Wittgenstein and Francis Skinner came at the end of the summer to stay with me for a couple of weeks. The arrangement was that the car which was to take my mother to Recess station should pick up Wittgenstein and Francis and bring them back to the cotta ,e. Wittgenstein had about twenty minutes talking to my mother while she was waiting for her train to arrive. Up to now, my mother had felt some suspicion of the influence Wittgenstein had over me, and my apparent need to consult him about everything. But after this short meeting she wrote me a letter by the first post saying that she now quite understood what an impressive person he was, and felt much happier about my being guided by him. I was struck once again by the way in which Wittgenstein's personality could in such a short meeting make a profound impression.

When Wittgenstein got out of the car at Rosroe, the first thing he said to me was, 'You have a beautiful country.' He and Francis had been amused at the very antiquated train that had brought them from Galway, with its Victorian rolling-stock. 'This', he said, 'is a country for horses, not railways.'

Thinking my guests would be hungry after their long journey and night crossing, I had prepared a rather elaborate meal: roast chicken followed by suet pudding and treacle. Wittgenstein rather silent during the meal.

When we had finished:

WITTGENSTEIN: Now let it be quite clear that while we are here we are not going to live in this style. We will have a plate of porridge for breakfast, vegetables from the garden for lunch, and a boiled egg in the evening.

This was then our routine for the rest of his visit.

The next day being fine and sunny, we walked over the hill to Tully sands.

WITTGENSTEIN: The colours of the landscape here are marvellous. Why even the surface of the road is coloured.

When we reached the sands we walked up and down by the sea.

WITTGENSTEIN: I can well understand why children love sand.

We discussed the plan that he and Francis were thinking of: that they should go and live and work in Russia. They had both been having lessons in Russian.

FRANCIS: I want to do something 'fiery'.

WITTGENSTEIN: That is a very dangerous way of thinking.

DRURY: I think Francis means that he doesn't want to take the treacle with him.

WITTGENSTEIN: Oh, that is an excellent expression: I understand what that means entirely. No, we don't want to take the treacle with us.

Wittgenstein had already[20] been to see the Russian ambassador in London, Maisky, in order to get a visa to visit Russia. He told me that this was the only time he had worn a tie instead of his usual open-neck shirt. He did this in case Maisky thought he was putting on an act in coming in unconventional dress. Maisky had asked him if he could speak any Russian and Wittgenstein had replied, 'Well, try me.' After they had been talking for some time, Maisky had said, 'Not bad at all' – Russian, said Wittgenstein, was a most beautiful language to listen to.

We talked for a time about Lenin.

WITTGENSTEIN: Lenin's writings about philosophy are of course absurd, but at least he did want to get something done. A most remarkable face, partly Mongolian in feature. Isn't it remarkable that, in spite of their professed materialism, the Russians have gone to such trouble to preserve Lenin's body in perpetuity; and to visit his tomb. You know I don't think much of modern architecture, but that tomb in the Kremlin is well designed.

On the way home from our walk we passed a cottage outside which a small girl, about five years old, was sitting. Wittgenstein suddenly stopped and said, 'Drury, just look at the expression on that child's face. You don't take enough notice of people's faces; it is a fault you ought to try to correct.'

We commented on the very primitive cottages in the area.

WITTGENSTEIN: I thought I had struck rock-bottom in Poland – but this is even more primitive. You know, there is only one thing I dread about going to live in Russia: bedbugs!

*

Several days of almost continuous rain. Wittgenstein suggested that I should read something out loud to him and Francis. I happened to have with me a copy of Prescott's *History of the Conquest of Mexico*. Wittgenstein said,'That will be just the thing.'

During the reading he would from time to time stop me and exclaim at Prescott's condescending attitude towards those whom he referred to as 'the aborigines of the American continent'. Wittgenstein found this superior attitude very offensive, pointing out that at the time Prescott was writing, slavery in the Southern States was still legally enforced.

When we came to the account of the reign of the Emperor Nezahualcoyotl (Book 1, Chapter 6) I was reading the translation of one of the Emperor's poems:

> All things on earth have their term, and, in the most joyous career of their vanity and splendor, their strength fails, and they sink into the dust. All the round world is but a sepulchre; and there is nothing, which lives on its surface, that shall not be hidden and entombed beneath it . . . Yet let us take courage, illustrious nobles and chieftains, true friends and loyal subjects, – *let us aspire to that heaven, where all is eternal, and corruption cannot come.*[21]

WITTGENSTEIN: Why, this is remarkable, this is what Plato dreamed of – that a philosopher should be king. It seems to me that, in every culture, I come across a chapter headed 'Wisdom'. And then I know exactly what is going to follow: 'Vanity of vanities, all is vanity.'

When I was getting the vegetables ready for lunch, Francis was washing and preparing the lettuce for a salad. I couldn't understand why every few minutes he would disappear into the garden. Then I saw that a very small slug or snail which he found in the lettuce was being gently taken back to the garden. This was very typical of Francis's gentle character. Later, when we were alone, I told Wittgenstein about this.

WITTGENSTEIN: Francis is extraordinary. He is a man who is quite incapable of talking nonsense. Sometimes his silence infuriates me and I shout at him, 'Say something, Francis!' But Francis isn't a thinker. You know Rodin's statue called *The Thinker*; it struck me the other day that I couldn't imagine Francis in that attitude.

The rain had at last stopped, and it was a warm and sunny

day. I suggested rowing Wittgenstein and Francis over to the other shore of the Killary, and that we should walk to the Mayo sands, a fine stretch of sands unapproached by any road and therefore nearly always deserted. We did this, and as we were walking along the side of the mountain a horse suddenly took fright and galloped up the hill. Wittgenstein stood looking at it in amazement. He said how much he loved horses; that when he first went to Cambridge as a student he used to hire a horse and go riding.

When at last we came in sight of the sands we saw below us the Mortimer family – the only inhabitants of this isolated district – out making hay in the small area of cultivatable land available to them. As soon as Wittgenstein saw this he turned round.

WITTGENSTEIN: We are going back. These people are working, and it is not right that we should be holidaying in front of them.

I thought of the many times I had been to these sands and such an obvious thought had never occurred to me.

Back in the cottage that evening I continued my reading out loud. The walls of the cottage are of a rough whitewash texture.

WITTGENSTEIN: (looking at Francis silhouetted against the wall) What an excellent background this wall would make for a photograph portrait. Professional photographers spoil their work because they will try to use an elaborate background. They won't see the importance of simplicity.

This morning the local fisherman had landed on the pier a large catch of mackerel. The usual brilliant colouring of fish just out of the sea, some of them still half alive.

WITTGENSTEIN: [in a low voice] Why don't they leave them in the sea! I know fish are caught in the most horrible way, and yet I continue to eat fish.

1935(?)

Easter-time at Woolacombe in North Devon. Wittgenstein had

come to spend the holiday there with me and the other members of my family. On Easter morning we all presented each other with chocolate eggs and Wittgenstein of course was included in the ceremony. He showed real pleasure at this. Afterwards when we were out walking he told me how much he liked keeping up these old customs. We walked up the hill to Mortehoe and then out along the point. I said to him that in earlier years the ceremonies of Holy Week and Easter had meant a great deal to me; and now I felt a sense of emptiness when I no longer took part in them.

WITTGENSTEIN: But Drury, when I wanted to dissuade you from becoming a parson I didn't mean that you should at the same time cease to attend your church services. That wasn't the idea at all. Though it may be that you have to learn that these ceremonies haven't the importance you once attached to them – but that doesn't mean that they have no importance. Of course it does often happen that, as one develops, a man's expression of his religion becomes much drier. I had a Protestant aunt, and the only religious observance she kept was to observe every Good Friday in complete silence and complete abstinence.

1936

Wittgenstein on a visit to my home in Exeter. He spent a certain amount of time reading in the library. He read James Joyce's *A Portrait of the Artist as a Young Man*. It was, he said, a remarkable piece of writing; and the account of the retreat taken by the Jesuit was particularly well done. He tried to read Sean O'Casey but soon put it aside: 'No one ever talked this sort of language.' He then mentioned to me that he had recently read *Journey's End*.

WITTGENSTEIN: Nowadays it is the fashion to emphasize the horrors of the last war. I didn't find it so horrible. There are just as horrible things happening all round us today, if only we had eyes to see them. I couldn't understand the humour in *Journey's End*. But I wouldn't want to joke about a situation like that.

DRURY: It may have been that they had no language in which to express their real feelings.

WITTGENSTEIN: Oh, I hadn't thought of that. That might well be true: no way of saying what they really felt.

*

There was in our dining-room a steel engraving of a portrait of Pope Pius IX. A very striking face.

WITTGENSTEIN: [after looking at the picture for some time] The last of the *real* Popes, I would think. If it was declared that, whenever the Pope sat on a particular chair, what he then pronounced was to be believed and obeyed by all Catholics – then I would understand what the doctrine of infallibility meant. But as long as the words *ex cathedra* are not defined, the doctrine of infallibility decides nothing.

He told me he had been reading Newman's *Apologia* and that he admired Newman's obvious sincerity. But when he came to read the last sermon Newman preached to his friends at Littlemore, he thought to himself, 'I wouldn't wish to speak to my friends like that.'

*

We went every morning to have our lunch together at Lyons, the café in the High Street. Several times he mentioned to me how much he admired the Lyons organization and the cleanliness with which the cafés were run. Pointing out to me the uniform the waitresses wore:

WITTGENSTEIN: Usually, in twenty years' time the old fashions of dress appear ridiculous; but these uniforms are so well designed that they will never look silly.

We are still living in times where a good tailor knows within a fraction of an inch how to cut his cloth. But you and I may live to see that art lost too. When people just don't know what to wear. Just as in modern architecture they don't know in what style to design a building. I was looking at a portrait of Kierkegaard the other day: the one in which he is depicted as standing at his high desk. A face just like a bird. And do you know, he was dressed as a real dandy. I imagine that he felt if he didn't do this he would have to become entirely slovenly.

DRURY: I have never understood why people have set so much value on wearing precious stones: diamonds etc.

WITTGENSTEIN: That is because you have probably never met anyone who knew how to wear them.

That evening we walked together in the gardens in front of Colleton Crescent.[22] It was a warm, still evening, just getting dusk. Wittgenstein was unusually silent and seemed in a very tranquil frame of mind. I had not often felt his company so restful.

DRURY: Dusk is one of the best times of day.

WITTGENSTEIN: I wish the light was always like this.

This will seem a very trivial incident; but it was one of those inexplicable moments that left a permanent impression on my mind.

*

Sunday morning. Wittgenstein and I went for a walk.

WITTGENSTEIN: I saw you and your mother coming back through the garden before breakfast this morning. Had you been to church?

DRURY: Yes, we had been to Holy Communion together.

WITTGENSTEIN: I wish I could have been with you,

That same evening we were walking back through the cathedral close as people were going in to Evensong.

WITTGENSTEIN: Let's go in with them.

We sat at the back of the nave listening to the service. When it came to the sermon the preacher chose as his text: 'It is expedient for you that I go away: for if I go not away, the Comforter will not come unto you.'[23] After a few minutes Wittgenstein leant over and whispered to me, 'I am not listening to a word he is saying. But think about the text, that is wonderful, that is really wonderful.'

As we walked home after the service he was very critical of the organist's ability, especially of the voluntary he had tried to play.

WITTGENSTEIN: Who of us nowadays has any idea of what a Bach fugue really meant at the time in which it was composed? When people lament the Reformation they must then condemn Bach's music. Bach's music is an expression of Lutheranism.

Art forms lose their meaning. For instance, why have all Shakespeare's plays five acts? No one knows. What does the number five signify here?

Once when I was listening to the short crowd choruses in Bach's Passion music, I suddenly realized, 'This is what the very short scenes in some of Shakespeare's plays mean.'

The next day we walked down the canal to beyond the Double Locks. When we were out of sight of the city I said to Wittgenstein, pointing, 'I know that Exeter is in that direction and Topsham in that.'

WITTGENSTEIN: That is an interesting use of 'know'. Here you are certain of something, but there is nothing in the nature of what might be called a 'sense-datum'.

On the way home we mentioned a student we had both known in Cambridge, who had been killed fighting with the International Brigade in Spain. Some of his friends had said to Wittgenstein, 'What a relief to know that this was the end of his sufferings and that we don't have to think of a 'future life''.' Wittgenstein said he was shocked at their speaking in this way. I tried to explain to him that for me the only perfect moments in my life were when I had been so absorbed in the object – nature or music – that all self-consciousness was abolished. The 'I' had ceased to be.

WITTGENSTEIN: And so you think of death as the gateway to a permanent state of mind such as that.

DRURY: Yes, that is how I think of a future life.

He seemed disinclined to continue with this conversation; but I had the feeling that he thought what I had said was superficial.

*

Today at lunch the conversation turned to discussing 'detective stories'. Wittgenstein said how much he enjoyed the stories of Agatha Christie. Not only were the plots ingenious but the characters were so well drawn that they were real people. He thought it was a particularly English talent to be able to write books like this. One of the company advised him to read Chesterton's 'Father Brown' stories. He made a grimace. 'Oh no, I couldn't stand the idea of a Roman Catholic priest playing the part of a detective. I don't want that.'

Afterwards, on our walk, we discussed humorous books. I was slightly surprised to find that he appreciated the writings of P. G. Wodehouse. He said that he thought that the short story called 'Honeysuckle Cottage' was one of the funniest things he had ever read. We went on to discuss how taste in humour varied from age to age.

WITTGENSTEIN: I remember reading in an old book how someone saw a man walking beside a river reading and bursting into fits of laughter. And he said, 'That man must be reading *Don Quixote*, only the Don could make a man laugh like that.' Now I don't find *Don Quixote* funny at all.

DRURY: Voltaire's *Candide* was considered a very amusing book, but I couldn't see anything amusing in it.

WITTGENSTEIN: I agree with you about *Candide*. Now a book I like greatly is Sterne's *Tristram Shandy*. That is one of my favourite books. You remember the incident where they are discussing infant prodigies, and after several have mentioned examples, one of the company caps the lot by saying that he knew an infant who produced a work on the day he was born. Whereupon Dr Slop replies that it should have been wiped up and nothing more said about it. Now that you could say about a lot that is written today. They should be wiped up and nothing more said about them. I am particularly fond of the character of Corporal Trim in *Tristram Shandy*, and especially the sermon he reads out.

Our walk had taken us up to Victoria Park Road, where my brother's house was undergoing extensive alterations. Wittgenstein insisted on climbing up the scaffolding on to the roof to inspect the work being done. He shouted down to me, 'Don't try to come up, it is very vertiginous.' When he came down he had a lot to say about the work being done, and I was impressed by the usual thoroughness with which he went into everything.

*

We called round at my brother's architectural office in Bedford Circus. My brother was out on a site, but Wittgenstein spent some time talking to the senior partner, Mr Tonar. They seemed to be having a lively conversation. I was amused afterwards when Mr Tonar said to me in private: 'That's a very intelligent young man.' One of the assistant draughtsmen was designing an altar cross. Wittgenstein became quite agitated: 'I couldn't for the life of me design a cross in this age; I would rather go to hell than try and design a cross.' We hadn't left the office for long when he turned back, saying, 'I shouldn't have said what I did about designing a cross; that can do no good. We must go back and tell the man not to take the slightest notice of what I said.'

*

When we were out walking a few days later, Wittgenstein began to talk to me about Lessing. He quoted with great emphasis Lessing's remark: 'If God held closed in his right hand all truth, and in his left the single and untiring striving after truth, adding even that I always and forever make mistakes, and said to me: Choose! I should fall humbly before his left hand and say: Father grant me! the pure truth is for you alone.'[24] Then he said he would like to read to me something of Lessing's. So we turned back and hurried up to the public library to see if we could find anything either in German or in English. We found nothing; and I had to regret that I never heard him selecting what it was he wanted me to know.

On the way home through the cathedral close we passed the statue of Richard Hooker. Wittgenstein asked me who he was.

DRURY: He was an Elizabethan divine who wrote a famous apologia for the Anglican Reformation, a book called *Laws of Ecclesiastical Polity*. In it he tried to steer a middle course between Catholicism and Calvinism.

WITTGENSTEIN: That sounds to me impossible. How could there be any compromise between two such completely divergent doctrines?

The next day he had obviously thought about this and said to me that he could now see that a thoroughly bourgeois culture might want some such compromise.

*

Our walk took us through a modern housing estate.

WITTGENSTEIN: Look at all these houses. They are grinning at you, as if to say, 'Look at me, how pretty I am.' What a silly custom it is to give houses names.

When we got back to Colleton Crescent I pointed out to him that at one time all the windows had had wooden shutters; these had become rotten and had had to be removed. This spoilt the appearance of the crescent.

WITTGENSTEIN: Yes, like a face that has lost its eyebrows.

*

Today he talked to me about his brother Paul Wittgenstein, the pianist. He said that his brother had the most amazing knowledge of music. On one occasion some friends played a few bars of music from any one of a number of composers, from widely different periods, and his brother was able without a mistake to say who the composer was and from which work it was taken.[25] On the other hand he did not like his brother's interpretation of music. Once when his brother was practising the piano and Wittgenstein was in another room of the house, the music suddenly stopped and his brother burst into the room saying, 'I can't play when you are in the house. I feel your scepticism seeping under the door.'

His mother, he said, had an amazing ability in reading music at sight. You could put any piece in front of her and she would play it at once without a wrong note.

They had a friend of the family who was a blind organist. This man could play all Bach's Forty-eight Preludes and Fugues from memory. This he thought was a remarkable thing to be able to do. Wittgenstein's father had an organ built as a birthday present for this friend. When Brahms's Fourth Symphony was first performed, this organist was in the audience and after the performance said to Brahms, 'That was a daring canon on the thirteenth that you attempted in the last movement'; and Brahms replied, 'Only you would have noticed that.'

*

I was now back in Dublin, preparing for my First MB examination. This involved the immense task of memorizing all the details of human anatomy. I wrote to Wittgenstein mentioning that I found this a tedious drudgery. In a letter replying to this he said, 'You ought to be glad of this drudgery. It is just the sort of discipline you need.' In the same letter he went on to say that he and Francis Skinner were seriously thinking of coming to Dublin and joining me in studying medicine, and he asked me to make enquiries about the possibility of the two of them entering the medical school. I went and asked my tutor about this, and he seemed astounded that a Fellow of Trinity Cambridge and a university lecturer should think of giving this up and starting all over again in the medical school!

*

Another letter from Wittgenstein, in which he suggested that if he did qualify as a doctor he and I might practise together as psychiatrists. He felt that he might have a special talent for this branch of medicine. He sent me as a birthday present a copy of Freud's *Interpretation of Dreams*. This, he wrote, was the most important of Freud's writings. When he first read it he said to himself, 'Here at last is a psychologist who has something to say.'

When we talked about this later, he said he would not want to undergo what was known as a training analysis. He did not think it right to reveal all one's thoughts to a stranger. Psychoanalysis as presented by Freud was irreligious. 'It is a very dangerous procedure; I know of a case where it did infinite harm.'[26]

*

Wittgenstein and Francis Skinner had come on a visit to Dublin. I took them to the front square of Trinity College.

WITTGENSTEIN: [looking round at the rather severe classical architecture] Now I understand what was meant by the phrase 'the Protestant Ascendancy'. These buildings have the appearance of a fortress. But now the gypsies inhabit the castle.

He said about the Georgian architecture of the Dublin streets: 'The people who built these houses had the good taste to know that they had nothing very important to say; and therefore they didn't attempt to express anything.'

In the evening, walking along the quays, we saw Kingsbridge station outlined against the sky. In the distance it looked impressive. Wittgenstein wanted to go nearer and see it in more detail. But when we came close he shook his head: 'No, the details are poor: that cornice for example. What have I always said to you? Night is the architect's friend!'

The next day we were in Woolworth's for some purchases. Wittgenstein noticed some cheap little cameras: 'What fun it would be to take some snaps of each other.' So he insisted on buying three cameras, one for each of us. Then he wanted to climb to the top of Nelson's Column to view the city from there. We took a lot of photographs but they didn't turn out very well!

*

Noticing the street names in Irish, we talked about the efforts being made to revive the language.

WITTGENSTEIN: It is always a tragic thing when a language dies. But it doesn't follow that one can do anything to stop it doing so. It is a tragic thing when the love between a man and wife is dying; but there is nothing one can do. So it is with a dying language. Though one thing is achieved by putting these notices in Irish: it makes one realize that one is in a foreign country. Dublin is not just another English provincial town: it has the air of a real capital city.

*

The Nazis were now in control of Germany.[27]

WITTGENSTEIN: Just think what it must mean, when the government of a country is taken over by a set of gangsters. The dark ages are coming again. I wouldn't be surprised, Drury, if you and I were to live to see such horrors as people being burnt alive as witches.

DRURY: Do you think Hitler is sincere in what he is saying in his speeches?

WITTGENSTEIN: Is a ballet dancer sincere?

*

I told him I had been asked to be godfather at the christening of my nephew.

DRURY: The godparents have to promise in the child's name to renounce the devil and all his works, the pomps and vanities of this wicked world, and all the sinful lusts of the flesh.[28] I feel it would be hypocrisy for me to speak those words. It is something that I haven't done myself.

WITTGENSTEIN: To renounce the pomps and vanities of this wicked world. Just think what that would really involve. Who of us today even thinks of doing such a thing? We all want to be admired. St Paul said, 'I die daily.' Just think what that must have meant!

1938

I was now doing my period of residence in the City of Dublin

Hospital. Wittgenstein came to stay in my previous lodgings in Chelmsford Road. Whenever I had time off from my hospital duties I spent the evening with him. The situation in Europe was becoming more and more serious. It struck me that in all the years I had known him I had never seen him reading a newspaper, indeed I could hardly imagine him doing so. But now, when I came in to see him his first question was usually, 'Any news?' One evening I told him all the papers reported that Hitler was poised to invade Austria.

WITTGENSTEIN: That is a ridiculous rumour. Hitler doesn't want Austria. Austria would be no use to him at all.

The very next evening I had to tell him that Hitler had indeed taken over Austria and seemed to be in complete control, without any fighting. He did not refer to his remark of the previous evening; and, to my surprise, did not seem unduly disturbed. I asked him if his sisters would be in any danger.

WITTGENSTEIN: They are too much respected, no one would dare to touch them.

*

We walked in Phoenix Park. I told him that my present work entailed periods of duty in the Casualty Department, and that I was disturbed at my clumsiness; also that when I had to carry out some delicate procedure, such as suturing a wound, I developed a disabling tremor in my hands. I reminded him that when I told Canon Cunningham at the theological college that I intended to train as a doctor, he had said to me: 'You have enough brains to become a doctor, but I very much doubt whether you have the right temperament.'

DRURY: I am worried at times whether I have made a mistake, and whether I will be any use as a doctor. Too nervous and hesitant to make the necessary decisions. But perhaps it is wrong even to allow myself to think about that.

WITTGENSTEIN: You lack the necessary experience: that is all that is wrong at present.

The next day at the hospital I had a letter from him.[29]

*

During his visit to Dublin Wittgenstein asked me if I could arrange for him to have discussions with patients who were seriously mentally ill. He said this would be a matter of great interest to him. I was acquainted with one of the resident doctors in St Patrick's Hospital, and I put this request to him – and it was soon arranged, after the Medical Superintendent, Dr Leper, had had an interview with Wittgenstein. Wittgenstein then went two or three days a week and visited some of the long-stay patients who had few to visit them. He became particularly interested in one elderly man, of whom he said: 'This man is much more intelligent than his doctors.'

WITTGENSTEIN: That elderly patient I was telling you about has a wide knowledge of music. I asked him what was his favourite instrument in the orchestra, and he replied, 'the big drum'. Now that is an excellent answer; I know exactly what he meant.

Before he left Dublin, Wittgenstein wanted me to meet this patient, so that I could continue to visit him; for he had now no relatives who came to see him. When the three of us met and I was introduced, the patient continued a previous discussion he had started with Wittgenstein, about the philosophy of Herbert Spencer. I was fascinated to see how gently and helpfully Wittgenstein was able to discuss with him. When at one point I tried to join in the discussion. Wittgenstein at once told me to 'shut up'. Afterwards, when we were walking home:

WITTGENSTEIN: When you are playing ping-pong you mustn't use a tennis racket.

*

On the way back from Dublin for the vacation I visited Wittgenstein in Cambridge. He told me that that evening he was due to continue a series of lectures and discussions he was having with some students on the subject of 'Aesthetics'. He asked me if I would like to come, and of course I was delighted to be able once again to listen to Wittgenstein lecturing. If I understood him rightly, on that occasion he was saying that you couldn't speak of the meaning of a work of art, say a particular piece of music, as if the meaning was something that could be separated from the work itself. 'Part of the pleasure in hearing Beethoven's Ninth Symphony is hearing the Ninth Symphony.'

During this lecture one of the students was rapidly writing notes. Wittgenstein told him not to do so. 'If you write these spontaneous remarks down, some day someone may publish them as my considered opinions. I don't want that done. For I am talking now freely as my ideas come, but all this will need a lot more thought and better expression.'

(This indeed is what was done later in the volume called *Lectures and Conversations on Aesthetics, Psychology, and Religious Belief*.)[30]

*

The situation in Europe was becoming increasingly grave. Wittgenstein said to me that in the event of war he would not want to be interned as an alien. He therefore asked me: Would my mother agree for him to use her name as a reference in applying for British nationality? Of course she agreed, and this is what he did.

*

G. E Moore was retiring from the professorship of philosophy at Cambridge. Wittgenstein was debating whether he would apply for the chair.

WITTGENSTEIN: I would never be elected. I am now only a 'has-been'. Nobody wants a 'has-been'. One of the electors is Collingwood of Oxford. Can you imagine him voting for me?

After his election, Wittgenstein told me that Broad had said: 'To refuse the chair to Wittgenstein would be like refusing Einstein a chair of physics.' Wittgenstein knew how antipathetic

Broad was to anyone of Wittgenstein's temperament, and he appreciated this tribute.

WITTGENSTEIN: Broad is a very just man. I have been reading *Five Types of Ethical Theory*. I thought he wrote that very well.

1939

It was some time before I saw Wittgenstein again. I had in the mean time qualified as a doctor and was working as an assistant to a general practitioner in the Rhondda Valley. War with Germany seemed certain now, and I had been informed that in the event of war I would be required to join the Royal Army Medical Corps at a moment's notice. In view of this, Wittgenstein and Francis Skinner came down to South Wales to see me. I got rooms for them in a hotel in Pontypridd. The night they arrived, a total blackout was enforced, although war had not yet been declared. Trying to find our way in the darkness we got lost and bumped into things.

WITTGENSTEIN: This blackout is absurd. Nothing will happen here tonight. It is not like the English to get into a panic like this.

When we eventually arrived at the hotel he was still grumbling about the blackout, as the manageress showed us up to their rooms. I said partly as a joke; 'We will be quite accustomed to this in three years' time.' At this both Wittgenstein and Francis Skinner laughed heartily; the manageress looked shocked.

The next morning war was declared. I went at once to the hotel and found Wittgenstein very agitated: he had been ordered to report at once to the local police station. I guessed that the manageress, noticing his foreign name and our jocularity of the previous evening, had been suspicious of our arrival and reported it to the police. All three of us went round to the police station, and were soon able to identify ourselves and our nationality. But Wittgenstein seemed upset and said that in the future he would have to be very careful.

*

I decided that I would return to Exeter for a few days before receiving my calling-up papers. Wittgenstein and Francis decided to come with me. During the few days we had together Wittgenstein was concerned about what he should do, now that war was declared. He did not want to remain at Cambridge but thought that possibly he and Francis might be able to join an ambulance brigade.

The day before he was due to leave we had a final walk together, Francis remaining behind.

WITTGENSTEIN: I have been reading Luther recently. Luther is like an old gnarled oak, as strong as that. That isn't just a metaphor.

DRURY: The little I have read of Luther made a deep impression on me.

WITTGENSTEIN: But don't mistake me: Luther was no saint. No, indeed, he was no saint.

DRURY: Certainly not in the sense that Francis of Assisi was a saint.

WITTGENSTEIN: Francis of Assisi, so far as we can tell, seems to have been pure spirit and nothing else. On the whole I prefer the English Authorized Version of the Bible to Luther's translation into German. The English translators had such reverence for the text that when they couldn't make sense of it they were content to leave it unintelligible. But Luther sometimes twists the sense to suit his own ideas. For instance, when Luther comes to translate the salutation of the Angel to Mary, *Ave gratia plena*, he uses a popular phrase from the market-place which reads something like 'Mary you little dear'.[31]

DRURY: Luther didn't hesitate to make his own selection from the canons of Scripture. He considered the Epistle of James, the Epistle to the Hebrews and the Book of Revelation as of little authority.

WITTGENSTEIN: Isn't it strange that such a book as Ecclesiastes was included in the canon? Speaking for myself, I don't care for the Second Epistle of St Peter. Peter there speaks about 'our beloved brother Paul', whereas it is clear that they were constantly in conflict.

DRURY: It is generally agreed that the Second Epistle of St Peter is a late document, and certainly not written by the apostle. Even Calvin, in spite of his great reverence for the Scriptures, agreed about that.

WITTGENSTEIN: Oh, I am glad to hear that.

When I was seeing Wittgenstein and Francis off at the station, we talked for a time about the present war situation.

WITTGENSTEIN: England and France between them can't defeat Germany. But if Hitler does manage to establish a European empire, I don't believe it will last long. People have accused Stalin of having betrayed the Russian Revolution. But they have no idea of the problems that Stalin had to deal with; and the dangers he saw threatening Russia. I was looking at a picture of the British Cabinet and I thought to myself, 'a lot of wealthy old men'.

1940

It was that wonderful summer of 1940. France had collapsed before the German blitzkrieg. The British Army had at the last minute been ferried to England from Dunkirk. There was a spirit of unity and determination in the country to resist, whatever the cost, a German attempt at invasion. I was stationed at a camp near Yeovil. Wittgenstein came down for a few days to visit me.

WITTGENSTEIN: You have often heard me speak of my dislike of many features of English life. But now that England is in real danger, I realize how fond I am of her; how I would hate to see her destroyed. I have often said to myself that William the Conqueror got himself a very good bargain.

I told him I was having great difficulties with my senior medical officer in the camp, a retired regular colonel, who in my opinion had forgotten what medicine he ever knew. He kept wanting to dispute my diagnoses and treatment, and of course could overrule me by his seniority. Wittgenstein gave me a lecture on the importance in an army of discipline and obedience to superiors, especially in a time of crisis like this. I felt he was speaking of his own experiences in the previous war.

WITTGENSTEIN: Remember, Drury, no one joins an army to have a good time.

January 1941

At Liverpool, doing a course in tropical medicine before being posted to the Middle East. Both Wittgenstein and Francis Skinner came to say goodbye to me and spent a few days in Liverpool. Two days before they came there had been a heavy air raid on the port and town. I was telling them about this.

WITTGENSTEIN: I wish you and I could have been together in an air raid. I would have liked that.

When the time came for me to say goodbye to them, Wittgenstein presented me with a silver drinking-cup.

WITTGENSTEIN: Water tastes so much nicer out of silver. There is only one condition attached to this gift: you are not to worry if it gets lost.

*

During the years I was in Egypt we kept in touch with regular letters. These were largely what Wittgenstein used to call 'hullo letters'. Just letting each other know where we were and that we were well. I regret now that I did not keep these letters, but in the uncertainty of those days one became careless about the future.

He wrote and told me he was now working in Guy's Hospital as a dispensary porter. He had made friends with a young man in the dispensary called Roy Fouracre.[32] Sometimes Wittgenstein would be rushed or agitated and Roy would say to him, 'Steady, Prof.' This he liked. One of his jobs was to prepare Lassar's paste in quantities for the dermatological department. The sister on the ward said no one had ever produced Lassar's paste of this quality before.

I wrote to Wittgenstein that, being anxious to read something in philosophy, I had managed to get hold of a copy of Bradley's *Essays on Truth and Reality* in a shop in Cairo. To my surprise I had found them very stimulating and they had given me much to think about. In reply Wittgenstein wrote that he was not at all surprised that I found Bradley to my liking. He had once looked into something of Bradley's (he didn't say what), expecting to find it very dull, and found him distinctly 'lively'.

In another letter he told me that he had been reading a Swiss theologian, Karl Barth. 'This writing must have come from a remarkable religious experience.' In reply I reminded him that years ago at Cambridge I had tried to read something of Barth's to him, and he had dismissed it as very arrogant. He did not refer to this again.

1941

One morning I received a letter from Wittgenstein telling me that Francis Skinner had died very suddenly from acute polio-myelitis. I could realize what a loss this must have been to him. I too felt the loss of Francis, whom I had come to know so well. [Professor R. L. Goodstein ends the Preface (dated 1949) to his volume *Constructive Formalism: Essays on the Foundations of Mathematics* (Leicester, 1951): 'My last word is for my dear friend Francis Skinner, who died at Cambridge in 1941, and left no other record of his work and of his great gifts of heart and mind than lies in the recollections of those who had the good fortune to know him (p. 10). Ed.]

*

A letter from Wittgenstein[33] telling me he was moving to New-castle. While working at Guy's Hospital he had been invited to have his meals in the doctors' mess. There he had become acquainted with Dr R. T. Grant, who was doing some work on the physiology of 'shock'. Dr Grant had found Wittgenstein's questions and the suggestions he made so relevant that he invited him to join his team when they moved to Newcastle.

I wrote back wishing him luck in his new work, and added the rather foolish remark that I hoped he would make lots of friends. This letter brought the stern reply: 'It is obvious to me that you are becoming thoughtless and stupid. How could you imagine I would ever have "lots of friends"?'

1943

After the end of the campaign in North Africa I was posted back to England to prepare for the Normandy landing. Having a period of disembarkation leave, I travelled up to Newcastle to spend a few days with Wittgenstein. I journeyed from Exeter on the night train, arriving at Newcastle in time for breakfast. Wittgenstein met me at the station. He seemed very distant and silent when we met, and our breakfast together, which I had been looking forward to, was something of an ordeal. He then took me to his room in the Research Department and showed me the apparatus which he himself had designed for his investigation. Dr Grant had asked him to investigate the relationship between breathing (depth and rate) and pulse (volume and rate). Wittgenstein had so arranged things that he could act as his own subject and obtain the necessary tracings on a revolving drum. He had made several improvements in the original apparatus, so much so that Dr Grant had said he wished Wittgenstein had been a physiologist and not a philosopher.

In describing to me his results so far he made a characteristic remark: 'It is all very much more complicated than you would imagine at first sight.'

Suddenly he suggested, 'Let's go out and take the train to Durham and walk by the river there.' This we did; and on the journey our former easy manner of conversation seemed to return.

WITTGENSTEIN: You haven't changed a bit; you are just the same person you always were.'

I then realized that he had been quite convinced that after four years in the army I would have grown away from our previous friendship, and that was the reason why our first meeting had been so strained. When Wittgenstein had formed a fixed idea in his mind about other people, it took a good deal of evidence to make him change his mind. I think he was inclined to see other people in terms of black and white; though in this connection I must mention that he was fond of quoting the proverb, 'It takes *many* sorts to make a world', adding, 'That is a very beautiful and kindly saying.'

As we walked by the river at Durham I began to tell him some of my experiences in Egypt. How on one occasion, when I had a period of leave, I had travelled down to see the temples at Luxor. A wonderful experience.

DRURY: One thing did surprise me and rather shocked me. On going into one of the temples there was on the wall a bas-relief of the god Horus with an erect phallus in the act of ejaculation and collecting the semen in a bowl!

WITTGENSTEIN: Why in the world shouldn't they have regarded with awe and reverence that act by which the human race is perpetuated? Not every religion has to have St Augustine's attitude to sex. Why, even in our culture marriages are celebrated in a church; everyone present knows what is going to happen that night, but that doesn't prevent it being a religious ceremony.

1944

The military hospital to which I was now attached was stationed at Llandeilo in South Wales. Wittgenstein was once again staying at Swansea , and I was able to see him from time to time. On one of these visits he told me that one of his pupils had written to him to say he had become a Roman Catholic.[34]

WITTGENSTEIN: I seem to be surrounded now by Roman Catholic converts! I don't know whether they pray for me. I hope they do.

*

I knew that we were soon to move to our points of embarkation for 'D-Day'. I was to be one of the medical officers on a landing-craft. I came to say goodbye to Wittgenstein.

WITTGENSTEIN: If it ever happens that you get mixed up in hand-to-hand fighting, you must just stand aside and let yourself be massacred.

I felt that this advice was one that he had had to give himself in the previous war.

When some time later we met again he asked me about the landing. I told him how wonderful the sound of the big naval guns was when they opened up behind us.

WITTGENSTEIN: Oh yes, I remember that well. Heavy artillery is a marvellous sound; there is nothing quite like it.

*

I was in camp near Bayeux after the Normandy landing. A letter from Wittgenstein telling me he was reading Plato's *Theaetetus*: 'Plato in this dialogue is occupied with the same problems that I am writing about.' A little later he sent me a copy of a translation of the *Theaetetus* and I tried to read it under the difficulties of camp life. I had to write back to him saying that I found it 'cold'. His reply was, 'It was very far from cold when it was written.'

1945

When the war was nearly over and the Russian armies were closing in on Berlin, I spent a few hours with Wittgenstein in London, on my way back to Germany after a period of leave in England.

WITTGENSTEIN: What a terrible position a man like Hitler is in now.

He said this with compassion. I thought it remarkable that at a time when we were all gloating over the fall of Hitler, Wittgenstein, although detesting everything that Hitler had stood for, could at the same time see the suffering involved in such a terrible situation.

WITTGENSTEIN: As soon as you moved into Germany the tone

of your letters changed at once. I could see that you were not happy.

After demobilization from the army, I took a post as house physician in a hospital at Taunton. Wittgenstein came down to see me from Cambridge where he was now lecturing again. It was his birthday, 26 April. I had remembered that some years previously he had said how much he liked nineteenth-century French travelling clocks – those clocks with brass pedestals and glass panels through which one could see the works. I had been able to obtain one of these clocks and gave it to him as his birthday present. It was a great pleasure to see how much he appreciated this gift and also that I had remembered his casual remark after all this time. (Years after, he mentioned this clock in his will, leaving it to Dr Richards.)

Our conversation on this visit turned on the subject of English literature. He said that whereas there had been no very great English musical composers, English literature would stand comparison with that of any other nation. He thought that English poetry was largely aristocratic in style – in comparison with Russian poetry, which sprang from a peasant tradition. Two of his favourite English poets were Cowper and Blake. Then he quoted from memory these verses from Blake:

> They look in every thoughtless nest,
> Where birds are cover'd warm;
> They visit caves of every beast.
> To keep them all from harm,
> If they see any weeping
> That should have been sleeping,
> They pour sleep on their head,
> And sit down by their bed.
>
> And there the lion's ruddy eyes
> Shall flow with tears of gold,
> And pitying the tender cries,
> And walking round the fold,
> Saying 'Wrath, by his meekness,

And by his health, sickness
Is driven away
From our immortal day.'[35]

When he had finished this he repeated again the lines.

If they see any weeping
That should have been sleeping,
They pour sleep on their head,
And sit down by their bed.

WITTGENSTEIN: Those are very beautiful lines.

He went on to say that Blake's 'Proverbs of Hell'[36] contained many profound thoughts. And then suddenly he quoted:

I am sure This Jesus will not do
Either for Englishman or Jew.[37]

1947–8

I did not see Wittgenstein again for over a year. It was a time of considerable emotional turmoil and indecision for me – finding it difficult to settle down after the experiences of the war. I felt for the first time that I did not want to discuss my problems with him, dreading the powerful influence he exercised over me, and wanting to make my own decisions. I think he appreciated what I was undergoing, for he wrote to me not to send him letters, but from time to time let him have a postcard telling him how I was and where to get in touch with me.

Eventually I obtained a post on the staff of St Patrick's Hospital in Dublin and decided to specialize in psychiatry. After some months in this post I received a letter from Wittgenstein, telling me he had made up his mind to resign his chair of philosophy in Cambridge. He felt that he would never get his writing finished if he still had to lecture. He was undecided where he would live; somewhere where he could find the quiet he needed for his work. In replying to this letter I reminded him that he had often expressed a liking for Ireland and I wondered if he couldn't find a place in Dublin or near it. So it was that he came over to Ireland, and I booked a room for him in Ross's Hotel, close to the hospital where I was resident.

Wittgenstein questioned me closely about the work I was doing.

WITTGENSTEIN: I wouldn't be altogether surprised if this work in psychiatry turned out to be the right thing for you. You at least know that 'There are more things in heaven and earth' etc.

DRURY: Some of the patients I am seeing present symptoms which I find extremely puzzling. I often don't know what to say to them.

WITTGENSTEIN: You must always be puzzled by mental illness. The thing I would dread most, if I became mentally ill, would be your adopting a common-sense attitude; that you could take it for granted that I was deluded.[38] I sometimes wonder whether you will have the right sense of humour for this work. You are too easily shocked when things don't go according to plan.

I lent him a book which was at the time the basis of our hospital treatment, Sargant and Slater's *Physical Methods of Treatment in Psychiatry* (the first edition),

WITTGENSTEIN: This is an excellent book. I like the spirit in which it was written. I am going to get Ben to read this book [referring to a medical student who was a friend of his]. I can quite understand that you would adopt the attitude 'Let's see now what these methods of treatment will accomplish.'

I don't want for one moment to underestimate the importance of the work you are doing; but don't ever let yourself think that all human problems can be solved in this way.

1948

Whenever I was free from hospital duties I went with Wittgenstein to look at possible lodgings which we had seen advertised. He used to laugh as we set out, using a slang American expression, 'We will go and case the joint.' Although we looked at many places, he did not find anything he thought would be congenial.

One evening when I was on duty at the hospital he came and had a meal with me in the doctors' mess. During the meal several messages came, saying that as soon as I was ready there were a number of patients needing to be seen that evening. Wittgenstein looked concerned at the amount I had to do, and got up from the table saying, 'I must go, I am only in your way here.' The next day when I went to visit him at the hotel, the first thing he said to me was: 'Drury, remember the sabbath.' He meant that I must give myself time to rest and think, and not live in a continual whirl of activity. 'It would be quite enough for you if you had only one old woman with bronchitis to look after.' I found it difficult to make him understand just what being resident in a busy hospital necessitated.[39]

Soon after this, I heard from a friend that a farmhouse at Red Cross, in County Wicklow, was prepared to take a permanent guest. Wittgenstein said he would travel down and inspect it. On his return he said he thought he could work well in that quiet surrounding.

WITTGENSTEIN: On my journey down in the bus I kept remarking to myself what a really beautiful country this is.

So it was arranged that he would move down to Red Cross. He was too far away for me to see him regularly now; only when I had a weekend free was I able to visit him.

*

On my first visit to Red Cross it had been arranged that Wittgenstein would meet me at the nearest bus-stop, at Arklow. Even before I got off the bus I could see from the expression on his face that all was going well. He told me at once that the place suited him better than he had anticipated and that he was working hard.

WITTGENSTEIN: Sometimes my ideas come so quickly that I feel as if my pen was being guided. I now see clearly that it was the right thing for me to give up the professorship. I could never have got this work done while I was in Cambridge.

He was full of praise for the beauty of the Wicklow countryside and took me for one of his favourite walks. As usual he questioned me about my work and wanted me to tell him about the type of cases I was treating.

WITTGENSTEIN: Always take a chair and sit down by the patient's bedside; don't stand at the end of the bed in a dictatorial attitude.[40] Let your patients feel they have time to talk to you.

I have been thinking about the physical methods of treatment that you employ. There is no contradiction between this approach and that of Freud. If I have a dream it may be due to some physical cause, something I have eaten for supper that has disagreed with me. But what I dream about, the contents of the dream, may have a psychological explanation. It seems to me that my dreams are always an expression of my fears, not, as Freud thought, my wishes. I could build up an interpretation of dreams just as cogent as Freud's in terms of repressed fears.

DRURY: The French psychologist Pierre Janet said very much the same thing.

WITTGENSTEIN: Freud's work died with him. No one today can do psychoanalysis in the way he did. Now a book that really would interest me would be the one he wrote in collaboration with Breuer.[41]

*

Wittgenstein went on living at Red Cross for some months still, and I visited him as often as I could. All seemed to be going well. Then one day I got a telegram from him asking me to book a room at Ross's Hotel and to see him urgently. As soon as he had arrived I went down to see him. He looked distressed and agitated.

WITTGENSTEIN: It has come.

DRURY: I don't understand; what has happened?

WITTGENSTEIN: What I have always dreaded: that I would no longer be able to work. I have done no work at all for the past two weeks. And I can't sleep at nights. The people under my room sit up late talking and the continual murmur of voices is driving me crazy.

He then went on to tell me that he had found a ruined cottage near the farm which he thought could be cheaply restored, and that might provide the quiet he needed. I reminded him that the cottage at Rosro in Connemara, where he and Francis had stayed with me, was now empty, and that he would be more than welcome to have the use of it for as long as he wanted. This thought seemed to give him some relief, and he said that that might be the solution to his problem. He then returned to Red Cross to think the matter over, and I prescribed some tablets to help him to sleep. I also wrote off to Rosro to have the cottage made ready in case he decided to go there.

*

Wittgenstein spent several months at Rosro. It was too far away for me to get time off from my work to visit him, but we wrote regularly to each other. I gathered from his letters that the location and the quiet of the place suited him and that he was able to work again. He told me he found great interest in observing the very varied bird life in the area: he had tamed some of the birds by putting out food for them, and some even came and ate out of his hand. I was able to send him several illustrated books on birds which helped him to identify the different species. He was having to do all his own housework, which he disliked doing but said it was a good discipline for him. Remembering how he had often commended Johnson's *Prayers and Meditations* to me and had given me a copy, I sent him a copy of Boswell's famous *Life*. In reply he said that there must have been something remarkable about Boswell if Johnson was able to feel such a close friendship with him. That in quoting Johnson Boswell would say when he may not have got the exact words right – this Wittgenstein praised especially. (This warning has been in my mind all the time I have been

writing these conversations, and the reader must remember
that such a warning applies to all I have quoted.)

In the following autumn Wittgenstein went to Austria to see
his sister, who was seriously ill with cancer. On his way back
he decided to spend a few days at Ross's Hotel before returning
to the cottage for the winter. But when we talked the matter
over we decided that if he got ill in Connemara, there would be
no one to look after him and no way of getting medical attention. He found the hotel comfortable and friendly, and he could
have a coal fire in his room, which was at the top of the house
and, above all things, quiet.

Autumn 1948

The hotel where Wittgenstein was now staying was only a
short distance from Phoenix Park and the Zoological Gardens.
I was a member of the Royal Zoological Society and was able to
propose him as a member. This enabled him to have free access
to the gardens and to have his meals in the members' room. He
liked this; and we had many walks and meals together there.
The young lady receptionist at the hotel was very attentive to
Wittgenstein's requests, and to show his appreciation Wittgenstein invited her on one occasion to have lunch with him in the
members' room. This caused quite a sensation among the hotel
staff.

On other occasions he would go to Bewley's Café, in Grafton
Street, for his midday meal – always the same: an omelette and
a cup of coffee. What pleased him was that when he became
well known there the waitress would bring him his omelette
and coffee without a word and without his having to order it.
'An excellent shop: there must be very good management
behind this organization.'

I was now able to see Wittgenstein nearly every day, and
when I had a day off I spent longer with him. He seemed to me
to be writing copiously; when I went up to his room he was
nearly always working and would continue to do so for some
time before we went out. Indeed I remember on one occasion
when we had planned to have lunch together he said to me,
'Just wait a minute until I finish this', and then continued to

write for two hours without saying a word. When he did finish he seemed quite unaware that it was now long past our lunch time.

*

I introduced him to the Botanical Gardens at Glasnevin, and he often went there alone. He found the heated Palm House very congenial to work in during the winter, and would often sit on a step there with his small notebook for long periods

*

Walking in Phoenix Park one afternoon:

DRURY: I sometimes regret the amount of time I spent in reading the great historical philosophers, at a time when I couldn't understand them.

WITTGENSTEIN: I don't regret that you did all that reading.

DRURY: But I have forgotten so much of what I spent so much labour on.

WITTGENSTEIN: The mind has its own secretory organ just as the body has; and that is a good thing too.

We talked for a time about the history of philosophy.

WITTGENSTEIN: Kant and Berkeley seem to me to be very deep thinkers.

DRURY: What about Hegel?

WITTGENSTEIN: No, I don't think I would get on with Hegel. Hegel seems to me to be always wanting to say that things which look different are really the same. Whereas my interest is in showing that things which look the same are really different. I was thinking of using as a motto for my book a quotation from *King Lear*: 'I'll teach you differences.' [Then laughing:] The remark 'You'd be surprised' wouldn't be a bad motto either.

DRURY: At one time reading Kierkegaard so disturbed me that I couldn't sleep.

WITTGENSTEIN: It may be that you ought not to read Kierkegaard. I couldn't read him again now. He is too long-winded; he keeps on saying the same thing over and over again. When I read him I always wanted to say, 'Oh all right, I agree, I agree, but please get on with it.'[42]

DRURY: It is remarkable that Kant's fundamental ideas didn't come to him till he was middle-aged.

WITTGENSTEIN: My fundamental ideas came to me very early in life.

DRURY: Schopenhauer?

WITTGENSTEIN: No; I think I see quite clearly what Schopenhauer got out of his philosophy – but when I read Schopenhauer I seem to see to the bottom very easily. He is not deep in the sense that Kant and Berkeley are deep.

DRURY: I have been trying to read Plato's *Parmenides*, and haven't been able to make head nor tail of it.

WITTGENSTEIN: That dialogue seems to me among the most profound of Plato's writings.

DRURY: Did you ever read anything of Aristotle's?

WITTGENSTEIN: Here I am, a one-time professor of philosophy who has never read a word of Aristotle!

*

I told Wittgenstein that I would like to give him a record player and some records of his own choice, so that when he wanted a rest from his writing he could listen to music.

WITTGENSTEIN: That would never do. It would be like giving me a box of chocolates; I wouldn't know when to stop eating. But you ought to listen to music when you are tired after your work.

And so the very next morning he had delivered at my rooms a wireless set.

*

I noticed in the paper that there was to be a discussion on the

Third Programme between Ayer and Fr Copleston on 'The Existence of God'. I mentioned this to Wittgenstein.

WITTGENSTEIN: [laughing] Oh, we mustn't miss that – Ayer discussing with a Jesuit, that would be too much to miss.

So on the evening concerned he came up to my room, and we listened to the talk. Wittgenstein said nothing while the broadcast was continuing, but the changing expression on his face was itself a commentary on what was being said. When it was over:

WITTGENSTEIN: Ayer has something to say, but he is incredibly shallow. Fr Copleston contributed nothing at all to the discussion.

1949

For the first time he talked to me about his present writing. He showed me the 'duck–rabbit' picture (P II 194).

WITTGENSTEIN: Now you try and say what is involved in seeing something *as* something; it is not easy. These thoughts I am now working at are as hard as granite.

DRURY: James Ward used to say 'Denken ist schwer.'

WITTGENSTEIN: Yes, that must have been a frequent remark of his. Moore quoted him as saying that. But I wouldn't say now 'Thinking is hard.' There is I believe a stage in philosophy where a person feels that. This material I am working at is as hard as granite but I know how to go about it.

Then we went for a walk in the park.

WITTGENSTEIN: Broad was quite right when he said of the *Tractatus* that it was highly syncopated. Every sentence in the *Tractatus* should be seen as the heading of a chapter, needing further exposition. My present style is quite different; I am trying to avoid that error.

I thought when I gave up my professorship that I had at last got rid of my vanity. Now I find I am vain about the style in which I am able to write my present book.

I would like it if some day you were able to read what I am writing now. My type of thinking is not wanted in this present age, I have to swim so strongly against the tide. Perhaps in a hundred years people will really want what I am writing.

It is impossible for me to say in my book one word about all that music has meant in my life. How then can I hope to be understood?[43]

Later on in the walk:

WITTGENSTEIN: I have been wondering what title to give my book. I have thought of something like 'Philosophical Remarks'.

DRURY: Why not just call it 'Philosophy'?

WITTGENSTEIN: [angrily] Don't be such an ass – how could I use a word like that which has meant so much in the history of human thought? As if my work was anything more than just a small fragment of philosophy.

The next day, he told me that he had dictated from his manuscript to a typist in Cambridge.

WITTGENSTEIN: What I was dictating to her must have seemed completely incomprehensible; yet she never asked me to explain what it was all about. An excellent trait.

*

One day, walking in the Zoological Gardens, we admired the immense variety of flowers, shrubs, trees, and the similar multiplicity of birds, reptiles, animals.

WITTGENSTEIN: I have always thought that Darwin was wrong: his theory doesn't account for all this variety of species. It hasn't the necessary multiplicity. Nowadays some people are fond of saying that at last evolution has produced a species that is able to understand the whole process which gave it birth. Now that you can't say.

DRURY: You could say that now there has evolved a strange animal that collects other animals and puts them in gardens. But you can't bring the concepts of knowledge and understanding into this series. They are different categories entirely.

WITTGENSTEIN: Yes, you could put it that way.

*

I told Wittgenstein I was reading some of the early Church Fathers, at the moment Tertullian.

WITTGENSTEIN: I am glad you are doing that. You should continue to do so.

DRURY: I had been reading Origen before. Origen taught that at the end of time there would be a final restitution of all things. That even Satan and the fallen angels would be restored to their former glory. This was a conception that appealed to me – but it was at once condemned as heretical.

WITTGENSTEIN: Of course it was rejected. It would make nonsense of everything else. If what we do now is to make no difference in the end, then all the seriousness of life is done away with. Your religious ideas have always seemed to me more Greek than biblical. Whereas my thoughts are one hundred per cent Hebraic.

DRURY: Yes I do feel that, when, say, Plato talks about the gods, it lacks that sense of awe which you feel throughout the Bible – from Genesis to Revelation.* 'But who may abide the day of his coming, and who shall stand when he appeareth?'

WITTGENSTEIN: [standing still and looking at me very intently] I think you have just said something very important. Much more important than you realize.

*

During this winter when Wittgenstein was staying in the hotel, he asked me from time to time to borrow books from The Royal Dublin Society's library, of which I was a member. It interested me to notice that what he generally wanted to read was history. Among the books I remember him reading were: Macaulay's *Critical and Historical Essays*, Livy's account of the (?second)[44] Punic War, Morley's *Life of Cromwell*, Ségur's *L'Histoire de*

* Now that Simone Weil has taught me how to understand Plato, I would bite my tongue out rather than make such a remark.

Napoléon and Bismarck's *Gedanken und Erinnerungen* (this latter was his own copy and not borrowed from the library).

Once when we were out walking and passed some modern houses he referred to a quotation from Southey's *Colloquies*, which Macaulay had ridiculed in his review of the book.

> WITTGENSTEIN: Southey was quite right. Concerning these houses: 'Time will not mellow them; nature will neither clothe nor conceal them; and they will remain always as offensive to the eye as to the mind.'

This remark of Southey's had obviously so impressed him that he could repeat it verbatim.

On another occasion he said how interesting it was that Livy could not conceal his admiration for Hannibal. He particularly liked the incident when, after the battle of Cannae, Hannibal had the field of battle searched for the bodies of the two consuls in order that he could show his respect for them.

*

An incident which seemed to me to illustrate two traits especially characteristic of Wittgenstein: one, his close observation of details, and second, the 'finality', once his mind was made up, which made it hard to persuade him that he had been mistaken. When I arrived at the hotel he was sitting in the hall waiting for me.

> WITTGENSTEIN: There is a woman staying here at the moment who dresses superbly. She can't be English, for no English woman would have such good taste. She must be from some Continental country. If we wait here a minute she will be coming down the stairs and I will point her out to you.

A few minutes later the lady appeared.

> DRURY: Oh, I know who she is quite well. She used to live in Exeter many years ago and is now married and living near Dublin. She is English.

> WITTGENSTEIN: [looking very sceptical] I find it hard to believe you.

And indeed I don't think he was convinced that I was not making a mistake.

Then we went out for our walk.

DRURY: I was listening, on the radio you gave me, to a recording of Pablo Casals playing unaccompanied cello.

WITTGENSTEIN: I once heard Casals playing in the Albert Hall; and do you know, he was able to fill that huge building with the sound of his cello alone. It was a wonderful performance.

DRURY: The present-day recording on long-playing records is a great improvement on the old recordings we used to listen to in Cambridge.

WITTGENSTEIN: It is so characteristic that, just when the mechanics of reproduction are so vastly improved, there are fewer and fewer people who know how the music should be played.

*

I went to see Wittgenstein in a state of considerable distress. What had happened was this. I had been admitting to the hospital a female patient for the treatment of chronic alcohol addiction. She was very drunk and on arriving in the ward had become very abusive to the nurses, using particularly obscene language. I tried to get her to drink a draught of paraldehyde to sedate her, but she managed to throw the glass and its contents in my face. I lost my temper completely and had to retire from the ward, apologizing to the nurses and asking one of my colleagues to take over. I described all this to Wittgenstein, and told him I felt I was unsuited to this work and should resign my post. I was grateful that he did not try to minimize the seriousness of what had happened.

WITTGENSTEIN: You were right to apologize to the nurses. But you shouldn't give up your work just because of this incident. One keeps stumbling and falling, stumbling and falling, and the only thing to do is to pick oneself up and try to go on again. At least, that is what I have had to do all my life. It has often worried me that if you should make a serious mistake in your work you would suffer terribly.

*

Walking in Phoenix Park:

WITTGENSTEIN: Drury, what is your favourite Gospel?

DRURY: I don't think I have ever asked myself that question.

WITTGENSTEIN: Mine is St Matthew's. Matthew seems to me to contain everything. Now, I can't understand the Fourth Gospel. When I read those long discourses, it seems to me as if a different person is speaking than in the synoptic Gospels. The only incident that reminds me of the others is the story of the woman taken in adultery.

DRURY: That passage is not found in any of the best manuscripts, and most scholars consider it a later addition. In some manuscripts it is found in St Luke's Gospel.

WITTGENSTEIN: When I spoke to S—— about my difficulty in understanding the Fourth Gospel, he looked at me with such a strange smile. I couldn't describe it to you. S—— is the most religious man I have ever met. I would see nothing wrong in it if he became a Roman Catholic priest – of course I know he can't now because he is married.

We continued to talk for some time about the New Testament.

WITTGENSTEIN: If you can accept the miracle that God became man, then all these difficulties are as nothing. For then it is impossible for me to say what form the record of such an event should take.

DRURY: One of the early Church Fathers, Lactantius I think, said something like that. Novels and plays must indeed be probable, but why should this, the scheme of man's redemption, be probable?

WITTGENSTEIN: I am glad to hear that I had the same thought as one of the Church Fathers. At one time I thought that the Epistles of St Paul were a different religion to that of the Gospels.[45] But now I see clearly that I was wrong. It is one and the same religion in both the Gospels and the Epistles.

*

We were walking in the Botanical Gardens, and began to discuss architecture.

WITTGENSTEIN: The Cathedral of St Basil in the Kremlin is one of the most beautiful buildings I have ever seen. There is a story – I don't know whether it is true but I hope it is – that when Ivan the Terrible saw the completed cathedral he had the architect blinded so that he would never design anything more beautiful.

I was so shocked by Wittgenstein's hoping that this horrible story was true, that I could make no adequate reply;[46] I merely shook my head.

*

Another day walking in Phoenix Park:

WITTGENSTEIN: Drury, you have lived a most remarkable life. First those years in Cambridge studying philosophy; then as a medical student; then the war experiences – and now all this new work in psychiatry.

DRURY: There is one thing about it that I feel is all wrong with me: I have not lived a religious life.

WITTGENSTEIN: It has troubled me that, in some way I never intended, your getting to know me has made you less religious than you would have been had you never met me.

DRURY: That thought has troubled me too.

WITTGENSTEIN: I believe it is right to try experiments in religion. To find out, by trying, what helps one and what doesn't. When I was a prisoner of war in Italy, I was very glad when we were compelled to attend mass. Now why don't you see if starting the day by going to mass each morning doesn't help you to begin the day in a good frame of mind? I don't mean for one moment that you should become a Roman Catholic. I think that would be all wrong for you. It seems to me that your religion will always take the form of desiring something you haven't yet found.

DRURY: You remember a long time ago when we talked about Lessing – Lessing saying that he would choose the gift in the left hand, the striving after truth, rather than the possession of absolute truth.

WITTGENSTEIN: That might be all right for Lessing to say. But I can see that there is a much deeper state of mind than Lessing expressed there.

DRURY: I don't think what you suggest about mass would help me. I still prefer the English liturgy, with which I have been familiar since childhood, to the inaudible service in Latin.

WITTGENSTEIN: Yes, I can understand that.

DRURY: However, I think a child brought up in the colourful symbolism of the Roman Catholic liturgy would get a stronger and deeper impression of religious awe than one brought up in the plainer Protestant tradition.

WITTGENSTEIN: I don't agree with you at all. I would much prefer to see a child educated by a decent Protestant pastor than by a greasy Roman Catholic priest. When I look at the faces of the clergy here in Dublin, it seems to me that the Protestant ministers look less smug than the Roman priests. I suppose it is because they know that they are such a small minority.

Later, on the same walk:

WITTGENSTEIN: I am glad that you raised that point about the education of children. I see the matter quite clearly now. I have recently been reading a book in which the author blames Calvin for the rise of our present bourgeois civilization. I can see how easy it would be to make such a thesis plausible; but I, for my part, wouldn't dare to criticize a man such as Calvin must have been.

DRURY: But Calvin had Michael Servetus burnt for heresy!

WITTGENSTEIN: Tell me about that.

So I told him at some length the story of Servetus's heretical book about the Trinity; and how he had deliberately come into the church at Geneva in the middle of Calvin's sermon.

WITTGENSTEIN: Whew! He deliberately courted his own death. What else could Calvin, believing as he did, have done than have Servetus arrested?

*

It was at this time that Wittgenstein complained to me that he was feeling ill. He complained of a recurrent pain in his right arm and a general feeling of exhaustion. I advised him to let me make an appointment for him to see the Professor of Medicine in Trinity College. I had at one time been taught by this doctor and had a high opinion of his diagnostic ability. Wittgenstein agreed to let me make this appointment.

WITTGENSTEIN: Yes, I will go and see this man; only I want you to tell him I am a man of intelligence who likes to be told exactly what is found wrong – to have things explained to me frankly.

The upshot of this consultation was that Wittgenstein was admitted to hospital for a full investigation. I went to visit him while he was in hospital. He talked to me about his previous experience, in Guy's Hospital, when he had his gall-bladder removed.

WITTGENSTEIN: I insisted that I should be given a spinal anaesthetic, although both the surgeon and the anaesthetist tried to persuade me to have a general anaesthetic. I also wanted them to fit up a mirror so that I could watch what they were doing, but this they absolutely refused to do. However, it didn't matter in the end, since I could see everything reflected in the lamp over the operating table. For several days after, I had an appalling headache, and was then told that this was often the case after a spinal anaesthetic. Now if only they had had the sense to tell me this beforehand I would have agreed to the general anaesthetic. There was a wonderful night nurse at Guy's. I used to tell her that if I was asleep when she came round, she was to wake me in order that I could have the pleasure of talking to her.

Wasn't it ridiculous that, when they built the York Clinic at Guy's for psychiatric patients, they made no provision for a garden in which the patients could walk. Every mental hospital ought to have a large garden where patients can stroll and rest.

The only findings made, as a result of the investigation in hospital, were that he had an unexplained anaemia. He was started on the necessary treatment for this, and from time to time had to go back to the laboratory for tests of improvement.

WITTGENSTEIN: What does please me is that when I go to have my blood test the doctor first examines the colour of my conjunctiva, before taking a specimen for the biochemical test. Nowadays doctors are so afraid of not being scientific that they neglect such simple procedures.

After he had been some time on treatment he expressed himself as feeling much stronger and no longer troubled by the pain in his arm. He told me that he had had an invitation to spend a long visit with a former pupil and friend of his in America, and that he had decided to spend the summer there and return to Ross's Hotel for the coming winter. I went down, the evening before he was due to leave Dublin, to help him to pack and decide what he would take with him. He was packing up his large pile of notebooks, manuscripts and typescripts.

WITTGENSTEIN: I have had a letter from an old friend in Austria, a priest. In it he says he hopes my work will go well, if it should be God's will. Now that is all I want: if it should be God's will. Bach wrote on the title page of his *Orgelbuchlein,* 'To the glory of the most high God, and that my neighbour may be benefited thereby.' That is what I would have liked to say about my work.[47]

*

I had at one time told Wittgenstein that if ever he needed to see a doctor when in Cambridge, he should consult Dr Edward Bevan. I had got to know Dr Bevan when we were in the same unit in the army, and he had impressed me as the ideal of what a general practitioner should be. On his way back from his stay in America.[48] Wittgenstein had been taken seriously ill when staying with Professor von Wright in Cambridge, and he went to see Dr Bevan. I then had a telphone message from Dr Bevan to say that he had made a certain diagnosis of carcinoma of the prostate gland. This is a type of cancer that often responds well to hormone therapy, and life can be prolonged for years.[49] Wittgenstein himself wrote to me that he would now not return to Dublin but remain in England, where his treatment could be supervised. He said he had a horror of the idea of dying in an English hospital, but that Dr Bevan had promised that, if it became necessary, he could spend his last days being looked after in Dr Bevan's own house.

1951

On my way back from my honeymoon in Italy I went up to Cambridge to see Wittgenstein, who was now living in Dr Bevan's house. He looked very ill, but was as alert and lively as ever.

WITTGENSTEIN: It was such a relief to me when the doctors told me that there was now no use continuing the hormone[50] and X-ray treatment; and that I could not expect to live more than a few months. You know that all my life I have been inclined to criticize doctors. But now at the end of my life I have had the good fortune to meet three really good doctors. First, the professor you introduced me to in Dublin, then the doctor Malcolm got me to see in America, and now Dr Bevan.

Isn't it curious that, although I know I have not long to live, I never find myself thinking about a 'future life'. All my interest is still on this life and the writing I am still able to do.

We talked for a time about my visit to Italy; and he told me about Goethe's visit to Italy and the deep impression it had made on him. Somehow – I can't remember quite how – the conversation came round again to talk about the Bible.

DRURY: There are some passages in the Old Testament that I

find very offensive. For instance, the story where some children mock Elisha for his baldness: 'Go up, thou bald head.' And God sends bears out of the forest to eat them.

WITTGENSTEIN: [very sternly] You mustn't pick and choose just what you want in that way.

DRURY: But I have never been able to do anything else.

WITTGENSTEIN: Just remember what the Old Testament meant to a man like Kierkegaard. After all, children have been killed by bears.

DRURY: Yes, but we ought to think that such a tragedy is a direct punishment from God for a particular act of wickedness. In the New Testament we are told the precise opposite – the men on whom the Tower of Siloam fell were not more wicked than anyone else.

WITTGENSTEIN: That has nothing to do with what I am talking about. You don't understand, you are quite out of your depth.

I did not know how to reply to this. It seemed to me that the conversation was distasteful to him, and I did not say anything further.

After a pause we began to talk about more trivial matters. When the time came for me to go to the station, Wittgenstein insisted on coming with me although I tried to persuade him he should not do anything to tire himself. On the way to the station he suddenly referred to our dispute over the Old Testament.

WITTGENSTEIN: I must write you a letter about that.

Just before the train pulled out he said to me, 'Drury, whatever becomes of you, don't stop thinking.' These were the last words I ever had from him.

*

I had only been back in Dublin a few days when I had a telephone message from Dr Bevan to say that Wittgenstein was dying and had asked me to come. I started at once. When I arrived at the house, Dr Bevan met me at the door, and told me,

'Miss Anscombe, Richards and Smythies are already here. Smythies has brought with him a Dominican priest whom Wittgenstein already knew. Wittgenstein was already unconscious when they came, and no one will decide whether the priest should say the usual office for the dying and give conditional absolution.'

I remembered the occasion when Wittgenstein had said he hoped his Catholic friends prayed for him, and I said at once that whatever was customary should be done. We then all went up to Wittgenstein's room, and, kneeling down, the priest recited the proper prayers. Soon after, Dr Bevan pronounced Wittgenstein dead.

There was then much hesitation about what arrangements should be made about the funeral. No one seemed ready to speak up.

> DRURY: I remember that Wittgenstein once told me of an incident in Tolstoy's life. When Tolstoy's brother died, Tolstoy, who was then a stern critic of the Russian Orthodox Church, sent for the parish priest and had his brother interred according to the Orthodox rite. 'Now', said Wittgenstein, 'that is exactly what I should have done in a similar case.'

When I mentioned this, everyone agreed that all the usual Roman Catholic prayers should be said by a priest at the graveside. This was done the next morning. But I have been troubled ever since as to whether what we did then was right.

M. O'C. Drury, 'Some Notes on Conversations with Wittgenstein'

1. On p. 160 the two remarks follow one another in the same conversation.
2. In the German edition this passage appears on p. 35. B. F. McGuinness's translation appears in Ludwig Wittgenstein, *Prototractatus: An Early Version of 'Tractatus Logico-Philosophicus'*, ed. B. F. McGuinness, T. Nyberg and G. H. von Wright, trans. D. F. Pears and B. F. McGuinness (London, 1971), p. 15, note 1 (the relevant part of this note is on p. 16).
3. Simone Weil, *Écrits de Londres et dernières lettres* (Paris, 1957), p. 74.
4. Psalm 119:131 in the Vulgate. The Authorized Version has 'I opened my mouth, and panted.'
5. On pp. 157–8 Wittgenstein's reaction to Kierkegaard appears in a different context.
6. In his translation (Harmondsworth, 1961) of the *Confessions*, R. S. Pine-Coffin renders this passage thus:

But you are Goodness itself and need no good besides yourself . . . What man can teach another to understand this truth? What angel can teach it to an angel? What angel can teach it to a man? We must ask it of you, seek it in you; we must knock at your door. Only then shall we receive what we ask and find what we seek; only then will the door be opened to us.

7. Otto Weininger, *Geschlecht und Charakter* (Vienna, 1903; photographic reprint, Munich, 1980; English trans., London and New York, 1906).

8. Weininger's quotation is from Pico della Mirandola's *Oratio de hominis dignitate*, written presumably in 1486 or 1487, first published in a posthumous edition of his works in 1495–6. (The text given here is taken from G. Pico della Mirandola, *De hominis dignitate, Heptaplus, De ente et uno*, ed. Eugenio Garin (Florence, 1942), pp. 104, 106.) Drury included his own translation of the passage in an earlier draft of 'Conversations with Wittgenstein', but left it untranslated here. It is better to leave it in Pico's own words. But Drury's translation is so much better than the one I have beside me that I will include it here.

'To you, Adam, we have assigned no fixed place in the scale of created beings; no one determined facial expression will characterize your race; you have no special service to perform. Thus it will be that whatever rank you select, what you want to express, what function you want to perform, by your decision, by your own wish, that you shall both have and keep. All other created beings are bound fast by the laws and ordinances we have laid down for them; but you are not hedged round with any restrictions, in order that by the free choice which is placed in your hands you may determine your own destiny. In the very centre of the universe are you placed, in order that you may survey the more easily whatsoever things there are in nature. You are neither an inhabitant of heaven nor of earth; neither mortal nor immortal have we created you; so that you freely and without reward may make and

mould your own image as it seems to you. You can if you
so wish it sink to that lower order of being such as animals are, you can also rise by the strength of your desire
towards the citizenship of heaven.'

Oh the unlimited generosity of God the Father, Oh the
boundless good fortune of man: to whom it has been
granted that he may have what he chooses and be what he
desires. The beasts of the field at the moment of their
birth bring with them . . . from their mother's womb all
that they can ever become. The company of heaven, from
the first moment of time or soon afterwards, are already
that which they will remain through all eternity. But man
is born having within himself, by the gift of God, the seed
from which any created being may arise. So that whatsoever seed he chooses to cultivate, that for him will grow
and bear fruit. If he chooses to lead a purely vegetative
existence, then his life will delight in sensuality, then he
can become as one of the animal creation. If he chooses
the way of understanding, then he can escape from his
brutish nature and be turned towards heavenly things. If
he becomes a true lover of wisdom, then he is like one of
the angels and a child of God. But if every form of separate
and individual existence fails to contain his spirit, then in
the very centre of his soul is he made one with the Holy
Spirit, in the mystery of God's unity which is the centre
of all things and before all things had its being.

M. O'C. Drury, 'Conversations with Wittgenstein'

1. Cf. a passage written in 1937:

In religion every level of devoutness must have its appropriate form of expression which has no sense at a lower
level. This doctrine, which means something at a higher
level, is null and void for someone who is still at the lower
level; he *can* only understand it *wrongly* and so these
words are *not* valid for such a person.

For instance, at my level the Pauline doctrine of predes-
tination is ugly nonsense, irreligiousness. Hence it is not
suitable for me, since the only use I could make of the pic-

ture I am offered would be a wrong one. If it is a good and godly picture, then it is so for someone at a quite different level, who must use it in his life in a way completely different from anything that would be possible for me. [C 32]

2. In a letter to Russell, dated 22 June 1912, Wittgenstein wrote:

> Whenever I have time I now read James's 'Varieties of religious experience'. This book does me a *lot* of good. I don't mean to say that I will be a saint soon, but I am not sure that it does not improve me a little in a way in which I would like to improve *very much*: namely I think that it helps me to get rid of the *Sorge* (in the sense in which Goethe used the word in the 2nd part of Faust). (L10)

3. In a manuscript of 1931 Wittgenstein wrote, with square brackets to separate it from the philosophical questions he was discussing: 'Within Christianity it's as though God says to men: Don't act a tragedy, that's to say, don't enact heaven and hell on earth. Heaven and hell are *my* affair' [C14].

4. Cf. p. 86 above.

5. Dawes Hicks was at that time Emeritus Professor of Philosophy in University College, London; he lived in Cambridge after retiring. The Moral Science Club is now called the Philosophical Society.

6. In Swansea, introducing a discussion on free will, I gave as an example: 'With a little effort I could have controlled myself, and not have spoken to him so sharply.' In the discussion Wittgenstein said, 'That is something that happens to me *every day*.' And later, 'And yet, you know that at the time you *couldn't* have.'

7. Years later Wittgenstein said to me: 'You know I said I can stop doing philosophy when I like. That is a lie! I *can't*.'

8. The question mark is Drury's. The first remark in quotes was probably in 1930, when Drury was still an undergraduate in Cambridge, anyway. The reference to Russell's exclusion from a professorship at the City College of New York must have been after the autumn of 1940.

9. *Prayers and Meditations* composed by Samuel Johnson,

LL.D. Third edition. H. R. Allenson, Limited, London: no date (but apparently 1826 or 1827). (The first edition appeared in 1785.) See above, pp. 94–5.

10. I intended to ask Drury about this sentence when I read it in the draft he showed me. I wondered if Wittgenstein had given a special emphasis to 'stand up to': whether these words should be in italics.

11. At the time of this conversation he was writing what is now in *Philosophical Remarks*.

12. Sir James Jeans, Cambridge, 1930. Wittgenstein's copy has a few pencilled comments in the margins; the last is on p. 53.

13. *A Course of Six Lectures on the Chemical History of a Candle* (London, 1861). Faraday gave these lectures for the sons and daughters of the Royal Institution of London in 1860. The lectures were published not by Faraday, who did not write them down, but by a young scientist, William Crookes, from a verbatim transcript made for him by a stenographer (*pace* the dons of Oxford and the TLS).

14. Later, e.g. in 1937, Wittgenstein said he wanted to avoid this way of speaking, since it led to perplexities and confusion. Cf. Ludwig Wittgenstein, 'Ursache und Wirkung: Intuitives Erfassen' ['Cause and Effect: Intuitive Awareness'], *Philosophia* 6 (1976), 391–445.

15. Although of course Wittgenstein had read it many times himself, and so had Moore.

16. Mr Raymond Townsend gave Wittgenstein a copy of the one-volume abridged edition in 1936.

17. Piero Sraffa, economist and Fellow of Trinity College, Cambridge. Wittgenstein, in his preface to *Philosophical Investigations*, speaks of his special indebtedness to conversations with Sraffa. And he valued Sraffa's judgements of practical affairs more than those of anyone else, I think.

18. Now the University of Newcastle.

19. This was in July and August 1920, at Klosterneuburg and in Hütteldorf; just before Wittgenstein started work as an elementary schoolteacher. See the two letters from Wittgenstein to Engelmann, dated 19 July 1920 and [20 August 1920] [E 34–7], and pp. 4–5 above.

20. This was in July 1935; see L 132–7. Drury's '1934' for this entry must have been a slip.
21. William H. Prescott, *History of the Conquest of Mexico* (3 vols, London, 1843), vol. 2, pp. 175–6.
22. The home of Drury's family.
23. John 16:7.
24. In Lessing's *Theologische Streitschriften*, 'Eine Duplik' (1778). See *Gotthold Ephraim Lessings Sämmtliche Schriften*, ed. Karl Lachman, 3rd revised ed. by Franz Muncker, 23 vols (Stuttgart, 1886–95; Leipzig, 1897–1907; Berlin and Leipzig, 1915–24; complete photographic reprint, Berlin, 1968), vol. 13 (Leipzig, 1897), pp. 23–4. Perhaps for the sense of Lessing's remark I should give the passage immediately preceding the one Drury quotes in translation, together with the original of the latter:

> Nicht die Wahrheit, in deren Besitz irgend ein Mensch ist, oder zu sein vermeinet, sondern die aufrichtige Mühe, die er angewandt hat, hinter die Wahrheit zu kommen, macht den Wert des Menschen. Denn nicht durch den Besitz, sondern durch die Nachforschung der Wahrheit erweitern sich seine Kräfte, worin allein seine immer wachsende Vollkommenheit bestehet. Der Besitz macht ruhig, träge, stolz –
>
> Wenn Gott in seiner Rechten alle Wahrheit, und in seiner Linken den einzigen immer regen Trieb nach Wahrheit, obschon mit dem Zusatze, mich immer und ewig zu irren, verschlossen hielte, und spräche zu mir: wähle! Ich fiele ihm mit Demut in seine Linke, und sagte: Vater gieb! die reine Wahrheit ist ja doch nur für dich allein!

An English version of the first paragraph might be:

> It is not the truth which anyone possesses, or thinks he does, but rather the pains he has taken to get to the bottom of the truth, that makes a man's worth. For it is not in having the truth but in searching for it that those powers increase in him in which alone lies his ever-grow-

ing perfection. The possession makes one placid, lazy, proud.

25. As Wittgenstein told it to me, it was a sort of game which Paul's friends often played with him. He was incredibly learned, and had a very large library of music scores. While he looked the other way, a friend would take some score from the shelves, open it and cover over all but two or three bars, and show him this bit. Paul Wittgenstein could always say in what work it came. Ludwig Wittgenstein's comment to me was a gesture and 'If you are learned, you are learned.' Although he disliked his brother's playing, he respected his 'phenomenal technique'; especially after he lost his right arm, but before then as well.

26. An isolated remark in one of Wittgenstein's manuscripts: 'Don't play with what lies deep in another person!' [C23].

27. Obviously this entry should have come earlier.

28. The actual wording in the Prayer Book is 'renounce the devil and all his works, the vain pomp and glory of the world, with all covetous desires of the same, and the carnal desires of the flesh'.

29. Printed above, pp. 95–6.

30. Edited by Cyril Barrett (Oxford, 1968). The editor emphasizes in his preface that these notes are nothing that Wittgenstein wrote or would have written.

31. Luke 1:28: 'Und der Engel kam zu ihr hinein, und sprach: Gegrüsset seist du, Holdselige!'

32. Wittgenstein left a small legacy to Mr Fouracre in his will.

33. This may have been at the end of March or beginning of April 1943. He wrote to me from Guy's Hospital on 1 April 1943, and came to Swansea for a week in the middle of April. I think he went to Newcastle soon after that. I visited him there in September 1943.

34. See above, p. 88.

35. The 3rd and 5th stanzas of 'Night', in *Songs of Innocence*.

36. In *The Marriage of Heaven and Hell*.

37. From *The Everlasting Gospel*.

38. Cf. two remarks of 1946: 'Madness need not be regarded as an illness. Why shouldn't it be seen as a sudden – more or

less sudden – change of character?' [C 54]; ' "It is high time for us to compare these phenomena with something *different*" – one may say. – I am thinking, e.g., of mental illnesses' [C 55].

39. I was in Dublin for a few weeks about this time, to see both Wittgenstein and Drury. Wittgenstein was worried for Drury's health (he had been ill about two years earlier), and he spoke to me about it: the intensity with which Drury kept his gaze fixed on hospital duties, day in day out, as though walking along a road with high walls on each side, and nothing to see ahead but the road.

In January 1949, Wittgenstein wrote in a notebook: 'The Sabbath is not simply a time for rest, for relaxation. We ought to contemplate our labours from without and not just from within' [C 80].

40. Wittgenstein may have been half remembering his own experience as a patient in Guy's Hospital after an operation for removal of the gall-bladder, in 1942. He spoke to me especially of the unimaginativeness of one young doctor who would 'make the rounds' of the ward in the morning: He would come and stand above my bed, and talk to me – a somewhat elderly professor – in a way in which *I* would never talk to a *schoolboy*:"Well; how are you?" ' As Wittgenstein imitated the tone of voice, it might have been a quartermaster-sergeant. He could not have imagined any such trait in Drury; at most he may have feared what hospital routine would do to him.

41. Josef Breuer and Sigmund Freud, *Studien über Hysterie* (1st ed., Leipzig and Vienna, 1895); in English, *Studies on Hysteria*, ed. and trans. James and Alix Strachey (London, 1956). In the course of a passage which Wittgenstein wrote in 1939 or 1940, he said: 'I have always believed – without knowing why – that the real germ of psychoanalysis came from Breuer, not Freud. Of course Breuer's seed-grain can only have been quite tiny' [C 36].

42. Cf. p. 88 and note 5 to that page.

43. Cf. p. 79 and note 1 to that page.

44. The only Livy I found among Wittgenstein's books is a school edition of Books 21–3. This was a second-hand

copy, which Wittgenstein could not have bought before 1929, and I imagine he got it in 1942. He has written German equivalents of some phrases between the lines. I think it was one of a half-dozen books which Wittgenstein left in Dublin.

In the autumn of 1942 he wrote to me that he was doing some reading, 'and *not* just detective stories'; that he was reading Cicero – 'which on the whole bores me' – and Livy's account of Hannibal's invasion of Italy: 'this interests me immensely'. He was still working in Guy's Hospital, going to Cambridge each Saturday to give a lecture. In November (1942) he wrote to me that he was lecturing on the foundations of mathematics; and 'I'm afraid I've no time now to read any Latin – not that that worries me.'

In 1944 – I think – he was reading something of Leopold von Ranke's. He was interested in the way in which Ranke would give a careful account of events leading up to some occurrence, and then say something like: 'In these circumstances it was inevitable that . . .', as though no one could have imagined things going in any *other* way. He was also reading in Eduard Meyer's *Ursprung und Anfänge des Christentums* (Stuttgart and Berlin, 1921–3) and his *Ursprung und Geschichte der Mormonen* (Halle a.S., 1912).

45. Cf. a remark written in 1937: 'The spring which flows gently and limpidly in the Gospels . . . ' [C 30].

46. At an earlier time Wittgenstein had spoken of this, when Drury and I were both present; and after 'I hope it *is* true' he added with great feeling, almost awe: 'What a *wonderful* way of showing his admiration!' Drury said, 'A *horrible* way', and I think I agreed. I now think this was irrelevant, i.e. that Wittgenstein might have admitted it, without in any way changing the feeling he'd just expressed. And what he felt about Ivan's move could not be separated from what he (Wittgenstein) felt in seeing and and remembering the cathedral. I think that his 'What a *wonderful* way of showing his admiration!' is akin to what he might have said of certain forms of human sacrifice as a gesture of deepest reverence. If we had said 'But it's horrible!' he'd have said this showed we didn't know what was taking place.

47. Cf. p. 78 above.
48. His way back to Ross's Hotel in Dublin. (He had already been seriously ill during his stay with Professor Malcolm in America. Cf. Malcolm's *Memoir*, p. 94.)
49. In a letter of 4 December – roughly a fortnight after the diagnosis – Wittgenstein wrote to me: 'I am getting slowly better and the doctor tells me that after some months I may be well enough to work . . . I am sorry that my life should be prolonged in this way. It was a great shock to me to hear of this possibility.' Cf. the passage from a similar letter printed in Malcolm's *Memoir*, p. 95. Earlier Wittgenstein had written that the cancer was inoperable. Drury told me later that this was because secondary cancerous growths had developed and had entered his spine.
50. About six weeks before his death (five weeks before this visit of Drury's) Wittgenstein found he was able to do good work again. From the end of November 1949 to, roughly, the end of February 1951, he was, as he wrote to me, 'letting the hormones do their work', and more often than not he felt that he could not write anything worth putting down. He recovered his power of mind when he left off the hormones.

1967 DUBLIN LECTURE ON WITTGENSTEIN[1]

It would be easy for me to spend a pleasant half hour chatting to you about Wittgenstein, with various anecdotes amusing or otherwise. I am not going to do this. For one of the things I learnt from him was that journalistic gossip is among the least attractive features of this present age.

It was a characteristic remark of Wittgenstein, and one he often repeated, that 'my father was a business man, and I am a business man too. I want my philosophy to be business like, to get something settled, to get something done'. And so this evening I would like to be business like in talking to you and try and get something done.

But what can one do in half an hour? Well I would like to try and get you all looking in a certain direction. To turn your attention away from certain common misunderstandings about the man and his work, and perhaps to help you see his writings from a new point of view.

So let me begin by saying something about these common misunderstandings. It is said that Wittgenstein knew little about the history of philosophy and spoke with some contempt about what had previously been called metaphysics. This is not true. Certainly he would not allow a philosophical discussion to be side tracked by irrelevant references to the statements of previous thinkers. And he thought it dangerous for a student of philosophy to spend a lot of time puzzling over say Kant or Hegel, when he should be thinking about what really puzzles him. Isn't it a great relief to read a philosophical text such as Wittgenstein's

---

[1] Obvious errors in Drury's typescript have been silently corrected by the editors, who have also added material in square brackets.

which is not weighed down by a mass of learned historicity? But that Wittgenstein was in any way arrogant towards the past or thought that he, or any of us, because we lived in the twentieth century were therefore more advanced in our thinking that is the very reverse of his belief. He shewed always a most remarkable and rare humility towards the past.

Soon after I had got to know him I was telling him about a book I was reading concerning the 'Desert Fathers', those heroic ascetics of the Egyptian desert. And with the typical shallowness of those days said something to the effect 'that I thought they might have made better use of their lives'. Wittgenstein turned on me furiously 'that is just the sort of stupid remark a bloody English person would make, how can you know what their problems were in those days and what they had to do about them'.

Again I remember him coming into my rooms at Cambridge saying 'just look at this'. It was the examination paper set for the current History Tripos. One of the questions set read as follows:

> Discuss the following statement 'The Pope shewed as little understanding in his negotiations with the Emperor as he had previously shewn in his dealings with Luther'.

'That's the sort of question', said Wittgenstein, 'that teaches people to be both stupid and conceited. How can a Cambridge undergraduate know what the Pope could or should have done about either Luther or the Emperor.'

Many years later here in Dublin he told me he was reading a book, I imagine it was the well known one by Tawney, in which the author blamed Calvin for the rise of the bourgeois capitalist culture of Europe. He said he could see the attractiveness of such a thesis, but then added 'I wouldn't dare to criticise a man such as Calvin'.

So please remember when you are reading Wittgenstein that you are reading a man who never thought of himself as an advanced thinker but was very conscious of the limitations which these present times impose on all of us and on him too.

A man who in the right sense of that word was truly humble.

That is what I wanted to say to you about Wittgenstein's attitude to the past. Now something about his relation to the present. There is talk of 'linguistic philosophy' which Wittgenstein is supposed to have originated and which has been carried forward by such writers as Professor Ayer, Gilbert Ryle, and the late J. L. Austin. I would beseech you to read Wittgenstein with such ideas completely out of your mind. For instance I find at the end of one of Austin's lectures the following:

> Is it not possible that the next century may see the birth, through the joint labours of philosophers and grammarians, and numerous other students of language, of a true and comprehensive science of language? Then we shall have rid ourselves of one more part of philosophy (there will still be plenty left) in the only way we ever can get rid of philosophy, by kicking it upstairs.[2]

Can you imagine Wittgenstein writing that? He is repeatedly reminding us that he is not building any new science, that he is not putting forward any thesis to be proved, and when he talks of grammar it has nothing to do with what grammarians are properly concerned with.

To make this point clearer I would like to quote to you some remarks written in one of his note books in 1930. He was at that time contemplating a book that was never completed. Some of the material that would have formed part of the book has since been edited and published by Mr Rhees under the title *Philosophische Bemerkungen*. The following sentences which I am going to read were obviously a rough draft for what would have been the introduction to this book. He writes:

> This book is written for those who are friendly to the spirit of it. This spirit is different, I think, from that of the great European and American civilisation

[2] See J. L. Austin, 'Ifs and Cans', in *Philosophical Papers*, ed. J. O. Urmson and G. J. Warnock (Oxford, 1970), p. 232.

I look on the stream of European civilisation neither with sympathy nor with an understanding of its aims, if it has any aims. So that I write for friends who are situated in various corners of the world.

Whether a typical scientist understands or admires me is no matter since he will certainly not understand the spirit in which I write.[3]

Our civilisation is characterised by the word 'progress'. Progress is its form: it is not one of its properties that it progresses. It is typical of it that it is building, constructing. Its activity is one of constructing more and more complex structures. And even clarity serves only this end, and is not sought on its own account. For me on the other hand, clarity, lucidity is the goal sought.

I am not interested in erecting a building, but rather in having the foundations of all possible buildings clearly before me.

So my way of thinking is different from that of the scientists, my way of thinking is other than theirs.

Gilbert Ryle in his introduction to *The Concept of Mind* says that philosophy is the replacement of category habits by category disciplines. Now compare this with what Wittgenstein writes in the *Philosophical Investigations*.

If the formation of concepts can be explained by facts of nature, should we not be interested, not in grammar, but rather in that in nature which is the basis of grammar? Our interest certainly includes the correspondence between concepts and very general facts of nature. (Such facts as mostly do not strike us because of their generality.) But our interest does not fall back upon these possible causes of the formation of concepts; we are not doing natural science;

---

[3] See Wittgenstein, *Culture and Value*, ed. G. H. von Wright (Oxford, 1980), pp. 6–7.

nor yet natural history, since we can also invent fictitious natural history for our purposes.

I am not saying: if such and such facts of nature were different people would have different concepts (in the sense of a hypothesis). But: if anyone believes that certain concepts are absolutely the correct ones, and that having different ones would mean not realizing something that we realize – then let him imagine certain very general facts of nature to be different from what we are used to, and the formation of concepts different from the usual ones will become intelligible to him.

Compare a concept with a style of painting. For is even our style of painting arbitrary? Can we choose one at pleasure? (The Egyptian, for instance.) Is it a mere question of pleasing or ugly?[4]

Wittgenstein is not trying to impose a stricter discipline on our conceptual usages, but to free us from thinking that our traditional concepts are the only possible ones, that one must see the world in this way. He is always substituting 'must' by 'can'. No, not more discipline but more freedom.

Wittgenstein is no more a linguistic philosopher than Plato was. He is deeply concerned with the whole mystery of language, not only the language of mathematics and the natural sciences, but the whole realm of communication between one person and another. The difference between spoken language and written language, the language of gesture and facial expression, of symbol and ritual, of music and poetry. And there's enough wonderment to keep you thinking for a lifetime.

Here perhaps also I should say something about a question which was a very live issue when I was an undergraduate. The relation of Wittgenstein to Logical Positivism and the Vienna circle. I imagine no one calls themselves a logical positivist nowadays. But in so far as logical positivism is a tendency in human thought which is as old as Protagoras,

---

[4] See Wittgenstein, *Philosophical Investigations*, trans. G. E. M. Anscombe (Oxford, 1967), p. 230 (pt 2, xii).

and will undoubtedly occur again under some new name, I would say something about it. Especially as in a recently published book Professor Pitcher seems to imply that the Vienna circle were more 'tough minded' and carried the teachings of the *Tractatus* to their real logical conclusion, and that Wittgenstein because of some mystical trait in him fought shy of doing so.

I remember when Moritz Schlick, one of the ablest of the Vienna circle, came to read a paper in Cambridge, Wittgenstein told me that I should go hear him, and then pointing to the title of Schlick's paper 'Phenomenalism', said to me 'that of course is what I am doing'. And again I was present at an early lecture where Wittgenstein actually used the words 'the meaning of a proposition is its method of verification'. Unfortunately some of us, myself included I am sorry to say, took hold of this isolated statement as if it was a magic key to open all the doors of philosophical puzzlement. Of course we should have known better. For one thing Wittgenstein had made it quite clear already in his lectures there was not, and never would be, one particular doctrine that would suddenly bring understanding. And if we had stopped to think a little more we would have seen how various the meanings of the word verification are. We took it to mean what might be described as direct sensory observation. But obviously we talk of verifying a sum in arithmetic, of a fact of history, of a scientific hypothesis. In what sense are Newton's laws of motion verified? Or say the principle of the conservation of matter? When it is stated that Fermat's last theorem has never been verified, what sort of verification are we even thinking of? You see a whole treatise would need to be written on the different uses of the concept of verification.

I am sure by now some of you are getting impatient with me. I keep saying that Wittgenstein's teaching is not to be confused with this, that, and the other, but have said nothing positive about its real content. There is a great and important difficulty here. We are living in an age in which the methods and steady achievements of the natural sciences

play an enormous part in our lives. And it is tempting to try
and see philosophy as a somewhat similar study. Now in the
natural sciences you can have the results of another's labour
without the pains of carrying out the investigation. I can, for
instance, look up the proper dose of a drug I want to use in
the pharmacopeia, and I don't have to worry about the
experiments by which that dose was determined. So you
might say: tell us something about Wittgenstein's conclusions, and if necessary we can check his proofs later. This is
a completely wrong analogy. There is no such thing as a
vicarious philosophy. Let me make myself clearer by giving
you three similes that Wittgenstein used at different times.

Philosophy he once said is like trying to open a safe with a
compound lock: each little adjustment of the various dials
seem to achieve nothing, it is only when all these are in the
right position that the door opens.

Or again. Philosophy is like trying to arrange in order the
books in a library. You have to put these two books together
and then these three, and later have to move these from their
original place to another. Each little movement seems to be
insignificant yet when they have all been done, then the
library is in order.

Thirdly philosophy is like teaching someone their way
about a strange town. You take him on many different
journeys, from A to B, from C to D, etc., and on many of
these journeys you pass the same place. There is no one
journey that is of crucial importance. But eventually after
much travelling he knows his way about.

Now these are only similes. We have a right to ask what
sort of procedure is it that corresponds to the setting of the
dials, the putting together of two books, one of the many
journeys. I will try and explain to you how I see it.

In one of his printed lectures Wittgenstein says that 'the
great difficulty in philosophy is to say no more than we really
know'. This for me is fundamental. Notice how this fits in
with the mottoes he chose for the title pages of the *Tractatus*
and the *Philosophical Investigations*. For the first 'All that
man really knows can be said in three words, the rest is

nothing but dressing up and over tones'. For the second book he chooses 'It is in the nature of any new discovery to appear more important than it really is'. Do you get the idea? Philosophy requires a mental asceticism, a firm resolve to ask constantly 'what do I really know?'. Here it is often a matter of the resistance of the will that has to be overcome and not merely of the intelligence. Wittgenstein once shocked Moore by saying that he thought character was more important in philosophy than intelligence.

I will try and make myself clearer by doing two fragments of philosophy with you now. But remember that these are only two of the many journeys that have to be made.

Many years ago Wittgenstein asked me to read out loud to him Frazer's *Golden Bough*. Now Frazer did a valuable piece of work in collecting from all over the world the rites and myths of very different cultures. If he could have been content to do just this and no more it would have been a great book. But Frazer has to make out that he understands perfectly well why these rites and ceremonies were carried out. He always refers to these earlier people as savages. He is sure that they carried out these strange proceedings because of erroneous scientific hypotheses. Listen to him for a moment.

> Therefore in reviewing the opinions and practices of ruder ages and races we shall do well to look with leniency upon the errors as inevitable slips made in the search for truth, and to give them the benefit of that indulgence that we ourselves may one day stand in need of.

Frazer completely fails to mention that these so called savages, these ruder ages, had alongside their myths and rites already made immense scientific discoveries. They knew something of agriculture, of metal working, of architecture, the use of the wheel, and how to make fire. If they thought it important to carry out an elaborate fertility rite before the Spring ploughing, it is also true that they could make a plough and knew the importance of ploughing. In pretending to understand the reason for these rites Frazer is saying more than he really knew. In looking down on them he is indulging his own vanity. He speaks of the Australian aborigines as the rudest savages as to whom we possess information. But could Frazer have made and used, let alone invent, a boomerang. Take Professor Frazer out of his college rooms and strand him in the Nullabor desert, and to these rude savages he would seem a veritable ignoramus.

I imagine that if Frazer was being introduced to a stranger he politely shook hands. If he entered the college chapel he removed his hat and lowered his voice. Being a kindly man he probably decorated a tree for the children at christmas. If asked why he did these things he would rightly say that in our culture they were expressions of friendliness, reverence, and celebration. It would be ridiculous to say they were based on some hypothesis concerning the nature of things. Yet when he finds similar expressive acts in a different culture he has to look down on them as a false and rudimentary science.

In Wittgenstein's notes I find this written 'Our language is an embodiment of old myths; and the rite of the old myths was a language'.

So now turn to an entirely different field of human knowledge, and again see the importance of saying only so much as we really know. To-day if you go into any bookshop you will find several books and magazine articles with some such title as 'The nature of the Universe'. You know the sort of thing I mean. Extra galactic nebulae millions of light years away and receding from us at speeds approaching that of light. But what do we really know concerning these things?

First turn your attention to these words 'The Universe'. Where do they come from? Originally they referred to the sphere of the fixed stars, that which turned as one, *unus versus*. That stately and constant movement of the stars that made such a deep impression on the Greek mind. But if you reject Aristotelian cosmology, as we all do, then you can't just take a term out of that realm of thought and suppose it carries its meaning with it without further definition. And so far as I can find out none of our popular writers on cosmology ever attempt to say what precisely this term 'The Universe' is now meant to denote.

Then secondly consider the actual figures of distances and speeds with which we are presented. What do we really know? Where have these figures come from, what is really measured? Let us take for example the statements about the enormous speeds that the distant Galacti are said to be receding from us. Listen for a moment to a serious astronomer saying what is actually done. He writes:

> First one point of light among thousands of others all around it had to be kept steadily fixed over the slit of a spectrograph attached to the telescope, perhaps for eight or ten nights. Then after all this concentrated effort the resulting picture might be no more than one tenth of an inch long and one thirthieth of an inch wide containing many closely packed lines.

As you know the speed of recession of the nebulae is calculated from the fact that these closely packed lines are shifted towards the red end of the spectrum. I am not deriding this work or these hypotheses for one moment. What I do insist on is that nothing in the spectrogram or in nature compels us to make this and only this inference. Many different inferences could be made. More important still no inference need be made. One might just say well this is what things look like when you carry out this complicated procedure. The spectra of some stars just happens to be different from that of others.

It used to be a standing joke against Hegel that he gave an explanation of why there were seven planets in the solar system. As a matter of fact Hegel never said anything so silly. But no astronomer considers it necessary to give an explanation of either the number of planets or their respective distances from the sun. It is just one of those things that are. In the same way there would be nothing unscientific or illogical in accepting the differences in stellar spectra as contingent facts not requiring either explanation or inference.

I will quote Wittgenstein, this time from the *Tractatus*:

At the basis of the whole modern view of the world lies the illusion that the so-called laws of nature are the explanations of natural phenomena.[5]

These two very abbreviated fragments of philosophical investigation were meant to illustrate what I meant when I said that the difficulty in philosophy is to say no more than we really know. Such a pruning and purging has to be carried out over the whole range of knowledge, and that is neither a short nor easy task. When it is done then one knows one's way about the city, the library is in order, the door of the safe opens.

Why is it so important to say no more than we really know?

I am going to risk going a step further, and here I must say that I speak without authority. For the expressions that I now want to use have formulated themselves in my mind since Wittgenstein's death. That I owe them to his influence I have no doubt, that he would approve of them I cannot assert.

For me from the very beginning, and ever since, and still now, certain statements in the *Tractatus* siezed hold of my attention. They were these:

What can be said can be said clearly. [4.116]
We shew what cannot be expressed in words by saying clearly what can be said. [4.115]
How the world is is completely indifferent to what is higher. God does not reveal himself in the world. [6.432]
There is indeed that which cannot be expressed in words. This shews itself; it is what is mystical. [6.522]

In a lecture on ethics which Wittgenstein gave to a society of undergraduates who were not specifically studying philosophy he made more explicit how the phrase 'it is what is mystical' is to be understood.

[5] See Wittgenstein, *Tractatus Logico-Philosophicus*, 6.371.

He began the lecture by saying he was going to use the word Ethics in the sense Moore defined it in his book of that name 'an enquiry into that which is good'. He said he could have used various synonyms instead, such as: an enquiry into what is valuable, or into, what is really important, or an enquiry into what is the meaning of life, or into the right way of living. He then goes on to explain that although we can discuss good in a relative sense, good as a means to something else we cannot make any judgement about what has absolute value, what is good in and for itself. His own words are:

> What I wish to contend is that although all judgements of relative value can be shewn to be mere statements of facts, no statement of fact can ever be or imply a judgement of absolute value.[6]

and later on in the same lecture,

> I can only describe my feeling by the metaphor that if a man could write a book on Ethics which really was a book on Ethics, this book would with an explosion destroy all other books in the world. [p. 7]

and towards the end of the lecture:

> I see clearly, as it were in a flash of light not only that no description that I can think of would do to describe what I mean by absolute value, but that I would reject every significant description that anyone could possibly suggest, *ab initio*, on the grounds of its significance. [p. 11]

I said earlier on in my paper that Wittgenstein was no more a linguistic philosopher than Plato was. I would ask you now to compare what I have just quoted from Wittgenstein with a well known passage from Plato's seventh epistle. Plato you will remember is replying to those who have claimed to have written a treatise expounding his teaching and even

---

[6] See 'Wittgenstein's Lecture on Ethics', *Philosophical Review*, vol. 74 (1965), p. 6.

doing it better. Plato replies:

> I know that certain others have written about these same subjects, but what matter of men they are not even themselves know. But this much I can declare concerning all these writers, or prospective writers, who claim to know the subjects I seriously study, whether as hearers of mine or of other teachers, or from their own discoveries: it is impossible in my judgement at least that these men should understand anything about the subject. There does not exist, nor will there ever exist, any treatise of mine dealing therewith. For it does not at all admit of verbal expression like other subjects, but as a result of continued application to the subject itself and communion therewith it is brought to birth in the soul of a sudden, as light that is kindled by a spark, and thereafter it nourishes itself.[7]

Alongside of this voice from a very different past I would like to quote this from a contemporary of Wittgenstein's, but one who certainly had never read anything by him. Simone Weil writes:

> A mind enclosed in language is in prison. If a captive mind is unaware of being in prison it is living in error. If it has recognized the fact even for the tenth of a second and then quickly forgotten it in order to avoid suffering, it is living in falsehood. In them intelligence is neither a good, nor even an asset. The difference between more or less intelligent men is like the difference between criminals condemned to life imprisonment in smaller or larger cells. The intelligent man who is proud of his intelligence is like a condemned man who is proud of his large cell. A man whose mind feels that it is captive would prefer to blind himself to the fact. But if he hates falsehood he will not do so. And in that case he will have to suffer a lot.

---

[7] See Plato, Seventh Letter 341.

One more effort to point in the direction I want to point.

   You are sitting in a room and it is dusk. Candles have been brought in that you may see to get on with the work in hand. Then you look up and try to see the garden that lies beyond. But all you see is the reflection of the candles in the window. To see the garden the candles must be shaded. Now that is what philosophy does, it prevents us from being dazzled by what we know.

Maurice O'Connor Drury, with his wife Eileen, Lucan, 1953